The Politics of Change
in the Middle East

The Politics of Change
in the Middle East

EDITED BY

Robert B. Satloff

Published in Cooperation with
The Washington Institute for Near East Policy

Westview Press

BOULDER • SAN FRANCISCO • OXFORD

Copyright © 1993 by The Washington Institute for Near East Policy

Published in 1993 in the United States of America by Westview Press, Inc., 5500 Central Avenue, Boulder, Colorado 80301-2877, and in the United Kingdom by Westview Press, 36 Lonsdale Road, Summertown, Oxford OX2 7EW

A CIP catalog record for this book is available from the Library of Congress.
ISBN 0-8133-8672-1 (hardcover)
ISBN 0-8133-8673-X (paperback)

Printed and bound in the United States of America

The paper used in this publication meets the requirements
of the American National Standard for Permanence of Paper
for Printed Library Materials Z39.48-1984.

10   9   8   7   6   5   4   3   2   1

Contents

Acknowledgments

This collection of essays benefitted greatly from the suggestions of members of The Washington Institute's Editorial Council, especially Martin Indyk, Yehudah Mirsky, Patrick Clawson, and Laurie Mylroie. John Hannah played a significant role in the conceptualization of the project. Becky Diamond ably provided research assistance.

The project was funded through a generous grant from the Lynde and Harry Bradley Foundation of Milwaukee, supporting research on U.S. strategic interests in the Middle East. The opinions expressed in this book have not been endorsed by the Bradley Foundation and should not be viewed as representing the views of either the Bradley Foundation or the Board of Trustees of The Washington Institute.

Editor's Note

To assist students and non-area specialists, the only diacritical marks included in the transliteration are 'ayns ['] and hamzas ['] when they appear in the middle of a word. Commonly accepted English forms are used for many personal and place names, such as King Hussein, Abdel Nasser, and Ibn Saud. The Arabic definite article "al" usually only appears when reference is first made to the subject in each chapter (e.g., Anwar al-Sadat, Hafez al-Assad).

The Politics of Change
in the Middle East

Introduction

Robert B. Satloff

In the contemporary Middle East, threats of political instability are both real and imagined, and differentiating between the two is no easy task. Myths, such as the region's near-congenital predisposition for instability, abound, but when rapid change (e.g., Iraq's invasion of Kuwait) does occur, Western governments are often caught off-guard and unprepared.

The "crescent of crisis," for example, boasts some of the longest-ruling rulers in the world, ranging from conservative monarchs like Jordan's King Hussein, with more than forty years on the throne, to more eccentric leaders like Muammar Qadhdhafi, whose revolutionary credentials have become increasingly difficult to maintain after more than two decades in control of his desert "republic of the masses." Of all the Middle Eastern regimes in place at the time of the 1973 Yom Kippur/Ramadan War, radical and often violent change has normally been the province of the periphery—Afghanistan, Somalia. In that time, a military coup has toppled one Arab state, Sudan; civil war and foreign intervention nearly dismembered another, Lebanon; and a third, South Yemen, was effaced through a peaceful union with its northern neighbor. But revolution, in the fullest sense of the word, occurred only in Persian, Shi'ite Iran, and its march was thereafter impeded by war with Iraq and by the resilience of the alarmed Sunni Arab regimes to Iran's west. Indeed, throughout the rest of the twenty-odd Arab states, longevity appears to be the rule, not the exception. Moreover, when leaders themselves pass from the scene, their regimes have proved remarkably resourceful at maintaining the levers of control in the hands of one of their own, as the examples of Tunisia, Saudi Arabia, and Iraq can attest.

Longevity and stability, of course, are not synonymous; the former is not necessarily a useful, predictive tool of the latter. Indeed, straight-line forecasting can be dangerous, and the Middle East is no exception. It took several years for the debacle of the Six Day War of June 1967 to reverberate throughout the region, but when it had, the Middle East witnessed a series of fundamental leadership challenges and changes unmatched since 1948. Within four years, Egypt and Syria had new presidents; Libya, the end of the Sanussi monarchy; Iraq, the restoration of the Ba'th regime; and Jordan, a showdown fight between King Hussein and a Palestinian resistance that did not previously exist in a military sense. A second wave, in the late 1970s and early 1980s, marked the emergence of Islamic political activism that had been first recognized as a social and economic response to the events of 1967. In that test between regimes and Islamic oppositions, there were some shaky moments—the 1979 takeover of the Mecca mosque, the 1981 assassination of Anwar al-Sadat, the 1982 civil revolt throughout Syria—but Arab regimes fought back ruthlessly and survived; only Shi'ite Iran fell to the Islamists. The third wave, less violent but no less of a threat to the existing order, is now underway in different guises in Algeria, Tunisia, Jordan, Saudi Arabia as well as in the West Bank and Gaza. Though incumbent regimes are likely to weather the storm, there is no certainty of that, and in any case, they will be changed for the experience.

Into this mix one needs to add the special ingredient of the Gulf War. Will the war reverberate among the current generation of Middle Easterners the way the 1967 war did to the previous one? The crisis certainly has all the makings of a cataclysmic event in the region's political psyche, an event which publicly broke taboos that had been previously broken only in silence on issues such as inter-Arab conflict, dependence on outside powers, and the true national priorities of various Arab regimes. Economic inequality, democracy, government accountability, military insufficiency, and the frailty of pseudo-states like Kuwait are now on the national and regional agenda in the Middle East; that the clock cannot simply be rolled back to August 1, 1990 is clear. But what is unclear is whether Middle Eastern regimes have grown so resilient over the last quarter-century that they will simply absorb or deflect these challenges or whether generational change will bring profound political change in its wake.

From an historical viewpoint, Washington does not have a stellar record of recognizing, let alone managing, change. The failure to differentiate between the U.S. national interest in the Iraq of 1980-1988 and the Iraq of 1988-1990 and to adjust policy accordingly is only the most recent of a number of analytical errors that have occurred over the past twenty years. Some, like the failure to acknowledge the depth of the domestic opposition to the Shah (or, perhaps, the Shah's unwillingness to deal forcefully with the opposition) had disastrous repercussions both for American interests and the lives of individual American citizens; others, like the failure to understand the strategic message behind Sadat's expulsion of Soviet advisors in 1972, had no long-lasting damage, because Sadat was bent on re-defining Egyptian national priorities even without an early American response. When successions have occurred in recent years in countries with close ties to Washington (e.g., Tunisia, Egypt), they have tended to work smoothly, but that has usually been a function of the ruling regime's institutional need to maintain order and stability, with American diplomats, soldiers, and politicians keeping largely in the wings. Overall, the United States can be justifiably proud of its status as the major power to whom the vast majority of Middle Eastern states—Arabs and Israelis, conservative monarchies and radical national-ists—now look for security, support, and patronage. But given the fact that the Carter, Reagan, and Bush administrations were all hobbled by misjudgments about the extent and nature of change in the Persian Gulf, it often seems that whatever Pax Americana exists in the region has developed no less by default than by design.

The essays in this book examine the politics of change, transition, and continuity in eight key regional actors and explore the real prospects for short-term and medium-term stability inside those regimes. The goal throughout is to use the events of recent years as a preamble to prepare policymakers for the task of understanding and, perhaps, managing change in a region that is, as Muhammad Heikal has noted, famed for "cutting the lion's tail."

In the eight chapters to follow, heavy emphasis is laid on developments in domestic politics. This reflects the fundamental notion that the quest for survival is the chief, overriding factor in understanding most political insti-tutions, Middle Eastern regimes being no exception. If survival (and not ideology or ambition) is the defining principle of politics, then what matters most is controlling what happens close to home; consequently, each chapter addresses itself first and foremost to the instruments each regime employs in fulfilling that task and the political dilemmas with which each is faced in the process. This includes discussion of the distribution of power in the existing regime, in terms of both individuals and institutions; of the sources of legitimacy for the regime and the challenges to it; and of the social, economic, and ideological trends militating for political change and the forces arrayed against them. In many instances, the authors have been able to offer sober and informed insight into the most speculative aspect of political analysis, regime succession.

Only eight regimes—seven states and one non-state actor—are examined in the chapters below, barely one-third of the total number of Middle Eastern states. By admission, therefore, this collection is not an exhaustive effort to analyze political change throughout the entirety of the region. The eight were chosen for the simple reason that they are the most central actors in the two great regional confrontations that have historically engaged Western, and particularly American, interests—the Arab-Israeli conflict and the battle for control of the Gulf. This is not to deny the importance of, for example, the seething internal transformation inside Algeria or the backdoor Islamic takeover in Sudan; rather, the decision to limit the scope of this book to these eight regimes is itself reflective of the political priorities that shape America's national interest.

At the same time, the chosen eight do cut across ethnic, political, and ideological divides and are in some ways representative of others. They include Arab monarchies (Jordan, Saudi Arabia) and Arab republics (Egypt, Syria, Iraq); two non-Arab states, one Jewish (Israel) and one evangelistically Islamic (Iran); and one non-state actor that nevertheless plays a critical role in the region's politics (the Palestine Liberation Organization). Other dichotomies are perhaps useful—between well-entrenched, highly institutionalized regimes (Egypt) and those considered illegitimate by the majority of their population (Syria, Iraq); between those that are revolutionary (Iran), those that claim revolutionary status but are, by their actions, status-quo players (Syria, the PLO); and those for whom revolution is a self-defeating strategy (Jordan, Egypt, Israel, Saudi Arabia). Another useful distinction is between those that have witnessed peaceful transitions of power (Israel, Egypt, Saudi Arabia); those that have known only violent political change (Iran, Iraq); and those that have no mechanisms or no real precedents for leadership change at all (Jordan, the PLO). Perhaps the most obvious distinction for American policymakers is between various degrees of allies (Israel, Egypt, Saudi Arabia, and perhaps Jordan); adversaries (Iran, Iraq); and those regimes whose relationship with the United States is ambivalent or, at best, in the process of definition (Syria, the Palestinians).

There is no single lesson to be drawn from these country studies, except perhaps what Itamar Rabinovich, in his assessment of Syrian politics, calls "the usefulness and the limits of such terms as 'stability' and 'change' as analytical tools" in the Middle East. That is indeed the case for virtually all the countries examined here. The "endemic problem of the personalized authoritarian regime" that Rabinovich describes in Syria is no less apt for Iraq, where, as Amatzia Baram points out, Saddam's years in power and establishment of an octopus-like system of intelligence agencies has not guaranteed him political stability. In Syria's case, Rabinovich notes, "the original formula" that combines elements of governance and control has remained sufficient to overcome the regime's "underlying instability"; in Iraq's case, Baram says, that formula is inexorably coming apart. As for Iran, Shaul Bakhash argues that it has settled down to a "post-revolution malaise, characterized by relative stability and massive, seemingly intractable problems." Even such stability, though, could not forestall mass rioting in the summer of 1992 which, he says, reflected "deep and widespread discontent" and the general state of dissatisfaction toward the Rafsanjani government. He concludes on a cautionary note no less applicable to Syria and elsewhere: "Severe political controls, once established, cannot be eased without threats to the ruling group."

Though the immediate problems may be less acute, similar judgments about inherent instability are made for Jordan, Saudi Arabia, and the Palestinian political community. In these three cases, the role of the single leader is paramount though not detached from the problems facing the regime each has built. In describing the historic "watershed" that confronts Jordan today, Adam Garfinkle speaks of a "gradually deepening crisis" that combines "acute and structural economic weakness, a new political activism ... and questions about the well-being of King Hussein." These, he contends, have placed the Hashemite regime in deeper jeopardy than it has known since 1948. The Palestinians of the West Bank and Gaza, writes Barry Rubin, are hamstrung by their allegiance to an organization (the PLO) and a leader (Yasser Arafat) whose basic interests differ from their own; at the same time, that organization has acquiesced in a peace process that almost assuredly will lead to institutional cleavage and possibly the organization's demise. The results of the Arab-Israeli peace talks, Rubin contends, "will determine whether [Palestinians] accept the PLO as a revolutionary vanguard in a continuing struggle; a government; an ethnic, interest group representative under a non-Palestinian regime; or an outdated group which no longer serves a purpose." For Saudi Arabia, a different political process is underway that will have similar ramifications for the stability of the Saudi regime. There, argues Emile A. Nakhleh, the pitfalls involved in the ruling house's efforts to accommodate the increasingly irreconcilable post-Gulf War demands of Islamic traditionalists and Western-leaning technocrats could sorely test the limits of the regime's ability to control the coalition of forces that has long been the bedrock of Saudi rule. Nakhleh not only suggests the likelihood of an "eruption" of "communal conflict" between political moderates and Islamic fundamentalists, but he goes so far as to apply the fate of the modernizing monarch to the Saudi king, raising the possibility, however remote, "that Fahd's brush with liberalization might bring about his downfall." That the possibility of regime change would be seriously entertained by these experts, despite the longevity of Hussein, Arafat, and Fahd, respectively, underscores the notion that there may be in the post-Gulf War era a spurt of intense political transformation that could replicate the post-1967 years.

In the last set of chapters, Ami Ayalon and Marvin Feuerwerger address the two countries with the region's deepest sense of nationhood and hence political stability, Egypt and Israel. Despite their vast differences in geography, demography, and political tradition, they have each found a formula to weather severe national challenges—economic, social, political, and military—and to maintain a fundamental political continuity despite a whirlwind of change. Given their proven ability to deal with acute crises and to manage political successions (in Egypt, from Nasser to Sadat and then to Mubarak; in Israel, from Labor to Likud and back again), both authors suggest that it may be the chronic problems of demography (for Egypt, the consequences of population growth; for Israel, mass influx of new immigrants) and economics that are likely to fuel the main sources of domestic instability in the future. Chronic problems, of course, have a certain penchant for combustibility, and the appeal of straight-line projection may prove to be more deceptive in Egypt—an authoritarian state with a liberal, proto-democratic veneer—than in any other Middle Eastern state. Yet, all in all, one cannot help but conclude that, in contrast to the former allies of the erstwhile Soviet Union, it is Washington's good fortune to have its Middle East policy focused so heavily on the strongest reeds in the region.

Taken together, these essays paint a portrait of a region in flux. In the absence of the Cold War, in the shadow of the Gulf War, and in the era of direct Arab-Israeli peace negotiations, governments and peoples across the Middle East are being forced to grapple with internal problems that have long been shunted aside. Whether they actually address those challenges or divert attention via foreign adventure is not yet known. The prospect of peace will almost surely force a reexamination of national priorities in countries like

Syria, Jordan, and Israel; the Gulf War experience has already begun to fuel an unprecedented debate inside Saudi society; other regimes, like Iran, appear to be seeking new outlets for foreign adventure to postpone that process. It is hoped that this volume helps make the politics of change across the region both more recognizable and comprehensible.

1

Stability and Change in Syria

Itamar Rabinovich

In a project exploring the themes of stability and change in the current Middle East, Syrian politics occupy a place of particular importance and interest. Not only does Syria play a crucial role in the region's affairs, but the evolution of the country's politics during Hafez al-Assad's tenure of power underlines both the usefulness and the limits of such terms as "stability" and "change" as analytical tools. Assad's regime, having held power for more than two decades in a country previously notorious for frequent changes of government, is obviously durable. Nor does the regime presently face any serious challenge from an organized opposition. But how stable is a regime considered illegitimate by a majority of the country's population and held together by and depending on one person who refuses to make any real arrangements for succession and transition?[1]

Since 1970 there has, naturally, been a considerable degree of consistency and continuity in the structure and conduct of Assad's regime. But sometimes patently and on other occasions more subtly, important changes have been introduced or have taken place. Thus, as will be shown later, Assad has operated since his early days in power through a small, intimate and informal

Editor's note: This chapter was written prior to Professor Rabinovich's appointment as chief of Israel's delegation to peace talks with Syria. The views expressed herein are those of the author and should not be construed as representing those of the Israeli government.

group that has served as the inner core of his regime. This has not changed, but the composition of that inner group has been altered more than once.

The relationship between the regime and Syria's population is another case in point. For over two decades, Assad has had to contend with an attitude of rejection or at least passive hostility by a large segment of his country's urban population. But the strategies he employed in order to obtain the latter's acceptance or at least acquiescence have been transformed more than once.

The Formation of Assad's Regime

Syria has been an independent state since 1945. For all but eighteen years of its independent existence it has been ruled by a Ba'th regime. Assad was an important figure during the Ba'th's first seven years in power and has held full power in Syria since 1970. With the passage of time, it becomes increasingly difficult to separate the country's history from those of the Ba'th party and Hafez al-Assad.

Assad seized power in Syria after a comparatively long period of preparation armed with a clear concept of what he wanted to accomplish and with a detailed plan of action. His strategy was formulated on a recognition of both the assets and liabilities inherent in his position as one of the leaders of the Ba'th regime and a member of Syria's Alawite community.

During his first three years in power, the Ba'th has developed an extraordinarily effective formula; marriage and cooperation between a military cabal and an ideological party that has worked more successfully than most previous attempts in the region to institutionalize the role acquired by the military in Arab politics (indeed, it was subsequently adopted in Iraq as well but was modified to suit Saddam Hussein's own choices).

At the same time, the Ba'th was rejected by the bulk of Syria's urban population as too radical, secular and sectarian. The issue was further compounded by the fact that Assad and most of his close associates came from the minority Alawite community. The value of solidarity and support by members of his kin group, region and community had to be balanced against the refusal of a majority of Syria's urban population to accept the legitimacy of a regime dominated by the sectarian Alawites.

Assad's strategy sought to preserve the Ba'thist formula and to continue the reliance on the effective and loyal core of his supporters but to minimize the Syrian public's opposition by cloaking the core of his regime with an institutional and constitutional mantle. The result can be described as either a series of concentric circles or as a dual regime.

Thus the inner core of the regime was made up of Assad and a dozen or so confidants. They were surrounded by a larger circle of trusted army officers and party apparatchiks who were enveloped by the formal institutions of army, party and state. The whole system was coated by a constitution, legislative assembly and a coalition with other "progressive" parties. This edifice was completed in 1973.

Closely affiliated with this structure was the regime's mode of functioning on dual tracks. Decisions made by Assad and the inner core were transmitted through the reliable informal network for execution by organs of the army, state, or party. In this fashion, Syrians who were willing to ignore the realities of Assad's regime could delude themselves to believe that they lived in a country ruled by a "national progressive" coalition in which the Ba'th party played a dominant, but not exclusive, role and in which a legislative assembly elected according to the 1973 constitution made laws and supervised a government run by the cabinet of ministers.[2]

During Assad's first years in power the inner core of his regime included such persons as his brother Rifat; the commander of the Air Force Naji Jamil; the foreign minister, Abd al-Halim Khaddam; the heads of the intelligence and security services; and the commanders of key units in the Syrian army. The other prominent names among Assad's close associates during the early years were Mustafa Talas, originally chief of staff and deputy commander-in-chief of the army and the air force and as of 1972 minister of defense; Hikmat Shihabi, originally head of military intelligence and as of 1984 chief of staff; Ali Duba, originally Shihabi's assistant as head of military intelligence and in 1974 his successor in that position; Ali Hayder, commander of the special forces (a position he was given when still a colonel); Muhammad Khuli, head of air force security (a position he was given when still a major in 1967); Tawfiq Jihni, commander of the first division; Ali Husayn, commander of the Ninth division; and Abdullah al-Ahmar, Assad's deputy secretary-general in the Ba'th party organization. In the 1970s the group was often referred to in Syria as the *jama'ah* (group, or band).

Phases in the Regime's Evolution

Assad's quest to mollify the urban Sunni population rested on much more than just an attempt to disguise the true nature of his regime. Assad moderated the social and economic policies of the Ba'th and introduced a new climate of relative openness. He invested great efforts in seeking an accommodation with the Sunni religious establishment and public which included an intriguing attempt to have the Alawites accepted as proper Shi'ite

Muslims. In the same vein, the constitution was drafted and adopted and Assad had himself elected as an ostensibly constitutional president. The drafting of the Syrian constitution in 1973 served to underline the complexity of Syria's political realities. The language of the article defining the president's religion generated widespread demonstrations by Sunnis who protested this formalization of Alawite supremacy. The regime had no real difficulty in quashing the opposition but preferred a peaceful political compromise.[3]

Domestic liberalization was reinforced by mending fences with Egypt and other Arab countries and after 1973 with the United States as well. The relative success of the 1973 war and subsequent foreign policy achievements particularly in Lebanon contributed to the enhancement of Assad's stature as the country's leader. By the mid-1970s he could, thus, offer the urban Sunni population a political and social contract of sorts. They would accept his rule and his regime's character and monopoly of power in return for stability, a considerable degree of freedom in the conduct of their affairs, and Syria's return to the regional and international mainstream.

But this *entente* was predicated on the condition that real political power and activity remained the regime's exclusive domain and the public could enjoy comparative liberalization and the patronage offered by the regime as along as it abstained from engaging in politics.

This strategy, aided by the economic expansion of these years, seemed very successful in the mid-1970s. Assad's regime had at least the passive support of that sector of the rural population which benefitted from its policies as well as of those parts of the bourgeoisie which thrived on its economic policies and relative openness. In fact, some members of the urban bourgeoisie became allied to members of the regime's new elite. One of the Ba'th regime's most astute students described it in this as a network of nepotism and patronage managed by Assad and his coterie.[4]

The regime's critics took a less academic view of the matter and denounced its conduct as mere "corruption" to the point of pushing the regime itself to launch an "anti-corruption campaign" which soon got out of hand. Indeed in 1977-1978, several forces and factors at work combined to produce a massive popular rebellion against the regime. These included contradictions inherent in its social economic policy; domestic and external criticism of its policies in Lebanon; the conflict with Iraq and the Palestine Liberation Organization; and, most importantly, the transformation of the Muslim Brotherhood and the rise of a new radical Muslim fundamentalist leadership which spearheaded the offensive against the regime.

In addition to the direct fundamentalist message, the rebels also articulated Sunni grievances against Alawite domination and general disenchantment with the regime's corruption. Given the passive support of large segments of the urban population, the boldness they displayed and the sophisticated technique they enjoyed, the rebels could not be contained and their offensive resulted in a full-fledged confrontation between the regime and the urban Sunni population which unfolded in Aleppo in 1980 and culminated in Hama in 1982. The events of Hama due to their lingering impact need to be explained in some detail. The crisis occurred when government forces were trapped in that city. In the process of extricating his forces and punishing the rebels and their hostile environment, Assad ordered massive killing and destruction. The end result was the devastation of a significant part of the old city and the killing of up to 20,000 of its residents. The suppression of the anti-regime insurrection in Aleppo in 1980 had been brutal enough and the predominantly Alawite troops did not spare that city's population. But the deliberate unprecedented violence used by the regime in Hama represented a conscious decision to teach a lesson when the backbone of the opposition had been broken. It also signified a decision to cease the effort to mollify the Sunni urban population; if that population could not be won over it had to be terrified into submission. The events of the 1970s and early 1980s had a dual effect. The opposition was eliminated and had not been able to regroup. Social groups, hostile to the regime that in the late 1970s provided sympathetic environment to the underground organizations were no longer willing to take the risk. But at the same time, the degree of acceptance that had been gained in the mid-1970s and was so important to Assad had been lost.

The next crisis occurred in early 1984 and was a direct result of Assad's illness of November 1983. Assad's incapacitation for several months and the absence of a proper institutional arrangement for an orderly succession resulted in an open struggle between Assad's brother Rifat and the latter's rivals and subsequently between the two brothers. A bloody confrontation was narrowly avoided. It took several months for Assad to recuperate physically, to eliminate his brother's supporters and bases of power and to fully reassert his authority before things returned to normal in 1985.[5]

Rifat al-Assad is still formally one of his brother's three vice-presidents, but except for a brief period he has been effectively in exile in Europe. (He returned to Syria for his mother's funeral in July 1992 and has since remained.) His principal power base, the Defense Companies, have been disbanded and their function assigned to the presidential guard headed by another relative, Adnan Makhluf. Rifat's main rivals such as Shafiq Fayyad and Ali Duba retained their positions as commanders respectively of an armored division and military intelligence. Likewise, Assad's son, Basel, was groomed by the late 1980s as a possible heir. This has been done cautiously and Basel was not given prominence and a power resembling those of his uncle in his heyday. Rifat's virtual elimination and the erosion of his power base were not the first major change to have occurred in the *jama'ah*. Some of the *jama'ah*'s members were quietly removed over the years. Their place taken by others, the most notable instance was the removal in the late 1970s of Naji Jamil. Jamil had been Assad's assistant and successor in the air force and was often mentioned as a possible successor. As such, he became Rifat's rival, and Rifat indeed played a major role in his retirement. Rifat's own ouster was done more obstreperously.

The intra-Ba'thist conflicts of the winter and spring of 1984 served to bring the issue of succession to the surface, but this remained a passing episode. Hafez al-Assad clearly regards any discussion or mention of the question of succession as a challenge to his authority and upon returning to full-time political activity he suppressed it. Formally, the issue is regulated by the 1973 constitution but no one familiar with the realities of Syrian politics expects Assad's eventual successor to be chosen according to that constitutional procedure. Consequently, the issue was submerged but did not disappear; it persists in the mind of the Syrian public and in the regime's own ranks as a matter of speculation and subtle preparation.

The domestic problems of 1984-1985 remained a purely internal matter of Assad's regime. The radical Islamic opposition had been exhausted and emasculated in the terrible aftermath of 1982. Other opposition groups did not fare better. Individual factions from earlier chapters of Ba'thist history and other Syrian parties sought every so often to form a united opposition front and published an occasional newspaper or pamphlet, but this did not amount to any meaningful challenge to the regime. Consequently, there was no effective opposition that could take advantage of the regime's crisis in the mid-1980s. Nor was there a meaningful opposition or alternative to the Ba'th regime when an accumulation of domestic and external problems combined to produce an acute sense of malaise in Syria during the decade's final years. Chief among the domestic problems was the endemic economic crisis. Externally, Assad had to contend with a series of difficulties running from the challenges to his Lebanon policy and the water conflict with Turkey to the more profound problems that will be discussed presently. Beyond these concrete difficulties lay more vaguely the sense that Assad's regime had run its course: that while it faced no direct challenge from the weak Syria opposition, it had lost the power to innovate and to formulate new policies suited to the realities of the 1990s.[6]

It was against this background that Assad and his men had to contend with the domestic dimension and repercussions of four main developments of the past few years—the collapse of the Soviet system, the end of the war between Iran and Iraq, the Gulf crisis and the renewal of the Arab-Israeli peace process. The description and analysis of these developments as such falls outside the scope of this paper but their impact on Syrian politics, on the regime's stability in particular, will now be examined in some detail.[7]

The Need for Reassessment

By 1987, many of the repercussions of Gorbachev's policies of *perestroika* and *glasnost* for the Middle East in general and for his country in particular had become apparent to Assad. He could see that the Soviet Union had conceded its defeat in the Cold War, that Gorbachev had decided to shift, in the new Soviet terminology, from a policy of "confrontation" to a policy of "a balance of interests" with the United States; he saw that, in the Middle Eastern context, this meant a reduced commitment to and lesser support for Syria and a better relationship with Israel. The import of these developments and their still more ominous sequels went well beyond the realm of foreign security policies. The relationship with the Soviet Union, its ups and downs notwithstanding, had been a cornerstone and a mainstay of the Ba'th regime since the mid-1960s and its gradual evaporation clearly threatened the very foundations of Assad's regime.[8]

In 1988, yet another threat surfaced when the Iraq-Iran War ended with an Iraqi victory. Ayatollah Khomeini's death soon thereafter magnified the effect of Iraq's victory by disrupting Iranian politics and by forcing the Ayatollah's successors to turn their attention and resources at least for a few years' transitional period to the home front. This left the victorious Saddam Hussein possessed with the vast military machine he had built in the 1980s and free to use it to promote his regional policies. From Syria's point of view this meant that the relief from Iraq's pressure it had enjoyed for eight years had ended, that the Iranian alliance, a crucial relationship in both the domestic and foreign spheres, had lost at least part of its value and that Saddam Hussein was well positioned to retaliate for Syria's alliance with Iran and hostility to Iraq.

While Saddam refrained from a direct confrontation with Syria, he did encourage and support her rivals in Lebanon and his new prominence in Arab politics tended to dwarf and isolate Syria. He could also be expected to revive his country's strategy of the mid and late 1970s and galvanize the dormant Syrian opposition. Even without a frontal Iraqi attack the prospect of a powerful and hostile neighbor, occupying center stage in Arab politics, championing the cause of radical Arab nationalism under the banner of the other Ba'th party and extending support and inspiration to the ever present Syrian opposition was quite appalling.

The collapse of several Communist and dictatorial regimes in Eastern Europe in autumn 1989 exacerbated the threat. Assad lost additional allies but more severe was the fact that an analogy could easily be drawn—and indeed was soon made—between the regimes of Ceaucescu and Honecker and that of Assad. And if the removal of the Soviet Union's protective mantle in Eastern Europe resulted in the immediate toppling of dictatorial regimes resting on a party cadre and an apparently formidable military establishment and security apparatus, why could the same not happen in Syria? The differences could be easily pointed out, but the fear that the East European example could serve as a source of inspiration to the opposition and undermine the self-confidence of the regime's cadres could not be lightly put to rest. The manner in which the Iranian Revolution had inspired the Islamic opposition in Syria a decade earlier to mount its offensive must have been fresh in the memories of the regime's leaders.

Indeed, in January and February 1990, several indications appeared that various Syrian opposition groups at home and abroad were renewing their activity. In January, anti-government leaflets were distributed and the establishment of unidentified committees for democracy and human rights was announced. The terminology clearly reflected the spirit of the time as did the demands for elections, democratization, the removal of emergency laws and measures and the release of political prisoners. The comparatively free parliamentary elections that had been held in Jordan and resulted in a Muslim fundamentalist plurality were cited in one such leaflet as an example worthy of imitation.[9]

In February, a National Front for the Salvation of Syria was formed in Paris. Another sign of the changed mood in Syria were interviews given during the same month by two leaders of the Syrian Communist Party, Khaled Bakdash and Yusef Faisal, to the Kuwaiti press in which they departed from the acquiescence of the previous years and criticized the Ba'th regime.

A reexamination and quite likely a reorientation of the Ba'th regime's domestic and foreign policies was clearly in order. The soul-searching in foreign policy had already been done in the late 1980s, and its effects were publicly felt at the end of 1989. The loss of the Soviet alliance and Syria's other losses were to be compensated by seeking a dialogue with Washington and by mending fences with Egypt and drawing closer to the conservative Arab states. But Syria was not simply going to join the American orbit and ally itself with the conservative Arabs. The residual relationship with the Soviet Union was to be maintained and the alliance with Iran to be cultivated. That alliance was to enhance Syria's leverage on the Gulf Arabs and, equally important, to enable the Ba'th regime to maintain a radical edge. That edge was important for the regime's self-image and as a hedge against criticism by the opposition and from within its own ranks that the Syrian Ba'th had lost its raison d'etre.

In December 1989, Syria renewed diplomatic relations with Egypt having abandoned its erstwhile persistent and vociferous demand that Egypt abrogate its peace treaty with Israel. Indeed, as his visit to Egypt (and to Sinai) early in 1990 and the messages he transmitted during the same period through visiting American dignitaries further indicated, Assad clearly understood that the shift from a Soviet orientation to a dialogue with Washington required also that a new and milder approach to the issue of an Arab-Israeli settlement be adopted.

By March 1990, Assad had also reached the decision that the domestic effervescence must be placated and that the recrudescence of the opposition's activity had to be addressed. The strategy chosen was familiar and disturbingly reminiscent of the 1970s—some political and economic liberalization, a series of measures offering greater participation and representation without actually affecting the regime's core, structure, and degree of control.

Assad himself referred to the change of policy in his customary Revolution Day address on March 8, 1990. The speech attracted considerable attention at the time due to the rather unusual discussion of the Jewish immigration from the Soviet Union to Israel—its most memorable sentence explained that "the Soviet Jews are neither Israelis nor Semites ... They are remains of the Khazars." It also included an interesting analysis of the impact of the changes in the international system, particularly the effect on the Arabs of the decline of the Soviet Union. But the address is particularly significant as a reflection of Assad's cautious approach to and his limited concept of the notion of change. Assad spoke at length about the importance of change, freedom and participation. He argued that these were all germane to his corrective movement and emphasized the importance of the Progressive National Front and of the People's Assembly.

He then spoke at some length about one issue on which he had already decided to make a concession: the emergency laws. Following a time-honored practice of dictatorial rulers, he was willing to admit that his government had erred on some marginal technical matters and promised correction and reform. With regard to the emergency law, he promised that "the government should soon study the idea of restricting the use of this law to more important matters such as state security and public order.

He subsequently alluded to a broader reform further down the road: "In any case, and as I said a few days ago, the Ba'th party congress will meet and will discuss the great state of affairs in a comprehensive manner. The Progressive National Front congress will do the same. This is an important step in developing the front's action. Attention will be given to everything that contributes to a national congress."[10]

These themes were then pursued and elaborated by the Damascus media. Thus, *Tishrin* and *al-Thawra* called for a return to the roots and original course of Assad's November 1970 "Corrective Movement." One such article went to the length of arguing that it was the Syrian Ba'th regime that had originally formulated the notion of *perestroika* some twenty years earlier. More concretely, Prime Minister Mahmud Zu'bi announced the abrogation of all emergency laws and measures.

The chief manifestation of the regime's policy of "democratization" was the May 22 elections to the People's Assembly. In preparation for the elections, the number of seats was raised from 195 to 250. Out of the total number, 166 (or 60 percent) were assigned to candidates representing the Progressive National Front. the nominal coalition formed by the Ba'th and several licensed parties. The other 40 percent were left to independent candidates and to those representing parties and factions that did not form part of the Front. Two other changes were made in the rules of the game—independent candidates were allowed to form political groupings and three factions were added to the front. One of the three had an Islamic orientation, thus representing the regime's latest effort to curry favor with Muslim opinion.

Close to 10,000 candidates competed for the Assembly's 250 seats. Of those elected, 173 turned out to be new members. The new Assembly met for the first time on June 11 and reelected the outgoing speaker.

As an act of political reform, the changes in the composition of the People's Assembly were very limited and they were so received by the Syrian public. The Assembly as such wields no real power in Syria and its opening to a somewhat broader section of Syrian opinion amounted to no more than a cosmetic change.[11]

The government's concomitant efforts to improve economic conditions in the country were facilitated by the fortuitous increase in oil production and export. The additional revenue and the corresponding decline in the expenditure on the purchase of oil accounted for the fact that 1989 was the first year in three decades to end with a positive trade balance. But this and the growth of Syria's gross national product did little to alleviate the endemic shortage of consumer goods. To this end, specific liberalization measures were taken. Thus, businessmen were now permitted to use foreign currency earned through export in order to import staple foods and other essential consumer goods.

Such specific measures were to be fitted into the broader policy of *infitah* (opening) entrusted to Minister of Economy Muhammad Imadi. Trained in the United States, Imadi had served in several Syrian cabinets as a professional rather than a political appointee. His was the task of formulating and implementing the economic policies that would complement the political liberalization embarked on by the regime and help bring Syria into harmony with what seemed to be the victorious trends in the international arena. But the actual implementation of the policy of *infitah* proved to be an arduous task. The very tern *infitah* evoked memories of the ill-fated liberalization of the mid-1970s that ended in disaster. In the Syrian reality of 1990 and 1991, all liberalization attempts were obstructed by the political system's lingering rigidity, by the Ba'th cadres' resistance to the ideological ramification of economic liberalization, by the weakening of their control of the public sector, and by the military's refusal to give up the economic privileges they had been enjoying under the existing system.

The Domestic Repercussions of the Gulf Crisis

Whatever consideration was given by Assad at the time to problems inherent in economic liberalization were soon overshadowed by Iraq's invasion and annexation of Kuwait. The ensuing Gulf crisis and Gulf War became the governing issue of the region's and Syria's politics and served specifically to further compound the policy dilemmas faced by Assad's regime since the late 1970s.

For one, the Iraqi threat to Assad's Syria became still more serious. Should Saddam Hussein's gamble succeed, his position would be dramatically enhanced and with it his ability to exert pressure on and settle scores with his Syrian rivals. The formation of the U.S.-led coalition, while creating unusual opportunities for Syrian policy, also presented new and significant problems. As the crisis unfolded, other problems were added. Thus, when war seemed more and more inevitable, the issue for Syria was transformed from the deployment of its troops alongside American and other Western troops on

Arab soil against an Arab party to the possibility of joining in battle against Iraq and perhaps even of contributing to Iraq's destruction. Furthermore, while Assad wanted Saddam Hussein weakened, he was not interested in destroying Iraq's military power to the extent that it would undermine the Arab—and, in that respect, Syria's—military posture *toward* Israel.

Surely there were considerable gains to be made by joining the coalition and by dispatching Syrian troops to the Gulf. Syria's participation in the coalition was very valuable to the United States and to the conservative Arab oil producers. It would not only guarantee a majority in the Arab League and other Arab forums but would also deny Saddam the ability to depict the coalition as an alliance of Western imperialists and Arab conservatives pitted against an Arab revolutionary alliance. This was a very valuable asset, and Assad knew that he would be rewarded handsomely for supplying it. An acceleration of the rapprochement with Washington and Cairo and financial renumeration by Saudi Arabia and other Gulf states were two obvious benefits.

But joining the U.S.-led coalition also exacted a price, primarily in Syrian domestic terms. By 1990 and in fact much earlier, Assad's regime could hardly be defined as revolutionary. Still, it was important for Assad to maintain the image and label of an ideological regime upholding the doctrine and legacy of the Ba'th party. Furthermore, while the regime's inner core may have abandoned its commitment to the Ba'th's ideology and outlook, there was a cadre of party *apparatchiks* and militants, important for the regime's smooth functioning, who did attach importance to matters of ideology and doctrine. As has already been noted, the strategy formulated by Assad in the late 1980s did not envisage a Syria placed squarely in the Western camp but rather saw the alliance with Iran and the residual relationship with the United States as a means of maintaining an independent posture. That posture was jeopardized by the new policy and the regime's rivals and enemies in and outside Syria were most likely to criticize and embarrass it for a stark deviation from the familiar and well-trodden path of Ba'thist foreign policy.

It would, however, be erroneous to reduce Assad's dilemma to a matter of image and posture. Assad flirted in the past with Washington (to Moscow's displeasure) and he had a relationship with Saudi Arabia, but an open and intimate military and political alliance with the United States and the conservative Arabs against the leader of a radical Arab regime did run against the grain of Ba'thist politics and policies. Time was not on Assad's side as it turned out not only that war was inevitable but that Saddam's claim to revive the themes of revolutionary Arab nationalism and to evoke memories of its Nasserist heyday resonated in large parts of the Arab world.

Indeed, criticism of the regime's new policy was soon voiced in Syria in several forms—graffiti, leaflets, and conversations with foreign correspondents. The latter reported that many Syrians listened openly to Baghdad's radio station and that many Syrians, representing a cross-section of Syrian society, expressed sympathy for Saddam and displeasure with their own government's conduct.[12] In this chorus of disapproval, three distinct strands could be discerned. These ranged from a particular resistance to the government's policies that was focused in northeastern Syria, close to the Iraqi border; to an effort by the lingering organized opposition (Muslim fundamentalist and other) to take advantage of the situation and resume its activity; to a general tendency by the large segment of Syrian society that had not reconciled itself to the regime to manifest its hostility by supporting Saddam Hussein and his cause. As the crisis wore on and the danger of war became more imminent, the criticism escalated. Most notably, a manifesto signed by more than 120 intellectuals was published in Cyprus in early March 1991. The signatories did not launch a direct attack on Syria's policies but their denunciation of the war against Iraq clearly implied that Assad's policies were at best misguided in that they served the "Zionist" and "imperialist" designs of which the war against Iraq formed an important part:

> The real aims of this war against Iraq and the Arab nation require that every Arab whatever his place and position to rise to the level of responsibility and to sense the gravity of the great dangers which threaten the future of the Arab generation. The slogans of the new imperialist campaign to defend the putative "international legitimacy" and to "liberate Kuwait" cannot disguise the true purpose of this war which seeks to redraw the political map of [foreign] control of the Arab homeland's resources.[13]

Earlier efforts by the Muslim Brotherhood to criticize and denounce Assad's policies were obstructed by bickering and dissention in the ranks of the fundamentalist opposition. That opposition had indeed been divided since its defeat in the early 1980s (and had also been penetrated by Assad's intelligence services), but its effectiveness during the Gulf crisis was also blunted by inherent contradictions. Whether supported by Iran or by Saudi Arabia, it was difficult to come out in support of Iraq's policies without antagonizing their benefactors.[14]

On the whole, Assad dealt cautiously and defensively with the criticism and the opposition. Critics, including the signatories of the Cyprus manifesto, were not prosecuted. The emphasis was laid on trimming the regime's policies and on their exposition to the Syrian public. The "trimming" was effected by occasional criticism of the United States (by way of demonstrating that a certain distance from Washington was kept), by going to great lengths to limit the role and visibility of Syria's troops in the Gulf, and by offering persistent and self-exonerating advice to Iraq to save itself from war and disaster.

The propaganda campaign designed to defend and explain the regime's policies was conducted on the familiar two levels, with one set of arguments directed at the party members and the other at the Syrian public. Assad himself set the tone in a speech delivered on September 12. He was patently apologetic: "There are those who wonder—within the framework of delusion, within the framework of erroneous thinking—they wonder how Arab forces can be present on Saudi Arabian territories while the foreign troops are there. Imagine the fallacy."[15] The rest of his speech was devoted to a detailed defense of his policy and to an equally detailed effort to counter Saddam's claim to promote the causes of Arabism and Islam. These themes were repeated during the next few months by Syria's written and electronic media and adapted to the changing circumstances. Thus, the need was felt after the war's outbreak to explain that the Iraqi missile attacks on Israel, rather than being a new Arab exploit, were rendering a service to Israel. Assad himself did not choose to deliver another major address in this vein and left the task to his deputy, Khaddam. On February 24, 1991, Khaddam spoke before "a forum of the Ba'th party and popular organizations" and offered a lengthy, apologetic, and generally interesting account of the Gulf crisis. Curiously, he chose to argue *inter alia* that Iraq had supported the Muslim Brotherhood in Syria and was therefore responsible for the bloodshed of the late 1970s and early 1980s:

> Who stood behind the problem in Hama? Was the blood spilt there not Arab? And who were the victims? Not leaders but hundreds and thousands of [ordinary] Syrians. Was the killing done for Palestine? Arab unity? ... They were killed because the state had opposed the Camp David Accords and its banner of unity and liberation remained hoisted.[16]

The net effect of domestic opposition to Assad's policies was limited. It constrained the regime's conduct of a policy about which it had itself been ambivalent and ambiguous. It did point to the fact that the cosmetic liberalization and democratization of the first half of 1990 did little to placate the widespread and diffuse opposition to the regime. It did not penetrate into the regime's own ranks nor did it enable the organized opposition to re-group and mount a fresh offensive. And, most significantly, while constraining the regime, it fell short of preventing it from pursuing the policies on which it had decided and embarked. As a backdrop to the unfolding course of events, it served as a reminder that in its twenty-first year in power, Assad's regime still had to contend with its rejection by a considerable segment of Syrian society.

The Resumption of the Arab-Israeli Peace Talks

The dilemma faced by Assad's regime at the outbreak of the Gulf crisis was replicated, albeit in a much milder form, by the resuscitation of the Arab-Israeli peace process as one of the by-products of the Gulf War. It has already been noted that by the late 1980s Assad had accepted the fact that a new, more pragmatic approach had to be adopted to the issue of settlement and peace with Israel. But this did not quite amount to a willingness to come to a public peace conference and to negotiate directly with Israel. Like the participation in the anti-Iraqi coalition, this seemed to Assad and his men as well as to their critics as a sharp deviation from the most seminal Ba'thist principles. Unlike the new partnership with the United States and Saudi Arabia, success and renumeration were not guaranteed, certainly not in immediate terms. The regime, in other words, ran the risk of appearing to have compromised on the hard core of its ideological stance and, still worse, to have done so in vain. Assad's main effort was invested in securing the success of his policy (by seeking a firm and explicit commitment from the United States) but efforts were also invested in explaining the new policy to the regime's own cadres and to the larger Syrian public.

It is curious to note in this context that in the February 1991 address quoted above, Vice President Khaddam was still proudly explaining Syria's politics in terms of the regime's firm resistance to the Camp David Accords. In February 1991, Syria had already renewed diplomatic relations with Egypt and was close to accepting the U.S. initiative of resuming a peace process modelled on the Camp David Accords. Khaddam's statements, like many other acts of Assad's regime, was thus indicative of its limited ability to respond to profound changes. Policies were adapted and trimmed but deeper changes of norm and attitude were slow and difficult. As the brief survey of developments in 1990 and 1991 has shown, this applies to domestic policies as well as to foreign policy.

The actual evolution of the new phase of Arab-Israeli diplomacy further exacerbated Assad's dilemma. Having obtained satisfactory clarifications from the Bush administration, he dispatched Foreign Minister Faruq al-Shara to Madrid. There, the Syrian delegation must have been dismayed by President Bush's reference to "territorial compromise," as opposed to the more widely accepted formula of "territory for peace," which implies a fuller withdrawal. This may have contributed to the adoption by al-Shara of a particularly aggressive line, out of tune with a tendency by all other delegations to seek to impress international public opinion with their pragmatism and openness.

During the next round of negotiations, Syria pursued a complex policy. On the one hand, it sought to contrast itself with other Arabs and to other Arab delegations by remaining committed to the traditional fundamental positions of Arab nationalism and to the code of conduct they entailed. Syria's delegates to the talks in Washington avoided any fraternization with their Israeli interlocutors, and Syria boycotted the multilateral round of talks in Moscow determined to indicate that normalization with Israel was not being considered. And yet, on the other hand, a close scrutiny of the Washington talks would reveal glimpses of pragmatism on Syria's part.

Syria's conduct during this period was naturally affected by the interplay with Israel's policies. Assad could not be confident that Israel's government of the time contemplated any meaningful concessions to Syria as part of the settlement, but a monitoring of the Israeli press would have brought to his attention the argument made there that, for a Likud government, it was preferable to make a deal with Syria rather than with the Palestinians. As 1992 wore on and Israel's parliamentary elections were announced and then drew nearer, it became clear that no progress could be expected in the negotiations before the Israeli voters made their decision.

It is curious but not really surprising that in the aftermath of Israel's June elections, Syria's spokesmen and media gave Yitzhak Rabin and his new Labor-led government a rather cool reception. For one thing, it could be gathered from Rabin's campaign that he intended to seek rapid progress in the autonomy negotiations with the Palestinians and preferred to deal with Syria at a later stage. Perhaps more significantly, Assad and Syrian government officials viewed Rabin as determined and likely to restore the intimate U.S.-Israeli relationship, thereby hampering Syria's own efforts to develop a dialogue with Washington at Israel's expense.

Nearly a year after Syria's decision to attend the Madrid conference, there were no signs either of agitation among the public or of any effort by the regime to prepare public opinion for a radical shift in position and policy toward Israel. Clearly, Assad felt that his hold on the country sufficiently firm and unchallenged for the conduct of his present policies. It would take a dramatic progress in the Syrian-Israeli negotiations or in Israel's negotiations with another Arab party, from which Syria is excluded, to test the regime's hold and freedom of action in an entirely different context.

Conclusion

Syria's domestic politics in 1991-1992 unfolded within a familiar pattern. Assad was elected for yet another term by a massive majority. On the eve of the elections, thousands of political prisoners were set free as a gesture of goodwill. Larger oil revenues and the economic fallout from the Gulf War contributed to an improvement of the economic situation in the country. Prime Minister Zu'bi and his cabinet resigned, but Zu'bi himself formed a new cabinet without introducing any significant changes.

Assad's health and the issue of succession remain a matter of rumor and speculation. These concern the movements and whereabouts of Assad's brother, Rifat, or the increased stature of Basel, the president's son. Press reports in this domain are important not as hard facts but as testimony to the endemic problems of a personalized authoritarian regime.

In more general terms, it can be stated that developments since the Gulf crisis have revealed the limited effect that the far-reaching changes in regional and international politics have so far had on the regime's stability. Despite successive challenges and difficulties, the original formula developed by the Ba'th, combined with Assad's personal skills, dominance, and mastery of the techniques of governance and control, proved sufficient to overcome the regime's underlying instability. And yet the personal and, in the final analysis, ephemeral nature of the successful formula became ever more apparent.

Notes

1. For biographies-cum-histories of Assad and his regime, see Patrick Seale, *Asad: The Struggle for the Middle East* (Berkeley: University of California Press, 1989) and Moshe Ma'oz, *Asad: The Sphynx of Damascus* (New York: Weidenfeld and Nicholson, 1988).

2. See Itamar Rabinovich, *Syria under the Ba'th 1963-1966: The Army-Party Symbiosis* (Jerusalem: Israel Universities Press, 1972), and "Syria," in Colin Legum and Haim Shaked, eds., *Middle East Contemporary Survey (MECS)*, vol. 1, 1976, (New York: Holmes and Meier, 1977).

3. Abbas Kelidar, "Religion and State in Syria," *Asian Affairs,* vol. 61, February 1974, pp. 16-22.

4. Yahya Sadowski, "Bathist ethics and the spirit of state capitulation," in P.J. Chelkowski and R.J. Praeger, *Ideology and Power in the Middle East* (Durham, NC: Duke University Press, 1988), pp. 160-186.

5. Alasdair Drysdale, "The Succession Question in Syria," *Middle East Journal,* vol. 39, no. 2, spring 1985, pp. 246-57.

6. For a fuller account, see Itamar Rabinovich, "Syria and Lebanon," *Current History,* vols. 86 (February 1987) and 88 (February 1989); and *Syria's Quest for a Regional Role,* The Woodrow Wilson Center for International Scholars, Occasional Papers Series (Washington: The Wilson Center, 1986).

7. For a detailed treatment of these issues, see Daniel Pipes, *Damascus Courts the West: Syrian Politics 1989-1991,* Policy Paper Number Twenty-six, (Washington: The Washington Institute for Near East Policy, 1991).

8. Alasdair Drysdale and Raymond A. Hinnebusch, *Syria and the Middle East Peace Process* (New York: Council on Foreign Relations, 1991), pp. 170-174 and 194-199.

9. For details and references, see Eyal Zisser's chapter on Syria in *MECS,* vol. 14, 1990 (Boulder, CO: Westview, 1992).

10. Radio Damascus, March 8, 1990.

11. See note 9 above. Also, in an article published in the winter of 1992, Volker Perthes, who teaches at the American University of Beirut, presented a slightly different interpretation of the May 1990 elections. While mindful of the regime's authoritarian character, Perthes does see the new parliament as more representative of a broader Syrian spectrum and expects that "those independent MPs who represent the commercial class will use parliament as a forum to call for economic reform and liberalization." This is quite likely, but his expectation that the same people will also "probably—in the long run at least—[be] claiming that private sector representatives should also share political responsibility" is more dubious. Volker Perthes, "Syria's Parliamentary Elections," *Middle East Report,* January-February 1992, pp. 15-18.

12. See for instance, *Wall Street Journal,* September 27, 1990; *Financial Times*, September 19, 1990; and Syrian Arab Television, August 30, 1990 (for a denial of "rumors").

13. *al-Hurriyya* (Nicosia), February 17, 1991.

14. See *al-Dustur* (Amman), August 17, 1990 and December 10, 1990; and *al-Quds al-Arabi* (London), December 7, 1990.

15. Radio Damascus, September 12, 1990.

16. *Tishrin,* February 12, 1991.

2

The Future of Ba'thist Iraq: Power Structure, Challenges, and Prospects

Amatzia Baram

Since its inception in 1920, instability and violence have been the two most salient characteristics of political life in the modern nation-state of Iraq. Despite its outward sense of continuity, the era marked by the two-and-half decades of Ba'thist rule—and especially the period since Saddam Hussein came to power in 1979—has been no exception. The unique contribution to Iraq's political culture that Saddam himself has made is an unprecedented degree of violence used both within the Sunni-Arab ruling circle and by this circle against the various other segments of Iraqi society. This chapter will examine the essential features of the core institutions of the Iraqi Ba'thist state, the internal and structural challenges to the current regime, and the prospects for political change.

The State's Institutions

At present, all the institutions that existed since 1968 (with the addition of a parliament) are still in place, and with minor changes they still have the same formal authority they originally had. In reality, since 1979 they have all been tools in the hands of Saddam Hussein. The Revolutionary Command Council (RCC) is the supreme decision-making and law-making institution. It is a self-appointed body, and it is the body that appoints also its chairman. Members should come from among the membership of the wider, and less important, Regional Leadership (RL) of the Ba'th party. As RCC chairman,

31

Saddam is by definition also the president of the Iraqi state, the secretary-general of the RL, and the commander-in-chief of the armed forces. Formally, his deputy, Izzat Ibrahim al-Duri, would replace Saddam as president should anything happen to him, although according to the interim constitution, a final decision on succession would be left to the RCC. To preserve a constitutional appearance, then, any prospective successor will have to control the RCC as, indeed, Saddam did on the eve of President Ahmad Hasan al-Bakr's "resignation." Since October 1991, there have been eight members of the RCC, the most important of whom are Saddam, Ali Hasan al-Majid, Taha Yasin Ramadan, Izzat Ibrahim, Tariq Aziz, and Muhammad Hamza al-Zubaydi.

Though party congresses allot the RL a higher standing than the RCC, it is, in fact, a subordinate body. Under Saddam, it became a mere legitimacy-bestowing institution, whose chief purpose is to support the decisions of the president and the RCC. As individuals, however, most of the seventeen RL members wield significant power, largely through other positions, such as RCC member, cabinet minister, or branch party secretary.

Directly under the RCC is the cabinet. Though it has been given some additional authority in recent years, the cabinet is still primarily a forum of bureaucrats charged with the execution of RCC instructions. Cabinet ministers are appointed, dismissed, and supervised by the chairman of the RCC.[1] Members of the RCC who are also cabinet ministers carry special weight, and due to their special relations with Saddam and the internal security apparatus, some cabinet ministers carry more weight than the prime minister (currently Zubaydi, a Shi'ite) and members of the RCC. Indeed, one's real influence over policy-making has less to do with official titles than it does with informal relations with the president and the various instruments of state power.

The 250-member Iraqi parliament, elected since 1980 every four years in a general election, carries very little political weight. First, candidates must be approved following a rigorous screening process, and only Ba'th party members or independents who "believe in the principles and aims of the 17-30 July [1968] revolution" are confirmed. Occasionally, parliament has criticized individual cabinet ministers and demanded their resignation, but it can neither criticize the president nor actually dismiss ministers. A glaring symbol of parliament's weakness is that the RCC has the power to disband it and call for new elections.[2] (Similarly, until Saddam became president in 1979, the judiciary had a certain degree of independence in criminal and civil matters, but this too has since disappeared.)[3]

The Instruments of Power

The Party

During its first period of rule (February-November 1963), as well as during the first years of its second period rule (since 1968), the Ba'th party governed in a totalitarian manner while maintaining a form of democracy in its internal workings. Decisions required majority voting; representatives were elected in a more-or-less democratic fashion; party meeting were often the scene of lively, occasionally chaotic debates; and, significant for Iraq, party members were never arrested or executed for their political leanings. But when Saddam emerged as a powerful political actor in the early 1970s, this picture began to change. By the 1980s, the last remnants of democratic procedures vanished.

When he assumed the presidency in 1979, Saddam faced a dilemma. On the one hand, he wanted the party to expand rapidly, because he saw in it the means to legitimize his rule and provide him with mass support. On the other hand, however, he wanted the party to serve as a docile tool of indoctrination, mass mobilization, surveillance, and control, with no real influence in the affairs of the state. His solution was both to expand and emasculate the party.

Today, there are some 30,000 full or "active" members in the party and over 1.5 million members of lower rank. The party is organized in a rigid hierarchical order from the local "cell" (consisting usually of fewer than ten people) up to the RL. Prior to the invasion of Kuwait, the party militia alone—the poorly-trained Popular Army—consisted of some 650,000 members. Despite these large numbers, the vast majority of party members joined out of opportunism, not principle, and the party's senior echelon only derive authority from its connections with the party's internal security bodies and with Saddam personally.

Theoretically, the party, acting through a general congress or the RL itself, could challenge the president and the RCC; in practice, however, Saddam's grip on power makes such a confrontation highly unlikely. In the event of Saddam's death or a similar political earthquake, senior party functionaries are most likely to splinter. Each is liable to seek the support of his own associates within the internal security apparatus and, less so, the Popular Army. Similarly, they are bound to attempt to forge coalitions with individual army units commanders.

The Internal Security Apparatus

Iraq's internal security apparatus consists primarily of four separate intelligence and surveillance organizations. The most important body is General Intelligence (*al-mukhabarat al-amma*), a 1972 derivative of the

Bureau of General Relations (*maktab al-alaqat al-amma*) which, in its own turn, replaced the Apparatus of Yearnings (*jihaz hanin*), the internal security apparatus established by Saddam Hussein in the underground years of the mid-1960s. General Intelligence has always been directly responsible to the RL and has supervised all the other organizations. As soon as Saddam became president in July 1979, he tightened his grip over this critical body by appointing his half-brother, Barzan Ibrahim, as director-general and another half-brother, Sib'awi Ibrahim, as Barzan's deputy. Due to a family quarrel, Barzan was replaced in late 1983 or early 1984 with a distant cousin, General Fadil al-Barrak, and Sib'awi left his post. Barrak himself was later replaced in October 1989, by Sib'awi Ibrahim, marking a partial end of the family quarrel. Since late 1991, the director-general has been Lt. General Sabr Abd al-Aziz Hussein al-Duri,[4] who was previously chief of military intelligence. Given the twelve-year period when it was under the control of Saddam's close relatives, however, this organization is likely to be fully permeated with members of Saddam's family and tribe, as well as with more distant Tikritis and Sunni Arabs with firm loyalty to Saddam and his clan.[5]

Military Intelligence (*al-istikhbarat al-askariyya*), also in charge of espionage and sabotage activities abroad, is manned mainly by army officers. Until 1991, it was headed by the much-decorated Sabr Abd al-Aziz Hussein al-Duri, a Sunni Arab from Dur, the hometown of Deputy RCC Chairman Izzat Ibrahim. Duri is an old-time Ba'thist, with close family and personal ties to Sadda, who enjoys the respect of both army officers and senior party leaders. Though his political views are not known, it may be assumed that he subscribes to the party's aggressive doctrine.

General Security (*al-amn al-amm*) is, alongside military intelligence, the oldest internal security organization in Iraq, with ties dating back to the monarchy. Though originally manned by professional police and army officers, it has since been thoroughly "Ba'thized" and "Saddamized," especially under the direction of Ali Hasan al-Majid, Saddam's paternal first cousin and minister of defense, who ran the service for several years prior to 1987. He was replaced by General Abd al-Rahman Ahmad Abd al-Rahman al-Duri, who was in turn replaced by Saddam's half-brother, Sib'awi Ibrahim.[6] Because of such control by a close Saddam relative, General Security cannot be viewed as a semi-independent state organization.

Special Security (*al-amn al-khass*) was established in the early 1980s by Saddam's paternal cousin, Hussein Kamil, to provide round-the-clock protection to the president, filling the gap created when the Republican Guard was transformed from Saddam's personal bodyguard into the army's strategic reserve. In addition, Kamil utilized the organization in his attempts to acquire illicit military technology from the West. Between 1988 and 1990 or 1991, the director of Special Security was Hussein Kamil's younger brother, Saddam, who is also married to the president's daughter, Rina; as of 1992, the director was Saddam's second son, Qusay.[7] In recent years, the privileged, tightly controlled, and extremely loyal organization has expanded rapidly, with its membership numbering a few thousand, most of whom hail from Saddam's tribe and hometown of Tikrit. Should Saddam's regime be threatened, they have the most to lose and will fight the fiercest to keep him and the regime in power. In the event of Saddam's death or overthrow, this organization will be the most potent weapon used by Saddam's family to assert one of its own his successor.[8]

In addition to these organizations, two entirely new security units were established in 1991 or 1992. The first, variously termed the "Golden Division" or the "Special Republican Guard," is apparently meant to service as a counter-balance for the Republican Guard should Special Security turn against Saddam in a strategy to cut the overall losses of ruling family. The second unit, comprised mostly of Sunni Arabs from Mosul, Tikrit, and other areas, is known as the "Emergency Forces."[9]

Army

In addition to intelligence services, the army—and the Republican Guard within it—is sure to play a central role in any power struggle, if only because it has the largest number of armed men at its disposal. So far, it appears that Saddam has managed to distance the top army brass from their traditional preoccupation with politics, employing a number of methods to keep them under control. The most important of these is the attachment of party commissars to every army unit down to the level of platoon; commissars not only lead indoctrination sessions but have veto power over the operational decisions of unit commanders. The commissars, in turn, are controlled by the Directorate of Political Guidance (*mudiriyyat al-tawjih al-siyasi*). In addition to the commissars, Saddam exercises control over the army by relying on a thick network of informers and by demanding frequent and humiliating public tribute from ranking officers.[10] Most importantly, he has engineered a series of purges since 1979 that weeded out any officer who showed too much independent thinking or who needed to serve as a scapegoat for military failures.[11] Through such means, the officer corps has been effectively cowed into subservience and docility.

There is only one known case of senior officers directly confronting Saddam, the episode in which army commanders demanded freer rein to conduct the war against Iran following the Faw and Mehran defeats in 1986.[12] This unique case, however, demonstrates the extents of the army's meekness. Not only has the army leadership stayed out of politics, but it waited through six disastrous years of a civilian president and his civilian lieutenants dictating military strategy before registering any objections. Only when the regime itself, and especially Saddam, were in mortal danger as a result of this strategy did the army commanders gather enough audacity to demand that the president allow them to save him.

Indeed, the experience of the Kuwait crisis syggests that the military command preferred not to risk a confrontation with Saddam rather than to warn him of the full implications of a showdown with the U.S.-led military alliance. Specifically, they meekly acquiesced in Saddam's strategy of concentrating troops in Kuwait, rather than to secure their right flank against a left-hook maneuver. They even continued to serve him docilely after the war destroyed half of the army and air force, saying nothing when Saddam fired the minister of defense and the chief of staff for failing to perform the impossible. Moreover, they remained willing to commit atrocities in Saddam's service while putting down the Shi'ite and Kurdish revolts in March 1991.

Such obedience may be explained in more than one way. Undoubtedly, fear of punishment is paramount. An officer who betrays the president may expect that his family will suffer whatever consequences (execution, perhaps) that will befall him. At the same time, the Shi'ite revolutionaries made the error of executing Ba'thist officials, many of them Shi'ites themselves, sometimes alongside their families, and of allowing infiltrators from Iran to assume a high profile. Both of these events were highlighted by Saddam's media and raised fears among the army officers that a Shi'ite victory in Baghdad would mean both mass executions and Iranian domination.[13] Though most of the army command is Sunni, with a heavy Tikriti influence, such fears were common even among the Shi'ites in the officer corps.

Enticement complements fear as a chief instrument of securing obedience. Saddam makes sure that his officer corps is rewarded for loyalty. Senior officers are paid well, receive plots of state land, enjoy grants and easy loans to build homes, and benefit from a number of other economic and social privileges and perquisites. As long as they stay away from politics and refrain from making major professional mistakes, they can expect a prosperous career. Excellence is not a precondition. Joining the party helps, but many army officers are only nominal party members. Abd al-Jabbar Shanshal, the longtime chief of the general staff under the Ba'th, never joined the party.

At present, it is difficult to visualize a field commander that would risk his and his subordinates' lives by attempting to lead an assault on the presidential palace. As long as the party's internal security system and other intelligence bodies are intact, and as long as the officers believe that Saddam's rule is not doomed, the army is unlikely to revolt. However, if there are signs of a systemic breakdown of the regime (e.g., massive food riots in central Baghdad) or evidence that the security apparatus is losing control (from internal rivalries, perhaps), the officers corps is a promising reservoir from which new leaders are likely to emerge. The public, including the Shi'ites and the Kurds, will readily forgive them for their collaboration with Saddam if they represent a somewhat less dictatorial system that stands a chance of improving economic hardship. Indeed, the fundamentalist Shi'ite parties would be ready to cooperate with the army once Saddam and his family are removed from power. Opposition leaders are aware that the distinction between the party and the army is somewhat artificial, but they are sure to welcome the army should it be the vehicle for Saddam's removal.[14] Furthermore, if and when they assume power, the opposition movements will need the army, and judging by their frequent references to the army as "the property of the whole Iraqi people," they will not repeat Khomeini's mistake of destroying their own armed forces.

Republican Guard

The Guard was born as a brigade (one armored and three infantry battalions) under Abd al-Salam Arif in 1963.[15] In 1968, it turned against its master and helped bring the Ba'th party to power. This lesson was not lost on Saddam, who took pains to build up the Guard's loyalty to him personally. Between 1968 and 1982, the Guard was upgraded to an armored brigade and was delegated to serve as the president's bodyguard. When Baghdad itself was threatened during the Iran-Iraq War, the Guard's commander, Kurdish General Hussein Rashid, was authorized to expand it to the strength of an armored division; between 1986 and 1988, it was expanded again in preparation for an offensive, reaching the size of an army group of twenty-five brigades, including an armored division.[16] At that stage, the Guard became the army's strategic reserve.

On the eve of the Kuwait crisis, the Guard consisted of no fewer than 100,000 troops, organized in eight army divisions (including four armored), equipped with some 1,200 Russian-made T-72 tanks. Many of the new recruits were university students who joined the Guard when faced with the option of volunteering or being drafted into the regular army. The benefits of serving in the Guard are numerous, including prestige, better pay, first-class equipment, personal contacts with high party and regime figures, and even the right to carry side-arms during after-duty visits to town; Guard officers are particularly privileged. Though the Guard suffered heavily during the Gulf War, losing around one-third of its tanks, it was able to regroup quickly and spearhead the crushing of the Shi'ite and Kurdish revolts. Since then, the regime has placed high priority on rebuilding the Guard to its previous proportions, chiefly by "cannibalizing" other army units. All signs indicate that most of the Guard remains staunchly faithful to Saddam; its senior officers, though all professional soldiers, are largely hand-picked for their loyalty to the president.[17] Its current commander is Major General Ibrahim Abd al-Sattar Muhammad, a professional officer who rose through the ranks of the Guard.[18] Its wartime commander—General Iyad Futeih Khalifa al-Rawi, a Sunni Arab bedouin from western Iraq and a party old-timer—has since been named chief of staff. The Guards' commander will be an important player in the event of Saddam's passing. Given the Guard's control of Baghdad, all contenders for the presidency will need his (and his divisional commanders') cooperation. If Saddam's whole inner circle is swept away, the Guard's officers, despite their conditioning against involvement in politics, will themselves be natural candidates for the leadership.

In early July 1992, U.S. media cited intelligence sources in reporting that, in late June, Saddam had exposed a coup d'etat planned by a Republican Guard brigade. He is said to have dismissed more than two hundred officers, some of whom were summarily executed. Reportedly, the punishments were carried out by Republican Guards units loyal to Saddam.[19] If true, this story shows that, as of summer 1992, Saddam could still rely on the bulk of the Guards as his main source of military power. At the same time, however, his position was more vulnerable than it had been before the invasion of Kuwait.

Saddam and His Family:
The Informal, Absolutist Monarchy

Though ostensibly ruled by a large and well-organized party via a plethora of republican institutions, Saddam's Iraq is, in fact, a state ruled by one person. The system he has developed to execute and implement his rule is itself a hybrid between a Stalinist-style dictatorship, and a traditional Middle Eastern society, where family, tribe, religious sect, and ethnic group play leading roles. Saddam permits members of his extended family and a few loyal Ba'thist old-timers into high-ranking offices, but he does not share power with them. Instead, save one person (Izzat Ibrahim), he usually shifts them from one position to another. By this means he plays them off against each other, prevents them from building independent power bases, and keeps them constantly guessing as to his next move. Some may have semi-independent power bases, but they are all permeated by Saddam's agents. Alone, none of them is powerful enough to challenge Saddam. Beyond this small circle of loyal—though not fully trusted—lieutenants, Saddam's rule rests on widening circles: his tribe; the city of Tikrit and its environs; and the Sunni-Arab triangle, lying west and north of the capital. Together, they rule the country with the help of some Shi'ite collaborators.[20]

The Majids: Saddam's Paternal Cousins

Most of Saddam's chief lieutenants are members of his extended family. Until November 1991, the most important among them was Lt. General Hussein Kamil al-Majid, his paternal cousin (whose father is Saddam's godfather) and son-in-law (married to Saddam's elder daughter, Ghard). Born in Tikrit in the late 1950s, he, like all the other members of this exclusive club of Saddam's closest associates started his ascendancy from the ranks of internal security. His first significant position was being in charge of security for the presidential palace, and in the early 1980s, he also assumed responsibility for the acquisition of arms production technology. Later in the decade he held the positions of minister of military industry and minister of industry. Until the invasion of Kuwait, he was the only person in Iraq, save the president himself, authorized to sign large-scale contracts with foreign companies without having to refer to the Presidential Palace Bureau, the supreme arbiter in all economic matters. After the Gulf War, he was made minister of defense, the second most important position after the presidency.[21] This was the first time in Iraqi history that a man lacking in military experience—he never served in the army—had been appointed to this post.

In November 1991, Hussein Kamil was removed in a sudden and humiliating way from "all his positions." The reasons were never disclosed, but it may be assumed that he paid the price for his meteoric rise to prominence and undisguised personal ambition. While around Saddam he behaved in a most docile and meek manner, as soon as the president was out of sight he was known to act in an arrogant and dictatorial fashion. Perhaps he paid the price for being perceived as Saddam's heir apparent. In any case, after a few weeks of anonymity, he reappeared in the role of advisor to the president, retaining his military rank. Shortly thereafter he was nominated as supervisor of military industries and of the ministries of industry, oil, and minerals, charged with responsibility for infrastructure reconstruction and very possibly the reconstruction of Iraq's mass-destruction weapons industry, too. That he was not completely out of favor was also evident from the fact that he often accompanied the president on tours of military plants and other installations.[22] By dismissing him in the way he did, Saddam demonstrated how easily he could remove and even humiliate the second most powerful man in Iraq. At the same time, however, it was in his interest to show that there was no real split in the family, which is his innermost power base, and that business remained very much as usual. Another important aspect of this incident was Saddam's careful balancing act: Kamil was replaced by his cousin (who belongs to the same side of the family), Ali Hasan al-Majid (see below), who had been minister of interior. To prevent one side of the family from becoming too powerful, the sensitive ministry of the interior was given to Saddam's half-brother, Watban Ibrahim.

Interestingly, Hussein Kamil is not a member of either of the two highest bodies of the state, the RCC or the RL; in fact, it is not clear whether he has ever joined the Ba'th party. His power rested solely upon his close association with his cousin and father-in-law, not with his credentials as an ideologue or political activist.

At present, the most important Majid and the second most powerful personality after Saddam is Ali Hasan al-Majid, cousin to Hussein Kamil and Saddam. Since November 1991, Ali Hasan has been minister of defense.[23] Born in Tikrit in 1941, he joined the party in 1958, one year after Saddam, and under Saddam's guidance, he has risen through the Ba'th (and later the state) internal security apparatus, serving as director of General Security from 1984 to 1987. At the same time, he has also risen rapidly in the official party hierarchy and was appointed in a 1986 Saddam-initiated purge as member of the RL in charge of all northern Iraq, including Kurdistan. It was in that capacity that he was responsible for the decision to use poison gas against the Kurdish town of Halabja in March 1988. After the ceasefire in the Iran-Iraq War five months later, he issued orders to use poison gas against the Kurdish villages on the Iraqi-Turkish border. Those decisions were decisive in breaking the backbone of the Kurdish rebellion; though he gained notoriety outside Iraq, among the ruling Iraqi elite he was a prime example of the tough and efficient "new Iraqi man."

Ali Hasan played a key role in the negotiations with Kuwait that preceded the August 1990 invasion. Though not the most senior delegate, he was the most important member of the team that met with Kuwaiti representatives in the crucial, final phase of talks in Jiddah on July 31, 1990. Considering his special relations with Saddam, it is very likely that he was the man whose advice carried the heaviest weight when Saddam decided to invade Kuwait. In September 1990, when Iraqi troops in Kuwait were faced with armed opposition, he was sent to Kuwait as governor with orders to eliminate dissent and expedite the "Iraqization" of the "nineteenth province." Within eight weeks he returned to Baghdad having achieved his goals through a combination of terror and an exchange of populations between Kuwaitis (forced across the Saudi border) and Iraqis, Palestinians, and Jordanians (invited to settle in the Kuwaitis' place). In March 1991, he was appointed minister of the interior with wide responsibility for crushing the internal rebellions.

In a succession struggle, Ali Hasan and his brother, a provincial governor named Hashim, may be expected to collaborate with Hussein Kamil against Saddam's half brothers, the Ibrahims (see below). He has a strong base of support in both General Security and, being a longtime Ba'thist, in the party, too. It is possible that many army officers will support him. Should he inherit power in a post-Saddam regime, Iraq is likely to be interested in improving relations with the West and with Gulf Arabs, but it will not be ready to do this at a cost of democratization or of other fundamental changes in national priorities.[24]

The Ibrahims: Saddam's Maternal Half-Brothers

The most important among Saddam's half-brothers is Barzan Ibrahim al-Hasan; Barzan's other brothers are Sib'awi, Watban, and Ghadban (another brother, Idham, died a few years ago). Generally, the Ibrahims are older than the Majids, with better established party records and close links to General Intelligence, the internal security body most intimately associated with the party. Relations between the Ibrahims and the Majids were soured in the early 1980s, when Saddam decided to elevate the latter at the expense of the former. According to some sources, the decline of the Ibrahims can be traced to the 1983 marriage of Saddam's daughter, Ghard, to the young Hussein Kamil, even though Barzan was under the impression that his own son would wed the president's daughter. Saddam's mother died that same year, and a very important link with his half-brothers was severed. In addition, there is some evidence that Saddam mistrusted Barzan, believing that Barzan and his younger brother, Sib'awi, had accumulated too much power.

A native of Tikrit, Barzan (b. 1949) joined the party in the late 1960s and worked as an agent of General Intelligence in Iraq's embassies in London and Geneva following the 1968 Ba'thist revolution. In 1977, he became the chief of the presidential bureau and deputy director-general of General Intelligence, and when Saddam became president two years later, he was elevated to director-general of General Intelligence. In late 1983 or early 1984, he fell from grace and was ignominiously appointed director of a large chicken farm. Apparently rehabilitated, Barzan was sent to Geneva in January 1989 to serve as head of the Iraqi delegation to the United Nations' European headquarters. From there, he is believed to have directed Iraq's European intelligence operations and to have managed Saddam's private funds abroad. In October 1989, Barzan's brother Sib'awi was made director-general of General Intelligence. Barzan himself participated in the negotiations between Tariq Aziz and Secretary of State James Baker in Geneva on January 9, 1991 and is likely that he contributed to Saddam's impression that Baker was bluffing in his threatened use force to expel Iraq from Kuwait. Barzan apparently wields great influence over his younger brothers, Sib'awi, who holds a doctorate in law from Baghdad University, and Watban, who minister of interior since November 1991.[25]

Barzan is usually described as ambitious, opportunistic, hedonistic, greedy, and—when necessary—extremely ruthless. When he ran General Intelligence, it was rumored that he aspired to become president, which may be the reason why Saddam removed him from office and even today prefers to keep him at arm's length. After the Gulf War, Barzan has endeavored to present himself both to the Iraqi public and to Western public opinion as the democratic, secular, and non-doctrinaire alternative to Saddam. In November 1991, he made statements suggesting a possible rapprochement with the United States and he published a number of articles in the Iraqi press in 1992 criticizing the dictatorial nature of all Arab regimes.[26]

In addition to these cousins, Saddam's own sons will participate in the scramble for power should Saddam pass from the scene. Both of them, Uday and Qusay, have periodically been described as prospective heirs, but given the relatively minor positions allotted to them, this possibility has seemed remote. However, Qusay's prospects have brightened considerably since his appointment as head of Special Security. As for Uday, his murder of one of Saddam's bodyguards in October 1988 did not improve the chances of his own succession.

Party Old-Timers

Though not members of his extended family, two other officials are critical players in the Iraqi leadership. The first is RCC Deputy Chairman Izzat Ibrahim al-Duri (b. 1942), a Sunni Arab from the town of Dur, north of

Baghdad, whose daughter is married to Saddam's son Uday. A civilian with no military experience and less than a secondary-school education, Ibrahim was appointed in March 1991 as deputy commander-in-chief of the armed forces and a general of the army; Saddam's apparent reasoning behind the appointment was to humiliate the army's professional officers. The second key official is Taha Yasin Ramadan al-Jazrawi, vice president and commander of the party militia. Ramadan (b. 1938) is a native of Mosul and an Arabized Kurd.[27]

In promoting these men, who technically hold the highest positions beneath the president, Saddam has shown himself to follow a pattern of fueling competition among subordinates in order to neutralize their threat to him. In the event of Saddam's death, they are likely to battle each other for the presidency, each of them trying to recruit support from Saddam's family, from the security agencies under their control, and from the army. Ibrahim and Ramadan are both ambitious, respected inside the party, and experienced in intra-party and intra-regime infighting; should one of them gain the presidency, he would be difficult to dislodge. Though each has been associated with various internal security organizations, Ramadan's main power base is the popular army and the city of Mosul, whereas Ibrahim's support centers around his hometown of Dur.

Ibrahim has always disguised his political views, but Ramadan has sounded his loud and clear. He objected publicly to Iraq's resumption of diplomatic relations with the United States in November 1984, as well as to the rapprochement with Mubarak's Egypt. He is a true Ba'thist hard-liner, and if he reached the top post he may also be expected to steer clear of any economic reforms or rapprochement with the United States and Britain. (He is likely, however, to be more flexible toward other European countries.)

There are a few other leading figures in the party, but they are less influential. Tariq Aziz, the Christian deputy prime minister and ex-foreign minister who has no hope of achieving real power because of his religion, but he would serve as a useful ally to any contender. The same can be said for General Iyad Khalifa al-Rawi, the chief of staff and former commander of the Republican Guard. Flight General Hamid Sha'ban, former commander of the air force and a very religious man, and Minister of Industry Lt. General Dr. Amir Hammudi al-Sa'di, a key figure behind Iraq's conventional military industries and missile development program, are other important players. Zubaydi, the Shi'ite prime minister, is himself a party apparatchick but could provide a more promising candidate with party backing.

It is important to note that if the army does eventually play a stronger role in politics, it may be represented by younger officers of whom relatively little is known. Given that the army has been discouraged from participating in politics for the last two decades, the political views of its officers are a total enigma.[28]

The Legacy of Saddam's Approach to Foreign Policy

Until the early 1970s, when Saddam became the single most important decision-maker in Iraq, the country's Arab and foreign policy highlighted extreme hostility towards the United States, Israel, Iran, and the pro-Western Arab Gulf states. Though not completely devoid of a pragmatic streak, this policy was essentially in line with traditional Ba'thist doctrine. The contribution of Saddam and his close circle to Iraqi policy-making was the introduction of two elements: first, the complete lack of ideological or moral principles, and second, a readiness to take great risks to achieve their main political goals. This combination led to Saddam and his clique to follow policies that fluctuated wildly. For example:

- The Ba'th refused to help the PLO against King Hussein in Black September but opted to send more than half the Iraqi Army to fight alongside the Syrians in 1973.
- Saddam engineered the April 1972 Iraqi-Soviet Treaty of Friendship and Cooperation only to initiate the near-complete severance of relations with the Soviet Union with the slaughter of Iraqi communists in 1978 and the denunciation of the Soviet invasion of Afghanistan in 1979. In the Kuwait crisis, though, Saddam relied on the Kremlin and Red Army "old guard" to come to his rescue.
- Under Saddam's guidance, Iraq headed the Arab world in ostracizing Anwar al-Sadat for his peace initiative, only to resume political (though not full diplomatic) ties with Sadat during the Iraq-Iran War and eventually to ease Egypt's re-entry into the Arab fold under Husni Mubarak.
- Saddam and his close circle never tired from promising "the liberation of Palestine," but when a viciously anti-American and anti-Israeli regime came to power in Tehran, they decided to invade Iran, not Israel.
- In August 1990, Saddam invaded Kuwait, a country which supported his war effort against Iran for eight years.
- On the peace process, Saddam supported the idea of Palestinian-Jordanian-Israeli peace talks in 1983, resumed diplomatic relations with the United States in 1984, and congratulated Washington when its navy entered the

Gulf to defend Kuwaiti shipping in 1987. The same man promised Arafat in April 1990 to "liberate Jerusalem" by military force and to eliminate "all traces of American influence" in the Middle East.[29]

All these policies were devoid of any ideological or other scruples, and they were aimed exclusively to secure the regime's survival and interests at the time. It may be concluded, then, that Saddam and his entourage introduced opportunism and adventurism, to a degree unprecedented even in the Arab world, into Iraq's regional and foreign policy. If Saddam's successors come from within the same circle that surrounds him today, most (but not all) of them may be expected to behave in the same way.

The Political Challenges to the Ba'th Regime

By far the most serious potential challenge to the ruling group around Saddam emanates from within the Sunni Arab, largely Tikriti element inside the army's officer corps, the internal security establishment, and the party officialdom. All these will not act, however, unless mass resentment and disillusionment in the larger Sunni Arab population reach a critical level—and even then, it is not clear whether they would turn against Saddam or fight a rearguard battle for survival against the "people." In any case, despite the difficult phase through which the regime has passed since the Gulf War, there is still no sign that such resentment has built up to tangible proportions.

Less threatening, but not insignificant, are the more than twenty different opposition organizations, some of which have recently moved elements of their operations to the safe-haven zone in northern Iraq. The most important groupings are Kurdish nationalists, Shi'ite fundamentalists, Communists, Arab nationalists (including Nasserists, pro-Syrian Ba'thists, and ex-Iraqi Ba'thists), and liberals. The Kurds and the Shi'ites are, by far, the most potent groupings.

Kurds

The most important Kurdish organizations are Mas'ud Barazani's Kurdish Democratic Party (KDP) and Jalal Talabani's Patriotic Union of Kurdistan (PUK), each of which can muster some ten thousand fighters and possibly more. Until the late 1980s, the two movements were at daggers drawn, with Talabani often collaborating with the Ba'th regime.

March and April 1991 saw a massive Kurdish revolt against the vanquished Iraqi army and the liberation of the whole of Iraqi Kurdistan, followed by a Kurdish military defeat and a retreat into the high, mountainous areas. In the wake of this retreat, some 1.5 million Kurdish men, women, and children fled towards the Turkish and Iranian borders.[30] After that military debacle, representatives of the Kurdistan Front (led by the KDP and the PUK) began negotiations on the establishment of Kurdish autonomy with the Baghdad government; soon thereafter both Talabani and Barazani met separately with Saddam.[31] At the time, the main Kurdish demands were for an independent militia; for the placement of oil-rich Kirkuk in the autonomous zone; for a share in the national budget commensurate with the Kurds' population; and for proportional allotment of positions in government, parliament, and the army.[32]

As months passed, many Kurds grew disenchanted with the prospect of progress in the talks and, in December 1991, Talabani began to openly call for armed struggle to topple Saddam and the Ba'th regime.[33] Given the economic embargo Saddam had by then imposed on Kurdistan, Talabani evidently concluded that Saddam was neither going to cede Kirkuk nor permit the Kurds real autonomy.[34] Even Barazani, who had argued for continuing the talks with Baghdad, was taken aback at the ruthlessness of the embargo, and negotiations soon came to a standstill.[35]

Paradoxically, by establishing a cordon sanitaire around Kurdistan, the Iraqi authorities both helped demarcate the borders of a *de facto* Kurdish state. The boundaries of the Kurdish zone extended roughly from the meeting point of the Syrian-Iraqi-Turkish borders west of Zakhu, southeast along the mountain slope west of Dohuk, east of Mosul, and west of Irbil, then south, leaving Kirkuk in government hands, then further south, leaving Kifri inside the Kurdish zone, then southeast to the Iranian border just south of Kalar. All the settlements mentioned, except for Kirkuk and Mosul, remained inside the Kurdish-controlled area.[36] Even though just over half their territory is located north of the thirty-sixth parallel, and thus officially under the UN umbrella, the Kurds have complete control over the whole area. Talabani's power base is primarily in Sulaymaniyya, whereas Barazani's is further north, in Irbil, Ranya, and Qal'at Diza.

Kurdish elections for an autonomous parliament, postponed three times due to the military and economic pressure from the Baghdad regime, were finally held on May 19, 1992.[37] Eight parties participated, including the KDP and the PUK; Turkoman parties boycotted the poll, apparently because they felt they were not promised adequate representation.[38] The vote itself was a near tie, with the KDP winning 50.22 percent and the PUK 49.78 percent. This translated into fifty seats for each of the parties, with none of the small parties passing the 7 percent threshold needed for representation; five other seats were allocated to Christian minorities. On the personal vote for the presidency, Barazani won 466,819, Talabani 441,057, and about 40,000 votes were divided among other candidates; neither party leader won the necessary 51 percent, but to avoid futher divisions, a second round of voting was deferred. Overall, despite some complaints of fraud and irregularity, all sides agreed not to protest the results of the elections so as not to threaten the legitimacy of the larger Kurdistan Front.[39]

Since its first session in Irbil in June 1992, the Kurdistan National Council has elected a government headed by the PUK's Fu'ad Ma'sum, a former professor of philosophy. As he defined it, the new government's priorities were to promote economic reconstruction, compose a constitution for Kurdistan, and establish a civil service.[40] While the small parties did not hesitate to say explicitly that the new democratic experience was a milestone on the way to complete Kurdish independence, both Barazani and Talabani were far more guarded in their words so as to allay Turkish, Iranian, Arab, and superpower fears.[41] Thus, for example, Barazani told the Turkish government that "elections are not aimed at setting up an independent state [but only] to fill a legal and administration vacuum."[42] Similarly, Talabani informed the Turks that Iraqi Kurdistan would "enjoy the right of self-determination within a [post-Saddam] democratic Iraq."[43]

The most important message of the elections was that, for the first time since the 1960s, the KDP and the PUK overcame their differences and worked in unison for a larger national objective. It is too early, however, to judge how durable is this achievement. In the interim, as long as Western forces continue to neutralize the Iraqi army, the Kurds are likely to concentrate on a quiet effort to build their military force and to promote economic reconstruction and development. As soon as the allies evacuate the area, the military confrontation against the regime will be revived; without massive arms supplies from the West, the Kurds have no chance of maintaining control of Irbil, Sulaymaniyya, and many smaller townlets. In the end, Kurdish military activities cannot be expected to overthrow Saddam's regime, though they will drain precious Ba'thist resources. Secular, pragmatic, and largely pro-West, the Kurds recognize that they must court the few friends they have and will avoid any moves that may antagonize Iran and Syria, who support them now. Should the United States adopt a more assertive posture on the Kurds behalf, acting through Turkey, the equation will shift significantly in their favor, and they may be able to turn their de facto independence into a more permanent existence.

All this is contingent, of course, on the eradication of Saddam and his regime. With Saddam and/or his clique still in power, the Kurds will remain targeted as a principal enemy of the regime; should the Western allies withdraw their protection from northern Iraq, Saddam would surely return to his genocidal program against the Iraqi Kurdish population. But in a post-Saddam, post-"Saddamist" Iraq, the Kurds will be in a strong position to demand precisely the kind of autonomy they want for Kurdistan as well as the proportional representation they seek in Baghdad.

The Shi'ite Fundamentalist Organizations

After more than a decade of minimum harassment from Baghdad, Shi'ite opposition groups were forced underground in 1970 when the Ba'th unleashed a crackdown that included mass arrests, torture, and even execution. Confrontation with the regime reached a peak after the Iranian revolution, when Khomeini called upon Iraqi Muslims, with a special appeal to the Shi'ites, to rise against their "godless" rulers. For the Ba'th regime, such propaganda was (and remains) a major challenge since it highlights both the secularism of the current regime and the disproportionate power Sunnis wield over Shi'ites.

At present, there are more than ten competing Shi'ite fundamentalist movements and organizations.[44] All their leaders live outside Iraq, from Iran to Syria to Britain and other Western countries. The most important group is the Tehran-based Supreme Assembly of the Islamic Revolution of Iraq (SAIRI), led by Muhammad Baqir al-Hakim, a descendent of a renowned, Najaf-based family of clerics. In Iran, Hakim has a fighting force of 4,000-10,000 regulars and paramilitary troops, and SAIRI itself is largely an Iranian front organization. The three other main movements are the Da'wa, led by a mixed group of *ulama* (the best known of whom is Shaykh Muhammad Baqir al-Asifi, the movement's spokesman) and laymen-intellectuals; al-Mujahedin, led by another member of the Hakim family; and the Islamic Action Organization (*Munazamat al-Amal*), led by the Mudarissi brothers, Mahdi and Hadi, hailing from an important *ulama* family from Karbala. Taken together, the membership of these three groups is just a few thousand, most of whom are outside of Iraq.

Despite their numerical strength, the chances of Iraqi Shi'ites achieving power are extremely slim. Even when they fought together with the Kurds in March 1990, they were defeated, and when Kurdish-Ba'thist negotiations started up again, cooperation between Kurds and Shi'ites virtually ceased. This relationship, however, has softened recently as Kurds and Shi'ites have jointly participated in the work of the Iraqi National Congress. The Shi'ite movements' chief problem is maintaining contact with the population inside

Iraq. The south suffers from lack of food, as the government is diverting food supplies to Baghdad to prevent food riots there.[45] Even if food riots break out in the south, the government will exploit them to repress the Shi'ites without mercy; the troops stationed in the south, having witnessed the massacre of Ba'thist officials at the hands of the Shi'ite revolutionaries in March 1991, will be more cruel than ever—regardless of the U.S.-imposed ban on Iraqi overflights.

This does not mean that the Shi'ite opposition has no chance at all. If Saddam is toppled or assassinated, and the Sunni Arab community is unable to settle amongst themselves the issue of succession, infighting may lead to gradual disintegration of the regime. Alternatively, if Saddam continues to refuse the UN offer of food for oil and he spends his remaining cash reserves, massive food riots may erupt in Baghdad itself. If the Shi'ites conduct their affairs more wisely this time, trying to create an alliance with the Sunnis, they may fare better than they did in 1991. Though most of Iraq's Shi'ites are not fundamentalist, the failure to resolve the Sunni-Shi'ite tension may promote the Iranian-backed fundamentalists to the fore of Shi'ite communal protest. Should Shi'ite fundamentalist organizations come to power, in collaboration with Kurds, Communists, Arab nationalists, and ex-Ba'thists, there is a reasonable chance they will choose not reneg on their newly declared commitment to democracy rather than risk a premature confrontation with their coalition partners. At the same time, they will take advantage of democratic freedoms to spread their message in preparation of the next phase of the competition for power. If, by some remote possibility, Shi'ite groups can gain power by themselves, possibly with Iranian support, their behavior is likely to be very different and much closer to that adopted by the Islamic Republic. To them and particularly to SAIRI, the notion of imposing Islamic law in every walk of life is far more important than democracy.

Communists and Ex-Ba'thists

In 1978-1979, the Ba'th introduced a wave of anti-communist terror. All party leaders who were neither executed nor jailed fled abroad, and the party in Iraq ceased to exist as a political body. Today, there are hundreds of members of the various factions of the Iraqi Communist Party in Europe, but they seem to have no grassroots organization inside Iraq itself.

There are a number of Arab nationalist and "socialist" opposition organizations, most conspicuous of which are the ex-Ba'thists. The best-known figure amongst them is Major General Hasan Mustafa al-Naqib (a/k/a Abu Falah). A native of Baghdad, Naqib (b. 1928) joined the party in 1952 and commanded the Iraqi Expeditionary Force in Jordan, where he was wounded in an Israeli air attack in the late 1960s. As deputy chief-of-staff at the time of the Jordan-PLO "Black September" fighting, he was among those Iraqi officers who wanted to side openly with the Palestinians. Because of this disagreement with the leadership in Baghdad, he was dismissed from the army and made ambassador first to Madrid and later to Stockholm. In 1978 he defected and took up a position as Yasser Arafat's military advisor, attacking Baghdad for failing to send troops to Syria to launch another war for the "liberation of Palestine." During the 1980s, he drifted away from Arafat and headed a small, Damascus-based paramilitary force called the Revolutionary Army of Iraq. In the Kuwait crisis, he worked closely with the Saudis, who lent him a clandestine broadcasting station to excoriate against Saddam's regime.[46] Though he is unlikely to retain any influence inside the army twenty years after his dismissal, Naqib is a fairly well-known officer who could serve as a figurehead of an alternative regime.

Another ex-Ba'thi often mentioned as a possible leader of an alternative regime is Salah Umar al-Ali. Born near the town of Tikrit in 1937, he joined the party in the late 1950s, became a member of the RL in the mid-1960s and joined the RCC in 1969. In March 1970, he was named both minister of culture and editor of the party daily newspaper; just four months later, after a thundering confrontation with Saddam, he was summarily dismissed and eventually dispatched as ambassador to Sweden and Spain. In 1978, he was appointed head of the Iraqi UN mission, but resigned in 1982 to seek asylum in the West, where he has resided as a businessman ever since.[47] He, too, is is touch with the Saudis but lacks meaningful support inside Iraq. In 1991, he established a political party and a newspaper in London.

The Independents

Following the Iraqi invasion of Kuwait, a few score of unaffiliated, anti-Ba'thist activists, many of whom were long-time residents in the West, decided to shed their veil of secrecy and publicly announce their opposition to Saddam. These people serve as a very useful link between the Iraqi opposition and Western governments. They met on many occasions, in private and in large groups, with officials of European foreign ministries and the U.S. State Department, trying to gain financial and military support in the opposition's bid to overthrow the Ba'th regime.

The independents' most important political conference was convened in June 1992, when some two hundred activists representing no fewer than forty (mostly small) organizations met in Vienna. They spanned the Iraqi demographic gamut: Shi'ite, Sunni, and Kurdish (KDP and PUK); secular and fundamentalist. Among the most prominent activists in this category are: Ahmad al-Chalabi, a London-based, Harvard-educated banker from an old, Shi'ite-Baghdadi family; Kana'an Makiya, a liberal Shi'ite author and leading intellectual; Shaykh Muhammad Bahr al-Ulum, the moderate and respected head of a Shi'ite cultural center in London; Layth Kubba, the conference's spokesman, a moderate, Shi'ite intellectual active in cultural institutions established by the late Grand Ayatollah Abu al-Qasim al-Kho'i of Najaf; Shaykh Fadil al-Sahlani, Khoi's representative in the United States; Muhammad al-Alusi, a leader of the small [Sunni] Islamic Bloc (*al-Kutla al-Islamiyya*) and scion of an old Baghdadi clergy family; and Salah al-Shaykhli, a leader of the secular, London-based Iraqi Patriotic Accord (*al-Wifaq al-Watani al-Iraqi*). But while the Kurdish parties gave their full support to the Vienna Conference, the two most important Shi'ite parties, the Da'wa and SAIRI, expressed strong reservations;[48] this was because the conference's calls for true democracy and a revised constitution could not have been welcome to the Tehran-backed fundamentalists.[49] In addition, the Communists also decided to boycott the meeting.[50]

The main outcome of the conference was the appointment of a seventeen-member executive board and an 87-member general board empowered to conduct all international contacts for the Iraqi people and thus serve as an "alternative to the dictatorial regime." Though some proposed to house the boards in Kurdistan and declare them an interim government, this resolution was never passed. The final resolutions did, however, promise Kurdish "self-determination" within the framework of a single Iraqi homeland.[51]

In sum, one can reasonably describe the the various opposition organizations inside Iraq (save the Kurds) as lacking any effective, central leadership. In the Shi'ite areas, they are capable of carrying out sporadic armed attacks on military and Ba'th party targets, but such attacks, while demonstrating a certain nuisance value, are unlikely to topple the regime. Southern Iraq is ruled by the Ba'thist troops as enemy territory, and despite the August 1992 imposition of a "no-fly zone" by the Western allies, there is no sign that this military occupation can be terminated through small-scale guerilla warfare.

Things would be different, however, if Saddam could not provide the basic necessities of life for Baghdad and the Sunni Arab heartland. At the moment, despite the fast-rising prices of basic commodities in the free (or "black") market, and the very limited increase in the salaries of the vast majority, the highly efficient food-rationing system (annual cost, $1.5 billion) prevents the spread of hunger.[52] As a result, when Sunnis consider the alternative of a violent Shi'ite takeover, and when the Shi'ites and Sunnis alike consider the perils involved in an anti-government revolt, they are likely to pause. As for the army, the economic conditions of soldiers and, especially, officers, are so far better than those of ordinary people that insurrection is unlikely. As many Iraqis see it, even the existing order is better than mass destruction, blood-shed, and chaos.

If, however, the UN is able to tighten the embargo around Iraq and expose Saddam's secret assets in the West, his chances of survival would be substantially reduced. Even if Iraq and the UN reach an agreement for the export of Iraqi oil under UN Security Council Resolutions 706 and 712, this may be for Saddam a mixed blessing. While it would improve the economic conditions of most Iraqis, thus relieving immediate pressure, it would also demonstrate that Iraq lacks control of its own oil. Furthermore, the UN inspection of food distribution will drive home the message that Saddam is no longer sole master even inside the Sunni Arab areas of Iraq; it will also lead to an end to the regime's embargo of Kurdistan.

Mid-Term Challenges to the Regime

Whoever rules Iraq in the late 1990s will have to start treating a number of cardinal issues that are currently being left to fester. On the socio-political level, the Kurdish and the Shi'ite problems need to be solved in a way that allows the Iraqi state to turn all its energies to economic reconstruction. A regime still headed by Saddam or his close associates has only one way to "pacify" Kurdistan—through force, as Saddam did in 1975, in 1988, and again in March 1990. A successor regime has two options: either to employ force or to concede to the Kurds real autonomy, including a local militia and an equitable share of Iraq's oil revenues (including, possibly, Kirkuk).

Much more difficult to solve is the Sunni-Shi'ite problem. At present, the Arabic speakers of Iraq are split in a way not seen since the 1930s. The most striking feature of the March 1991 uprisings was the extreme hate and violence unleashed during the few days when central control disintegrated in the south. This hate was, no doubt, directed against a ruling party, but it is difficult to separate it from more general Shi'ite resentment of Sunni rule and its Shi'ite collaborators. That this occurred after more than twenty years of gradual economic improvement under the Ba'th—and after eight years of war when Shi'ites fought side-by-side with Sunnis against Iran—confirms the notion that Shi'ite acquiescence to Ba'th rule was a product of fear, not compliance.[53] Even if Sunnis control a post-Saddam Iraq, unless they wish to maintain an iron fist over the south they will have to offer the Shi'ites a partnership in governance and politics. The prospect of economic revival and national integration will itself diminish the influence of Shi'ite fundamentalists.

Perhaps even more daunting will be the economic difficulties ahead. Iraq is, at its core, a very rich country. Not only is Baghdad's claim to 100 billion barrels of oil reserves plausible, but Iraq also rightfully claims some of the finest agricultural land in the world—all this with a relatively low population. Yet, despite its abundant resources, Iraq may expect serious difficulties in the medium term in bringing enough oil to market and in producing enough food to keep balance of payment deficits in check.

Just prior to the invasion of Kuwait, Saddam himself testified that Iraq owed non-Arab countries $40 billion (apparently including debts for military supplies) and, according to Western sources, Iraq owed a similar amount or more to Arab Gulf states.[54] Taken together, such debts in 1990 amounted to some 60 percent of the GDP.[55] And while Iraq had a good chance of being forgiven the Arab debt before the invasion of Kuwait, it is more likely that the Gulf Arabs will press their case now, even in the event of Saddam's own passing. In 1991, the Iraqi government reported to the UN that, on average, full servicing of its debt (probably excluding some Arab debt) for each of the five, subsequent years would require $15 billion, while another $28 billion in foreign exchange would be needed for reconstruction and ordinary consumption.[56] An additional burden will be war reparations to Kuwait and others; if UN Security Council resolutions are any guide, reparations and other UN expenses could equal 30-35 percent of Iraq's oil revenues. In order to generate the $43 billion that the Iraqi government says it needs each year and to pay UN charges at 30 percent, Iraq would need to export $61 billion each year. It is difficult to foresee circumstances under which Iraq could achieve this level of income.

But even the best-case scenario is not an easy one for Iraq. Assuming that Iraq manages to convince creditors to defer debt on Latin-American-style terms and to wheedle the UN to reduce reparations payments to 15 percent of oil revenues, Iraq will still need oil revenues higher than their pre-war levels to meet its own estimates. For instance, if debt payments were $2 billion per year, oil exports would have to be $21 billion per year. While theoretically that could be achieved—with 3.1 million barrels per day exported at $18.50 per barrel—that would require exceptionally good market conditions as well as a re-modeled international environment in which to operate.

First, Iraq will need to cultivate good relations with countries it depends upon for the transit of Iraqi oil, namely Turkey and Saudi Arabia. Ankara wants improvements in contract terms in return for the re-opening of its pipelines; similarly, the Saudis will probably be reluctant to re-open pipeline that runs through their territory and would probably not do so without re-negotiating the generous terms that prevailed before the Kuwait crisis.[57] Better ties with Riyadh will also be essential to secure Iraq's interests in OPEC. Iraq will be interested to keep low the overall OPEC production level and, at the same time, to increase its own quota, which can only be done at the Saudi's expense.[58] But just cultivating the Saudis will not be sufficient. Iraq will also need to develop working relations with the United States, with whom the Saudis are now in closer consultation than ever before.

To generate more funds, Iraq will try to win fresh medium and long-term loans from international agencies and private banks. To convince the international business community of its credit worthiness, Iraq will also need to change radically its national priorities, most important of which is the need to decrease defense spending. In this regard, continued UN supervision over Iraq's military industry will assist any new Iraqi regime interested in changing its spending priorities, because it will be able to present such change as a UN-imposed mandate.

Moreover, to assure prospective lenders that it has forsworn military adventures, Iraq will also have to normalize its relations with Kuwait. This will be far more difficult than improving ties with Iran and Turkey, both because Iraq still does not recognize Kuwait as a sovereign state and because Kuwait is such a tiny and vulnerable neighbor.

Only under optimistic assumptions (debt service covered largely with fresh loans or rescheduling; a 15 percent cap on reparations; the return of all oil outlets "back on line"; and reconstruction and consumption below hoped-for levels) will the Iraqi balance of payments avoid deficits. Perhaps some deficits could be met with reserves frozen by the UN or by hidden reserves, but such reserves have limits. The bottom line is that—barring an oil-price boom—Iraq is very likely to experience a few years of very high rates of inflation and unemployment even after the embargo is lifted.

Given the experience of high economic expectations of the late 1980s, Iraq's economic strife may push the regime toward significant foreign policy modifications. One direction may be a fundamental shift toward the West, as was accomplished by Anwar al-Sadat when radical pan-Arab and military options no longer promised rewards and when the public became fully aware of it after a long and bitter experience under Gamal Abdel Nasser. On the world scene, similar shifts were undertaken by postwar Germany and Japan. But there is an alternative, less positive model. After the 1956 Suez campaign, Nasser and the Egyptian people in general surveyed the American-Soviet support they received and drew the conclusion that radicalism pays off, a conclusion that eventually led to Egypt's military intervention in Yemen and later in the Six Day War. Similarly, after eight years of devastating war against Iran, Saddam opted again for military adventure, in Kuwait, as a way out of economic recession. He would not have done so had he believed he lacked massive popular support.

Therefore, in light of its economic recession, the direction of Iraq's foreign policy during the next five years will depend on two factors: first, the Iraqi people's collective memory of the events of the last war and its aftermath and second, the Iraqi people's assessment of the chances that radical policies will improve its lot. If Iraqis regard the Gulf War as even a limited success, and if they believe that radical foreign policy can bear fruit, then economic difficulties will push them to political radicalism. Should the country continue to be ruled by an offshoot of the present regime, the likelihood of military adventurism will then remain very high, with the leadership adopting Saddam's April 1990 strategy of wooing pan-Arab support through anti-American and anti-Israeli radicalism. In that scenario, even another incursion into the rich Arab Gulf states cannot be discounted. But if, in a post-Saddam Iraq, increasing numbers of Iraqis admit to themselves that the war against Iran was a strategic blunder, that Saddam's threat to "burn half of Israel" only isolated Iraq in Western eyes, and that the invasion of Kuwait led to disaster of immense proportion, then chances for a belligerent and aggressive foreign policy will be greatly reduced.

Over time, there is a good chance that such critical thinking will eventually emerge, because most Iraqis recognize that theirs is a rich country. Given the vigilance of the UN and the international community, the Iraqi people will eventually derive the conclusion that economic prosperity and national integration are better achieved through peaceful development. Iraqis will therefore choose the post-World War II German and Italian models, not their Nazi or Fascist antecedents. In that case, it is difficult to imagine even a despotic tyrant able to convince an entire nation to opt for still another suicidal war.

Notes

1. *al-Dustur al-mu'aqqat* [Interim Consitution] (Baghdad: Ministry of Culture and Information, 1970), clauses 42, 43, 44, 56-58.

2. *Qanun al-majlis al-watani* [Laws of the National Assembly] 55 of 1980, in *al-Waqa'i al-Iraqiyya* [Iraqi Documents], no. 2764, March 17, 1980, pp. 486-496.

3. This was symbolized by the case of Saddam's elder son, Uday, who murdered one of Saddam's bodyguards, was exiled to Switzerland for one week's service as his country's envoy to the United Nations Human Rights Commission, returned home and was then reinstated as head of the Iraqi Olympic Committee, the Football Federation and as chairman of the boards of two newspapers.

4. *al-Thawra* (Baghdad), October 24, 1991.

5. There exists a smaller body within General Intelligence called the "Special Apparatus for the [Preservation] of the Security of the Party and the Revolution" (*al-Jihaz al-khass li amn al-hizb wal-thawra*) which is designed to spy on party members.

6. Baghdad Radio in Arabic, January 11, 1992.

7. *al-Qadisiyya* (Baghdad), January 16, 1992.

8. This survey of internal security organizations is based on *Thawrat 17 Tammuz, al-Tajriba wal-afaq* (The 17 July Revolution, Practice and Horizons, the resolutions of the Eight Regional Iraqi Party Congress), Baghdad, January 1974, p. 139; *al-Thawra,* January 24, 1977; Uriel Dann and Dina Qehat, "Foundations of the Ba'th Regime in Iraq, [and] Nazim Kazzar's Coup d'etat Attempt," [in Hebrew], Moshe Dayan Center for Middle Eastern and African Studies, Tel Aviv University (August 1974); Iraqi News Agency, June 25, 1980, as reported in British Broadcasting Corporation (BBC) radio broadcast, June 27, 1980; Samir al-Khalil, *Republic of Fear* (Berkeley: University of California Press, 1989), pp. 12-16; *International Defense Review*, May 1991; and interviews.

9. *al-Hayat* (Beirut and London), May 10, 1992, quoting Western diplomats; Voice of the Iraqi People, June 1, 1992, as reported in *Foreign Broadcast Information Service-Near East and South Asia (FBIS),* June 3, 1992; Baghdad Radio, April 12, 1992, as reported in *FBIS,* April 6, 1992.

10. For more information on domination mechanisms used by Saddam and the party to keep the army under check, see, for example, *Hurras al-watan* [Guards of the Nation], April 1987, pp. 8-11, an interview with Ali Hasan al-Majid; Uriel Dann, "Foundations of the Ba'th Regime in Iraq: 1968-1973," [in Hebrew], Moshe Dayan Center for Middle Eastern and African Studies, Tel Aviv University (December 1974), pp. 2-6; Marion Farouk-Sluglett and Peter Sluglett, "From Gang to Elite: the Iraqi Ba'th Party's Consolidation of Power 1968-1975," *Peuples Mediterraneens,* no. 40 (July-September 1987), pp. 94-96.

11. Following the 1982 retreat from Khoramshahr, for example, Saddam executed three army generals.

12. See Stephen C. Pelletiere and Douglas V. Johnson II, *Lessons Learned: The Iran-Iraq War* (Carlisle Barracks, PA: U.S. Army War College, 1991), pp. 37-39.

13. These facts are not contested by either side of the Sunni-Shi'ite and government-opposition divides. This is based on an interview with a senior Da'wa activist, July 15, 1991, and an interview with CBS correspondent Bob Simon, August 12, 1991. During a visit to Baghdad and southern Iraq in late May 1991, Simon was told by government officials that Shi'ite revolutionaries executed Ba'th officials (mostly Shi'is) inside al-Husayn's tomb in Karbala; there is some evidence there to support this claim.

14. Interviews with a senior activist in the Da'wa Islamic Party in Europe, September 10, 1990, and July 15, 1991. The Iraqi Shi'i fundamentalist press published in Tehran (the Da'wa weekly *al-Jihad* and *Liwa al-Sadr,* the weekly issued by the Supreme Council of the Islamic Revolution in Iraq) relates to the army in a very different way from that in which they relate to the Ba'th party, terming the former "the property of the people" and calling for its preservation. Nowhere have I found in that press a call for purges of the officer corps after Saddam is toppled.

15. Hanna Batatu, *The Old Social Classes and the Revolutionary Movements of Iraq* (Princeton: Princeton University Press, 1978), p. 1028.

16. See *The Military Balance 1980-81* (London: International Institute for Strategic Studies, 1981), pp. 42-43; *The Military Balance 1988-1989*, pp. 101-102; Stephen C. Pelletiere, Douglas V. Johnson II, and Leif R. Rosenberger,

Iraqi Power and U.S. Security in the Middle East (Carlisle Barracks, PA: U.S. Army War College, 1990), pp. 15-17.

17. Based on Pelletiere, Johnson, and Rosenberger, pp. 14-18; Pelleitere and Johnson, *Lessons Learned,* pp. 37-39; and interviews in Europe and the United States with Iraqi opposition activists and Western officials between September 1990-July 1991.

18. *al-Qadisiyya,* October 20, 1991.

19. See *Ha'aretz* (Tel Aviv), July 8 and 10, 1992, quoting the *New York Times,* July 7 and 9, 1992.

20. For details see Amatzia Baram, "The Ruling Political Elite in Ba'thi Iraq, 1968-1986: The Changing Features of a Collective Profile," *International Journal of Middle East Studies,* vol. 21, no. 4 (November 1989), pp. 447-493.

21. Iraqi News Agency, April 11, 1991, as reported in *FBIS,* April 11, 1991.

22. *al-Qadisiyya,* November 7, 1991; Baghdad Radio, March 3, 1992, as reported in *FBIS,* March 6, 1992; Baghdad Radio, May 18, 1992, as reported in *FBIS,* May 22, 1992; Iraqi News Agency, June 7, 1992, as reported in *FBIS,* June 10, 1992.

23. *Ha'aretz,* November 14, 1991; *al-Qadisiyya,* January 16, 1992.

24. For example, *Hurras al-watan,* April 1987, pp. 8-11; *al-Jumhuriyya* (Baghdad), June 4, 1989; Iraqi News Agency, August 1, 1990, as reported in *FBIS,* August 2, 1990; *al-Thawra,* October 15, 1990; Iraqi News Agency, March 22, 1991, as cited by BBC, March 25, 1991; and interviews.

25. *al-Thawra,* November 12, 1991.

26. For example, *al-Jumhuriyya,* April 8, 9, 11, and 12, 1992, as reported in *FBIS,* April 15, 1992.

27. Ramadan was made vice president following the Gulf War. See, *Alif Ba* (Baghdad), April 3, 1991. For more personal details on both people, see Amatzia Baram, "The Ruling Political Elite in Ba'thi Iraq," pp. 481, 485.

28. For more details on some of these and other party leaders and army officers, see Amatzia Baram, "The Ruling Political Elite in Ba'thi Iraq."

29. Saddam Hussein in a closed meeting with Yasser Arafat in Baghdad on April 19, 1990, in *al-Muharrir* (Beirut and Paris), May 8, 1990, as reported in *FBIS*, May 9, 1990; also see, *al-Thawra*, June 22, 1990.

30. *L'Express* (Paris), February 28, 1992.

31. French News Agency, April 18, 1991, as reported in *FBIS*, April 19 and 22, 1991; Iraqi News Agency, April 24, 1991, as reported in *FBIS*, April 25, 1991; Radio Amman, May 6, 1991, as reported in *FBIS*, May 7, 1991.

32. See the text of the Kurdish propositions in *al-Hayat*, June 26, 1991. For an optimistic progress report on the possible merger of Kurdish fighters (*peshmerga*) with the national border guards and police, see Mas'ud Barazani's interview with the Voice of Iraqi Kudistan, June 16, 1991, as reproduced in *Baghdad* (London), July 12, 1991.

33. Broadcasts by Talabani's PUK clandestine radio, December 20, 1991, as reported in *FBIS*, December 20 and 26, 1991.

34. Talabani's claim was that the main issue was neither Kirkuk nor territory but democratization (*Turkish Daily News*, September 18, 1991, as reported in *FBIS*, September 23, 1991). Yet it is quite clear that while there is a possibility of meeting limited territorial demands, Saddam could never accept real democratization. It would seem, then, that Talabani, for his own reasons, decided that he could not trust Saddam, regardless of the results of the negotiations. For confirmation that territorial issues were the main stumbling block to an agreement, see Barzani's account over the Voice of Iraqi Kurdistan, April 12 1992, as reported in *FBIS*, April 13, 1992, and an interview with Barzani in *al-Majalla* (London), April 1-7, 1992, as reported in *FBIS*, April 9, 1992. Barzani also demanded the lifting of the siege.

35. Barazani evidently still held out the prospect of talks following the May 1992 parliamentary elections in Kurdistan. Voice of Iraqi Kurdistan, May 24, 1992, as reported in *FBIS*, May 26, 1992; interview with *Kurier* (Vienna), May 20, 1992, as reported in *FBIS*, May 21, 1992.

36. *L'Express*, February 28, 1992, p. 30. See also an interview with a Kurdish commander in *Ikibin'e Dogru* (Istanbul), May 31, 1992, as reported in *FBIS*, June 8, 1992.

37. Voice of the People of Kurdistan, May 19, 1992, as reported in *FBIS*, May 20, 1992.

38. Voice of the Kurdistan Revolution, mouthpiece of the KPDP, April 11, 1992, and The Voice of Iraqi Kurdistan, April 15, 1992, as reported in *FBIS*, April 16, 1992. See also Agence France Presse, May 22 and June 2, 1992, as reported in *FBIS*, May 26 amd June 2, 1992, respectively; and Vienna Oesterreich Eins Radio Network, May 21, 1992, as reported in *FBIS*, May 21, 1992.

39. Vienna Oesterreich Eins Radio Network, May 21, 1992, *op. cit.;* and Voice of the Iraqi People, June 3, 1992, as reported in *FBIS*, June 4, 1992. A few days after the elections, three of the small Kurdish parties announced a merger, apparently in order to have better chances in future elections. See Kurdistan Voice of Unification, June 8, 1992, as reported in *FBIS*, June 9, 1992.

40. Voice of the People of Kurdistan, June 8 and 16, 1992, as reported in *FBIS*, June 9 and 17, 1992, respectively; and *Ha'aretz*, July 7, 1992.

41. See, for example, the communique issued by the three small Kurdish parties, broadcast by Kurdistan Voice of Unification, June 8, 1992, as reported in *FBIS*, June 9, 1992. "The Kurdistan people ... will realize independence in the final stage."

42. Agence France Presse, May 17, 1992, as reported in *FBIS*, May 18, 1992.

43. *Ikibin'e Dogru*, May 31, 1992, as reported in *FBIS*, June 9, 1992.

44. For more details, see Amatzia Baram, "From Radicalism to Radical Pragmatism: the Shi'ite Fundamentalist Opposition Movements of Iraq," in James Piscatori, ed., *Islamic Fundamentalism and the Gulf Crisis* (Chicago: American Academy of Arts and Sciences, 1991), pp. 28-51.

45. Interview with CBS correspondent Bob Simon.

46. For example, *al-Jamahir* (Baghdad), July 9, 1963; *al-Waqa'i al-Iraqiyya,* November 7, 1976; *al-Thawra,* Feb. 17, 1978; *al-Safir* (Beirut), June 28 and September 7, 1978; Voice of Palestine (Baghdad), September 6, 1978, as reported by BBC, September 8, 1978; and interviews.

47. *al-Thawra,* March 30, 1970; *al-Hayat,* July 3, 1970; Middle East News Agency (Cairo), July 4, 1970 and June 25, 1978; and interviews.

48. *al-Jihad* (the Da'wa weekly magazine, Tehran), June 15 and 22, 1992; *al-Hayat,* June 9, 1992, interviewing Muhammad Baqir al-Hakim, as reported in *Iraqi File* (*al-Muliff al-Iraqi*) (London), no. 8, July 1992, p. 10.

49. Talabani interview in *al-Ahram* (Cairo), June 18, 1992, as reported in *FBIS,* June 23, 1992.

50. *Iraqi File,* p. 9.

51. *Iraqi File,* pp. 4-7; also, Radio Monte Carlo, Voice of the Kurdistan Revolution, and Kurdistan Voice of Unification, June 20, 1992, and Middle East Broadcasting Corporation (London), June 21, 1992, as reported in *FBIS,* June 22, 1992.

52. *al-Thawra,* March 15, 1992. At the official rate, this would amount to more than $4.5 billion; at the black market rate, just about $150 million.

53. See, for example, the communique of the Islamic Movements following Saddam's invasion of Kuwait, *al-Jihad,* September 17, 1990.

54. *Mahdar muqabalat al-sayyid al-ra'is saddam husayn ma'a al-safira ibril klasbi yawm 25.7.90* (Minutes of the Meeting Between President Saddam Hussein and Ambassador April Glaspie on July 25, 1990), p. 4. The text was published by the Iraqi embassy in Washington in mid-September 1990. According to then-Prime Minister Saadun Hammadi, Iraq's debt to non-Arabs reached, by the end of 1990, $42.1 billion (*Middle East Economic Digest,* May 31, 1991, p. 5) Western sources vary in their assessment of the Iraqi foreign debt. According to *The Financial Times,* by mid-1989 debt had reached $65-$80 billion, half owed to Arab states and half to foreign countries (September 8, 1989). The *Christian Science Monitor* reported (April 17, 1989) that Iraq owed to Western banks alone some $30 billion and to the Gulf Arabs between $50-60 billion. For Iraqi insistence that their Arab debt is, in fact, a

grant, see Saddam's interview with Glaspie and Ambassador Nizar Hamdoon to the *Christian Science Monitor,* April 17, 1989.

55. When calculated according to the official $3.2 to ID1 rate. According to the Economist Intelligence Unit, Iraq's 1989 gross domestic product was $66 billion. EIU, *Country Report-Iraq,* No. 1, 1990, p. 3.

56. Permanent Mission of Iraq to the United Nations, Document No. 73, April 29, 1991, p. 5.

57. According to the original terms, Iraq pays nothing for the passage of its oil through Saudi Arabia. See Economist Intelligence Unit, *Country Report-Iraq,* No. 2, 1991, p. 19. On January 21, 1991, Iraq cancelled "all charters and agreements concluded between the Republic of Iraq and the Kingdom of Saudi Arabia since July 17, 1968." See *Middle East Economic Survey,* April 22, 1991, p. A2.

58. See *Middle East Economic Survey,* April 22, 1991, p. A1.

3

Iranian Politics Since the Gulf War

Shaul Bakhash

Iran reaped considerable benefits from the 1990-1991 war in the Gulf. Iraq, Iran's most dangerous rival in the region, emerged from the war greatly weakened. To secure his eastern flank, Saddam Hussein early in the Kuwait crisis offered Iran highly favorable terms for a peace treaty formally ending the eight-year Iran-Iraq War. Iran's president, Ali-Akbar Hashemi-Rafsanjani, was able to use the cover of the Gulf crisis to advance his often controversial foreign policy aims, and his able handling of the crisis strengthened his hand at home. However, in the aftermath of the war, Rafsanjani did not win for Iran the international recognition or the level of foreign investment that the government had desired. The future of relations with Iraq, and Iran's own role in the Gulf and in future Gulf security arrangements, remained uncertain.

At home, hardliners continued to seek to hobble the government's domestic and foreign policy. Rafsanjani succeeded in greatly diminishing the weight of the hardliners in the *majlis* (parliament), when his supporters managed a sweeping victory in the spring 1992 parliamentary elections. But a legacy of revolutionary ideology and attitudes, combined with bureaucratic lethargy and pressures from entrenched interests, continued to constrict the government's freedom of action. Popular discontent, both economic and political, remained high, rendering any attempt to open up the political system risky for the regime.

63

Iran and the Gulf Crisis

Saddam Hussein's invasion of Kuwait in August 1990 posed a serious threat to Iran's vital interests. Not only did Iraq annex Kuwait, acquire access to Kuwait's Persian Gulf ports, and gain control over Kuwait's oil and financial resources, but it also inspired mass popular Arab support that might have crowned Saddam's success. Together, these achievements would have upset the regional power balance and given the Iraqi president considerable freedom to shape Gulf politics. Saddam would have been in a position to cow the Arab states of the Gulf and to set the agenda for the Organization of Petroleum Exporting Countries (OPEC).

Moreover, at the time of the invasion, Iraqi troops were still in occupation of Iranian territory. Given Iraq's considerable advantage in armaments, Iran could not have hoped by force of arms to expel these Iraqi contingents. Saddam seemed unlikely to withdraw unless Iran agreed to concede to Iraq complete sovereignty over the Shatt al-Arab, thus abrogating the 1975 Algiers agreement under which the two countries had agreed on joint sovereignty over the narrow waterway that constitutes Iraq's only outlet to the Gulf. It was to undo the Algiers agreement that Saddam had invaded Iran in 1980. His grab for Kuwait, therefore, confronted Iran with the prospect of territorial losses and a sharp shift in the regional balance of forces.

When President Bush deployed U.S. troops in the Gulf, Iranian officials thus made noises critical of the massive Western military buildup. But Iran's fundamental policy was not in doubt.[1] The government never wavered in condemning the invasion of Kuwait, demanding unconditional Iraqi withdrawal, and rejecting any changes in international frontiers through the use of force. Alarmist prognostications notwithstanding, Iran did not break the UN-sanctioned trade embargo against Iraq. When Saddam Hussein sought safe haven for Iraqi military and civilian aircraft in Iranian airfields, Iran went through the motions of protesting the violation of Iranian airspace and quietly accepted the aircraft, but it showed no inclination to help Saddam in any other way. If Saddam hoped to persuade Iran to break the UN embargo by dangling before its leaders the possibility of a peace treaty favorable to Iran, he was badly disappointed. Throughout the Gulf crisis and at least until the outbreak of hostilities, it is true: Iran sought to maintain reasonably good relations with Iraq in order to nail down a peace treaty. But on the critical issue of recognizing or facilitating Iraq's annexation of Kuwait, Saddam Hussein's apparent readiness to offer Iran favorable peace terms did not materially alter the Iranian position.

To mollify anti-American sentiment at home, to blur the fact that Iranian and U.S. interests happened to coincide on the need to stop Saddam, and to maintain standing with an Islamic constituency in the Middle East and elsewhere to which Saddam was also appealing, the government did make a number of symbolic gestures. It pretended to neutrality between two equally "arrogant" and unjust states, Iraq and the United States. It routinely condemned the size of the U.S. military presence in the Gulf, although Rafsanjani also said that the military buildup, however unwelcome, might be tolerated if it served a positive end. The government expressed concern over the scope of U.S. and allied bombing of Iraqi urban centers and provided some humanitarian aid, in the form of food and medical supplies, to Iraq's civilian population. In the middle of hostilities in February 1991, Rafsanjani even sought to cast Iran in the unlikely role of mediator between Iraq and the alliance of states ranged against it.

Iran also declared itself opposed to the physical dismemberment of Iraq. On this issue, the government was probably not seeking merely to mollify international opinion. Despite the hopes the Islamic Republic had entertained in the 1980s of seeing a Shi'ite regime installed at Baghdad, by the time of the Kuwait crisis, Iran's leaders appear to have concluded that the dangers resulting from the breakup of Iraq would have far outweighed any advantages that might have accrued to Iran. From the beginning of the crisis until virtually the end of the fighting in February 1991, Iran did not revive the call for an Islamic government to replace the Ba'th regime. The government kept on a tight leash the Iraqi Shi'ite leader and head of the Supreme Assembly of the Islamic Revolution of Iraq (SAIRI), Ayatollah Muhammad Baqer Hakim, living in exile in Iran.

When the Shi'ites in the south rose up against the Ba'th regime at the end of the Gulf War, Iran did provide some assistance. It allowed armed contingents faithful to Ayatollah Hakim and recruited in Iran from among Iraqi Shi'ite prisoners of war to cross over into Iraq. It no doubt provided financial and some military assistance to the uprising; and it began once again to call for the overthrow of Saddam Hussein. Given the Islamic Republic's long-standing commitment to the Iraqi Shi'ite community and the powerful emotions aroused in Iran by the bloody repression of the Shi'ites, the Iranian government could hardly have done less.

What is striking, though, is the limited nature of the Iranian response.[2] Rafsanjani wished to avoid getting deeply involved in the morass of Iraq's internal politics, committing Iranian troops to the Iraqi Shi'ite cause, and exacerbating Iran's relations with Saddam Hussein. Moreover, he did not wish to be accused of conspiring with the United States at the break-up and destruction of another Muslim country. The restraint shown by Iran, moreover, was fully in keeping with the overall thrust of Rafsanjani's foreign policy. He had no desire to damage the image he had been carefully nurturing of an Iran that could be a responsible member of the international community.

The Gulf crisis did result in an unexpected windfall for Iran. Though fighting between Iran and Iraq ended with a ceasefire in August 1988, negotiations towards a peace agreement, with the UN secretary-general serving as an intermediary, deadlocked over the issue of sovereignty over the Shatt al-Arab and were discontinued. In June 1990, negotiations resumed, this time direct and face-to-face. This came about largely at Saddam Hussein's initiative and also because Iran concluded that the Iraqi leader was willing to be more flexible. In retrospect, it seems clear that when he reopened talks with Iran, Saddam Hussein was already planning the invasion of Kuwait and desired to secure his eastern flank before moving his army southward. But again, the negotiations stalled because of the Shatt question, when Iraqi troops crossed into Kuwait on August 2, 1990.

On August 14, twelve days after the invasion of Kuwait, Saddam wrote directly to Rafsanjani. In that letter, he announced a unilateral withdrawal of Iraqi troops from Iranian territory, offered to begin an immediate exchange of prisoners of war, and—although his wording here seemed deliberately imprecise—implied he would settle the Shatt issue on Iran's terms. "Oh President Ali-Akbar Hashemi-Rafsanjani," he wrote, "everything you wanted and on which you have been concentrating has been achieved."[3] Within weeks, Iraqi troops withdrew unilaterally from most, and eventually from all, occupied Iranian territory, and all but a few thousand of the POWs held on each side were exchanged. Iran and Iraq reestablished diplomatic relations and exchanged ambassadors. Discussions on a comprehensive peace agreement were resumed.

Rafsanjani also used the cover of the Gulf crisis to advance the foreign policy aims he had already been pursuing. In 1988, Rafsanjani had secured Khomeini's approval for an initiative to improve Iran's relations with European states. This initiative was derailed when Khomeini, in February 1989, called for the assassination of Salman Rushdie, whose book, *The Satanic Verses*, was considered offensive to Muslim sensibilities. After Khomeini's death in June 1989, Rafsanjani resumed his attempt to reintegrate Iran into the international community, to build fences with the Persian Gulf states, and to attract foreign investment to Iran. For example, he resumed diplomatic relations with Great Britain, without insisting, as the Iranians had done in the past, that the British government denounce Rushdie and either ban *The Satanic Verses* or remove it from circulation.

Under cover of the Gulf War, Rafsanjani also resumed diplomatic relations with Egypt and Jordan and laid the groundwork for a resumption of diplomatic relations with Saudi Arabia. Iranian-Saudi relations were reestablished shortly after the end of the Gulf War. All these were controversial measures in domestic politics. Under Khomeini, Jordan was deemed a "reactionary" Arab monarchy with which the Islamic Republic said that it saw no need to maintain relations. The break in diplomatic relations with Egypt in 1979 had been ordered by Khomeini himself to signal displeasure with the Camp David Accords. Relations with Saudi Arabia had been ruptured in 1987, after clashes between Saudi police and demonstrators in Mecca during the *hajj* pilgrimage left four hundred dead, most of them Iranian. The large, radical faction in the *majlis* opposed the normalization of relations with all three of these countries.

Moreover, in April 1991, Rafsanjani finally managed the release of an Englishman, Roger Cooper, who had been held in Iran for several years as a spy. The radicals in the *majlis* had also persistently resisted Cooper's release. After the Gulf War, Rafsanjani acquiesced in the extension of the Syrian military presence, and eventually in a considerable degree of Syrian control, in Lebanon. This implied diminished Iranian support for the most radical of Iran's Shi'ite proteges in Lebanon; and, during 1991, Rafsanjani used Iran's influence with these groups to secure the release of all the remaining American and British hostages held in Lebanon.

Rafsanjani's Lebanon policy underlined the split in the Iranian leadership between the pragmatists, whom he led, and the radicals, who continued to urge the export of the revolution and militancy in the confrontation between Islam and the "arrogant" world powers, particularly the United States. Iran had invested considerable effort and resources in Lebanon's Shi'ite community. It funded welfare services, including schools, mosques, and clinics. It helped train younger clerics and reinforced the prominence of established Shi'ite religious leaders like Shaykh Muhammad Hussein Fadlallah, who in turn reinforced Iran's claim to leadership of the Shi'ite community outside Iran's borders.

Beginning in summer 1982, Iran also kept a contingent of Revolutionary Guards in the Biqa' Valley. It supported the most radical of Lebanon's Shi'ite factions, including Hizbollah and Islamic Jihad, and helped fund and train one of Lebanon's many armed militias. Lebanon had been the scene of America's humiliation, where U.S. citizens could be taken hostage with seeming impunity and from where U.S. marines were forced to beat an unseemly retreat in 1983. Lebanon was the base from which the armed struggle against Israel could be continued. It was to be the first country after Iran in which an Islamic Republic would be established. Even a partial Iranian disengagement in Lebanon was, therefore, highly controversial in terms of domestic politics.

The overriding consideration driving Iranian foreign policy was economic. Following the end of the Iran-Iraq War, Iran faced a massive task of reconstruction which it could not hope to carry out without foreign investment and technical assistance. The five-year development plan, launched in 1990, called for $28 billion in short and long-term foreign credits (the government still avoids the term foreign "borrowing") for a host of ambitious industrial projects in oil, gas, petrochemicals, steel, copper, motor vehicle assembly, dams, electric power generation, consumer durables, and construction materials production.[4] With a population of sixty million and a birth rate of around 3.7 percent, the task of providing food, housing, schools, university places, jobs, and health care for nearly two million more Iranians each year appeared formidable. These harsh realities persuaded Rafsanjani and his advisors that it was time to rein in revolutionary fervor and attend to domestic problems.

After a decade of massive state intervention in the economy, disillusion had set in. Rafsanjani and his people concluded that the state was a cumbersome engine for economic development and were anxious to encourage greater private sector activity and to attract foreign investment to the country. In 1988, Rafsanjani secured Khomeini's approval for a limited move in this direction, but he could not pursue these goals without control over the radical factions and radical ideologies at home. His foreign policy goals thus generated their own domestic imperatives.

The Limits of Success

Rafsanjani's attempt to reorient Iran's foreign policy was assisted by the Gulf crisis, but there were limits to his success in the critical areas of Gulf security, relations with Iraq, relations with the United States, and the attraction of foreign investment.

First, little came of initiatives, including those promised by the White House, for Persian Gulf security arrangements. Iran continued to press for regional security arrangements based exclusively on the Gulf states and excluding outside powers. This formula appeared to serve Iranian interests by providing a means for containing Iraq, ensuring Iran a dominant military role in the Gulf, denying the United States or non-regional Arab states such as Egypt and Syria a significant military presence in the region, and perhaps also permitting, by mutual agreement, lower expenditures on armaments. However, interest in regional security arrangements receded into the background once the Gulf War was over. In the immediate aftermath of the war, the United States was preoccupied with the Kurdish uprising in northern Iraq and the Shi'ite uprising in the south, as well as with the task of dismantling Iraq's nuclear, biological, chemical, and offensive war-making capacity. In subsequent months, the energies of the Bush administration were absorbed by the Arab-Israeli peace initiative. Saudi Arabia and Kuwait seemed more interested in the protective shield offered by a U.S. military presence than in regional security arrangements; at the same time, Saudi Arabia launched its own, massive armament acquisition program which it pursued outside any framework of regional agreements. Indeed, the Arab states of the Persian Gulf probably concluded from the Gulf War that they alone were incapable of containing Iraq without outside assistance. Iranian ideas for cooperative military arrangements among the Gulf states were not highly developed. Iranian and American ideas regarding Gulf security arrangements continued to diverge. Moreover, the survival of Saddam Hussein made more problematic any regional security arrangements, with or without Iraq.

Second, U.S.-Iranian relations did improve, but in small increments and not dramatically. There were a number of positive signs. During the Gulf War, Iran and the United States communicated frequently through Swiss and other intermediaries. Iranian criticism of the U.S.-Kuwait military basing agreement, concluded in September 1991, was surprisingly muted.[5] Iran persisted in a harsh anti-American rhetoric, especially following the start of U.S.-sponsored talks between Israel, the Arab states and the Palestinians in October 1991,[6] but this did not hamper the release of U.S. hostages in Lebanon. In the autumn, the United States finally released $270 million in Iranian funds related to arms purchased and paid for before the revolution but never delivered. Washington also eased restrictions on Iranian imports, and the release of the last American hostages in Lebanon was expected to clear the way for the lifting of the remaining restrictions on bilateral trade.

Nevertheless, on both the American and the Iranian side, normalization of relations was hampered by the combination of past burdens and current sources of friction. In the United States, the taking of American hostages in Tehran and Lebanon, the bombing of the marine headquarters in Beirut, and other acts of terrorism with which Iran was associated were not easily forgotten. Several other sources of friction emerged in the aftermath of the

Gulf War. Some attempt by Iran to reequip its military forces was to be expected, but administration sources voiced concern over the size of the Iranian military buildup. The administration also concluded that Iran was attempting to develop a nuclear capability (although the evidence here was in dispute) and tried to discourage the sale by third-countries to Iran of nuclear-related equipment that might be diverted to military purposes. Also standing in the way of any U.S. initiative to improve relations were Iranian attempts to organize opposition to the Arab-Israeli peace talks; Iranian support for the radical Islamic movement in the Sudan; evidence that Iran was involved in the assassination of Iranian opposition figures living abroad; and Iran's human rights record at home.

Inside Iran, revolutionary propaganda had associated America with hostility to the revolution for over a decade. The United States was blamed for Iraq's 1980 invasion and for supporting Iraq during the subsequent war; for permitting Saddam Hussein to crush the Shi'ite uprising in Iraq in 1991; and for blocking European investment in Iran. The American downing of an Iranian civilian airbus in the Persian Gulf in 1989, killing over 290 passengers and crew, was not easily forgotten. U.S. opposition to the sale of nuclear and other technology to Iran combined with Iran's perception that Washington stood in the way of possible World Bank loans for development projects also exacerbated relations.

Third, the withdrawal of Iraqi troops from Iranian territory and the exchange of POWs did not result in the conclusion of a formal peace treaty with Iraq. A close reading of Saddam Hussein's August 14, 1990 offer to Iran suggests that the Iraqi president did not intend to revert to the arrangements for shared sovereignty over the Shatt al-Arab agreed under the 1975 Algiers accord. Rather, he was only offering Iran shared administration of the Shatt in exchange for a recognition of full Iraqi sovereignty over the waterway. But his deliberately vague wording tended to obfuscate the nature of the Iraqi offer. Saddam, in any case, made his peace offer to Iran hoping that the Iranians would assist him in breaking the UN-imposed embargo. When Iran refused, Iraq had little incentive to make further concessions. Relations between the two countries deteriorated further following the Shi'ite uprising in southern Iraq. Saddam accused Iran of instigating and supporting the uprising; Iran strongly criticized the harsh repression of the rebels, the killing of fellow Shi'ites, and the damage done by Iraqi troops and artillery to the holiest of Shi'ite shrines in Najaf and Karbala. By April, relations were once again badly strained, and there was still no sign of a peace treaty.[7]

Fourth, the investment Iran expected from Europe and Japan did not materialize. Many projects were discussed, but few reached the stage of actual implementation or led to the commitment of substantial external funds to Iran. This derived only in part from lingering concerns in the West regarding Iran's international behavior. The slow pace of foreign investment was due in large measure to domestic conditions in Iran itself.

Consolidation at Home

Rafsanjani's deft handling of the Gulf crisis accelerated the pace of consolidation of his authority at home. His position was also more secure because of a series of domestic developments: approval of constitutional amendments that enhanced the authority of the president, the post Rafsanjani held since July 1989; widespread national fatigue with years of revolutionary turmoil and experimentation; heightened appeal of Rafsanjani's foreign and domestic policies to a significant middle class constituency; and Rafsanjani's ability to translate these sentiments (and his control over the election machinery) into electoral victory in the 1992 parliamentary elections.

In the years before Khomeini's death, Iran's politics were characterized by competition among three factions. A faction led by Rafsanjani—who, for want of a better term, are herein described as the "pragmatists"—emphasized economic development at home, a larger role for foreign investment and the private sector in the economy, and normalization of Iran's relations with the international community; export of the revolution had a relatively lower priority. This group controlled about half the votes in the *majlis* and was strongly represented in the foreign ministry and by technocrats in some of the other government organizations, such as the Central Bank and the Plan and Budget Organization. It had wide appeal to the middle and propertied classes. Its main media outlets were state radio and television, which was under the direction of Rafsanjani's brother, and the sister newspapers *Ettelaat*, one of the two largest in the country, and the *Tehran Times,* which generally reflected the views of the Rafsanjani faction and the foreign ministry.

Khomeini often listened to Rafsanjani's advice, particularly on foreign policy issues and increasingly in economic matters. But Rafsanjani headed no organized party or movement. His strength derived from his proximity to Khomeini, his ability to secure the services of technocrats with important skills and to place them in key positions, his intelligent use of patronage, and his success in forming loose coalitions in support of his key policies.

A second faction represented the views of conservative clerics, such as Ayatollah Ahmad Azari-Qomi, publisher of the Tehran newspaper *Resalat*.

The conservatives sought a strict application of Islamic law in matters affecting women and social behavior and the application of strict Islamic standards in legislation. They were upholders of private property and favored private sector activity in the economy. They were strongly represented in the Council of Guardians, the powerful watchdog body of senior Islamic jurists and experts in Islamic law that is empowered to strike down legislation considered in violation of Islamic or constitutional law. The smallest of the factions, the conservatives derived their strength from within the clerical hierarchy and the following that individual clerics sympathetic to conservative views could themselves mobilize.

A third faction represented radical elements among the clerical hierarchy, government officials, and political activists. Like the faction identified with Rafsanjani, the radicals were a loose and often shifting coalition, not an organized movement. But in the last years of Khomeini's life, the radicals came to constitute a formidable group, controlling half, and perhaps more, of the votes in the *majlis*. The prime minister, Mir-Hussein Musavi, was one of their men, as were members of his cabinet in such key ministries as interior, labor and industry. Among their clerical spokesmen were Interior Minister Ali-Akbar Mohtashami and Muhammad Musavi-Khoeniha, the mentor of the "students of the Imam's line" who had seized the American hostages at the U.S. embassy in 1979. Chief Justice Abd al-Karim Musavi-Ardabili articulated views close to those of some in the radical camp on the necessity of distributing wealth and property.

The radicals also enjoyed the backing and close cooperation of Khomeini's son, Ahmad. *Kayhan*, *Ettelaat*'s rival, reflected their positions, as did another Tehran daily, *Azadegan*. By 1991, Mohtashami was publishing his own magazine, *Bayan*, while Khoeniha was publishing another weekly, *Salaam*. Both these publications reflected radical views. The radical constituencies were to be found among university students, some elements in the civil service, in some of the Islamic associations established in workplaces, and particularly in the revolutionary organizations, such as the Revolutionary Guards, the revolutionary committees, the Crusade for Reconstruction, the Foundation for the Disinherited, and the Martyrs' Foundation. One of the radical *majlis* deputies, Muhammad Ebrahim Asgharzadeh, who had participated in the seizure of the U.S. embassy, established a network of *vahdat* (unity) committees through which he sought, with some success, to organize and enlist university students and seminarians in the radical cause.

The radicals remained hostile to the private sector and efforts to normalize relations with either the West or conservative Arab regimes. At home, they were committed to state control of the economy, more radical measures of distributive justice, power for the revolutionary organizations, and the maintenance of revolutionary spirit. They were hostile toward foreign investment and any enhancement of the role of the foreign and domestic private sector in the Iranian economy. Abroad, as already noted, they favored export of the revolution, support for radical Islamic movements, and opposition to Israel and the United States.

While alive, Khomeini sought to maintain a degree of balance between the pragmatists and the radicals. After his death, the Rafsanjani-led pragmatic faction made progress at the expense of the radicals. This shift occurred in part because of amendments to the constitution to which Khomeini gave his approval in 1988 and which were formally enacted in July 1989. These amendments considerably enhanced the powers of the president. The office of prime minister was abolished, and his extensive powers were transferred to the president, who until then had played a largely ceremonial role. As president, Rafsanjani named the cabinet, headed the National Security Council, a body charged with setting broad defense and internal security policy, and was directly responsible for the Plan and Budget Organization, one of the key economic organizations in the government.

Supreme authority, as under Khomeini, continued to be vested in the *faqih*, or the supreme Islamic jurist, in his role as heir to the mantle of the Prophet. But Ali Khamene'i, Khomeini's successor, lacked Khomeini's charisma, scholarly eminence, and the authority Khomeini could claim as the leader of the revolution. As a result, Khamene'i was in no position to exercise the vast powers vested in the *faqih* by the constitution. In fact, the requirements for the office of *faqih* had to be downgraded in the amended constitution to permit a cleric of lesser eminence such as Khamene'i to succeed Khomeini. The selection of Khamene'i as *faqih* weakened the overall authority of the state, whose very legitimacy was supposed to derive from the scholarly eminence and knowledge of Islamic law of the supreme Islamic jurist. But it meant that within the government structure itself, the balance of authority between the *faqih* and the president had shifted in latter's favor. Following Khomeini's death, it was evident that Rafsanjani, not Khamene'i, ran the government and made the major policy decisions.

Rafsanjani also consolidated his position through the power of appointment. He co-opted or neutralized many of his radical rivals by dropping them from the cabinet and other important positions, or by appointing them to largely ceremonial posts and advisory positions lacking executive authority. He established firm control over economic policy, naming his own men to run the key economic organizations, such as the Central Bank, the ministries dealing with economic affairs, finance, industry, commerce and oil affairs, and the Plan and Budget Organization. His minister of education introduced sweeping changes in the personnel of his ministry, sweeping out the radicals. His minister of interior, Muhammad Yazdi, introduced similar changes in the appointees to the posts of governor-general down to the district officer level in the provinces. This implied more central control over provincial governments and also over *majlis* elections.

At Rafsanjani's behest, the *majlis* approved legislation placing the heretofore separate organizations of the army and the Revolutionary Guards under a single command structure. It also approved the merger of the revolutionary committees with the national police and gendarmerie into a single security organization. This did not mean that the troublesome Revolutionary Guards and committees were fully under government control; the Guards particularly continued to enjoy considerable autonomy. But the legislation was, nevertheless, a clear signal of the government's intentions regarding these revolutionary bodies.

Two years after Khomeini's death the shift in the balance of power between the radicals and the Rafsanjani camp was evident in many spheres. The radicals had lost control of the cabinet and its key ministries. With Khomeini's death, the political weight of his son, Ahmad, was considerably reduced. Khamene'i, the new *faqih*, worked closely with Rafsanjani. The radicals were amply represented in the awkwardly-named but potentially-powerful Council for Determining the Interests of the System of the Islamic Republic, a body established by Khomeini in 1988 to adjudicate differences between the Council of Guardians and the *majlis* over legislation. However, during the first two years of Rafsanjani's presidency, it was convened only rarely, and in May 1991, Khamene'i further diluted the influence of the radical members of the body by appointing three of his personal representatives to the council, shifting the weight of the membership against the radical faction. The Islamic associations and the "unity" committees remained radical strongholds in the workplace, the universities, and the seminaries, but they appeared less powerful than in the past.

In the *majlis,* the strength of the radical bloc remained intact, at least until the spring 1992 elections. But even there, the weight of the radicals appeared somewhat diminished. For example, the radicals were able to unseat Rafsanjani's minister of health on a no-confidence vote in January 1991, but a similar move to unseat the minister of education several months later was decisively defeated. In 1990, changes were made in the qualifications for candidates to the Assembly of Experts, a body that has the critical role of selecting the *faqih*, that can depose an incompetent supreme leader, and that will choose Khamene'i's successor; such alterations effectively blocked the candidacy of many radical clerics. A number of aspiring radical candidates were, in fact, disqualified when elections to the Assembly of Experts were held under the new regulations in October 1990, and delegates identified with Rafsanjani and Khamene'i swept the vote. The radicals had been threatening to utilize a hoped-for majority on the assembly to control the actions of Khamene'i as *faqih*.[8] The composition of the new assembly took on added significance, since it could be in a position to select the successor to the ailing Khamene'i if he had to be replaced before his eight-year term ran out. The government's ability to exclude the radicals, or many of them, from the Assembly of Experts was a further sign of their diminishing influence.

More seriously, some of the radicals sought to challenge the authority and qualifications of Khamene'i as *faqih*. Such a challenge, though indirect and implicit, was mounted in autumn 1990, during the controversy over the election of the Assembly of Experts. The challenge was considered sufficiently serious for the pro-Rafsanjani, pro-Khamene'i faction to secure statements of support for Khamene'i from the army, the Revolutionary Guards, the Islamic propaganda organization, and *majlis* deputies.[9] Another grave attempt to weaken Khamene'i and, by extension, Rafsanjani, came in autumn 1991, when a number of deputies openly began to court Ayatollah Hussein Montazeri, Khomeini's former successor-designate, as supreme leader.[10] Khomeini had disqualified Montazeri from the succession in 1988, criticizing him for lacking leadership qualities. Montazeri was disgraced and ended up living under quasi-confinement in Qom. Montazeri had a reputation of militancy on foreign policy issues, and by courting him, the radicals were clearly seeking ways of undermining Khamene'i and blocking Rafsanjani's foreign and domestic policy programs. The approach to Montazeri was perhaps an indication of the desperation of the radicals and the extent to which they were prepared to go stop Rafsanjani. This attempt fizzled out, too.

More dramatic evidence of Rafsanjani's growing dominance came during *majlis* elections held in two stages in April and May 1992. As in the Assembly of Experts elections, several radical candidates were disqualified, this time on the basis of a ruling by the Council of Guardians, which appropriated to itself a heretofore unclaimed authority to vet all candidates. Protests from the radical camp led only to a partial reinstatement of the disqualified candidates. During the election campaign, the divisions within the ruling group were much clearer, particularly in the all-important Tehran constituency, with its twenty-eight seats. The supporters of Rafsanjani generally appeared under one list, the radicals under another. The issues between the two camps were clearly posed, at least in the large urban constituencies. The election results proved a virtual rout for the radicals. In Tehran, the entire list associated with the radical camp was defeated; and such leading radicals as Karroubi, Mohtashami, and Khoeniha failed to win seats. By contrast, men closely associated with Rafsanjani did well. In the provinces, a number of radicals were returned; nevertheless, Rafsanjani was assured of a clear majority. The government's control over the election machinery clearly helped determine the results and voter apathy was widespread, but the vote also appeared to indicate a rejection of radical formulas for the economy and foreign policy, as well as an endorsement of Rafsanjani's more pragmatic line.

Yet if the radical challenge to Rafsanjani in the post-Khomeini period was insufficient to derail the president's foreign and economic policies, it often forced Rafsanjani to revert to a radical rhetoric on a number of foreign policy issues and to move with greater caution in pursuing his policies both at home and abroad. This remained the case both before and following the parliamentary elections. The persistence of a radical lobby within the ruling group contributed to the general air of instability and incoherence, of zigzag policies that often seemed to characterize the government's activities.

Abroad, the image Rafsanjani sought to convey of a more moderate and pragmatic Iran was blurred by a frequent reversion to a radical, anti-American, revolutionary rhetoric. In October 1991, for example, government officials joined the radicals in organizing a conference in Tehran to condemn in the harshest terms the Arab-Israeli peace initiative. The conference coincided with the opening of the Madrid peace conference, and some speakers at the Tehran conference called for the assassination of all participants in the peace talks. The following month, Rafsanjani promised assistance to the Islamization program in the Sudan, where a civil war between the largely Muslim north and the largely Christian south has been raging for years. The government did not necessarily act in a meaningful way on these declarations, but they reinforced an appearance of policy inconsistency.

At home, the government haltingly eased social controls over the general population, but to please Islamic conservatives, it acquiesced in recurrent waves of strict application of the Islamic dress code on women. Radicals, like bureaucrats in government organizations, were in a position to hamper the government's privatization program. The ability of the radicals to act as spoilers was thus diminished, but not eliminated.

Structural and Bureaucratic Barriers

Nevertheless, the hands of Rafsanjani and of his government appeared tied not so much by the organized radical opposition as by the still fragmented nature of power; by entrenched interests in the nationalized sector and in the cumbersome, over-inflated bureaucracy; and by widespread corruption that often seemed to make economic programs hostage to special interests. The government's policy of privatization continued to be marked by a great deal of incoherence. And the narrow nature of power prevented the government from mobilizing broad middle or working class support behind its policies.

These structural problems were highlighted over the vexed issue of privatization and the policy of attracting foreign investment to Iran. In November 1991, Rafsanjani reiterated the government's intention to sell off nationalized and state-managed industries to the private sector, to do away with multiple exchange rates and permit the rial to float, and to remove restrictions on private sector investment and imports.[11] As part of this program, the government passed a law greatly facilitating foreign investment in Iran, established a free trade zone on the island of Kish, and eased foreign exchange and import controls. It courted governments and potential firms in all the principle countries in Western Europe, as well as Japan, China and South and North Korea. In the summer of 1991, the governor of the Central Bank and the minister of economic affairs invited several hundred emigre Iranian businessmen to meet with them in New York.

Seen against the background of policies pursued during the first decade of the revolution, the New York conference was an altogether extraordinary affair. Among the invitees were major industrialists, like members of the Lajevardi family, whose numerous industries and trading companies had been expropriated after the revolution because the owners were considered allies of the former regime who had made their monies in illicit ways. These industrialists had been repeatedly denounced as exploiters of the poor, plunderers of the public treasury, and worse. Four years earlier, a suggestion by Ayatollah Montazeri, then Khomeini's heir apparent, that Iranians with expertise living abroad (not businessmen, but doctors, engineers, economists, and other professionals) be invited back to Iran was shot down by the radicals, and in no uncertain terms, as a plot to bring "counter-revolutionaries" back to the country. If the meeting in New York was not widely publicized in Iran, reports about it were not censored either.

The meeting in New York between Iranian government officials and the emigre businessmen thus constituted a sharp reversal of the anti-private sector, anti-entrepreneurial policy of the first decade of the revolution. The initiative, however, produced only meager results. Few businessmen felt sufficiently secure to return to Iran. The once highly profitable expropriated industries were for the most part overstaffed, undercapitalized, unprofitable and loaded down with debt. Plant had deteriorated. Former owners were being held liable for debts resulting largely from post-revolution turmoil and mismanagement. Even with the best of goodwill, the return of property was tied up by red tape engendered by a mass of legislation passed since the revolution, cumbersome court procedures, and competing bureaucratic fiefdoms. Revolutionary organizations, such as the Foundation for the Disinherited, charged with managing these industries, resisted privatization of enterprises providing salaries and employment for a vast, new government state bureaucracy. And decision-making was everywhere slow and complicated. Foreign investors seeking to do business in Iran faced similar problems, a factor which helps explain the reluctance of foreign governments and firms to commit themselves to long-term projects in Iran. Rafsanjani's inability to bring about dramatic change in the economy, even following his dramatic victory in the parliamentary elections and the defeat of the radicals, underlined the fact that Iran's economic problems were structural and did not derive merely from an obstructionist opposition within the ruling group.

The Repressive Politics of Elites

Commentators on Iran have remarked on the liveliness of its politics, as compared with that of other regional states. Parliament is a vigorous debating body and the deputies are not ciphers of the state. The government does not fully predetermine the outcome of parliamentary elections. A range of views is represented in the press. The government does have a monopoly over radio and television and controls several newspapers and magazines, but both the conservative clerics and the radicals at the two ends of the political spectrum can air their views in newspapers and weeklies they either control directly or which reflect their positions.

Many mistake this for political freedom. It is not. No political parties or groups outside those of the ruling group are permitted. Even the Iran Liberation Movement, headed by the former prime minister, Mehdi Bazargan, is barely tolerated. Bazargan was part of the original revolutionary coalition that overthrew the Shah and Khomeini's first premier. But he earned the ire of the ruling elite by criticizing the absence of press and political freedoms and the suppression of civil rights. He took Khomeini to task for concentrating power in his own hands. As a consequence, meetings of Iran Liberation Movement have been routinely attacked by stick-wielding *hizbollahis*, or "partisans of the party of God." The organization's newspaper has been closed down. In June 1990, over thirty members of the group and others associated with Bazargan were arrested as signatories to an open letter to President Rafsanjani critical of civil rights violations and other government policies; a number were still serving out jail sentences over a year later.[12]

Women are repeatedly subject to harassment in the street, sometimes even in the privacy of their homes, because of alleged violations of the Islamic dress or behavior code.[13] Flogging of women for these violations is not uncommon. Although some improvement has reportedly taken place in the treatment of political offenders, repression can still be savage when the regime feels threatened. When Iraqi-sponsored members of the Mujahedin-e Khalq opposition group were given the green light by Saddam Hussein to move armed contingents across the Iraqi frontier into Iran in the closing days of the Iran-Iraq War in 1988, the government charged members of the group inside Iran of assisting the invaders. Over one thousand of the Mujahedin, many not part of the invading force and some in prison at the time, as well as members of other opposition groups, such as the Tudeh and the Fadayan-e Khalq, were executed in a brief six-month period. Another 900 persons were executed in 1989, when the new drug-trafficking law came into effect.[14]

Following the death of Khomeini in June 1989, several prominent Iranian opposition figures living in exile abroad were assassinated. Among them were Kurdish Democratic Party leader Abd al-Rahman Qassemlu; former prime minister Shapour Bakhtiar and his aide, Abd al-Rahman Borumand; Mujahedin-e Khalq activist Kazem Rajavi; and Cyrus Elahi, a member of a royalist group active in Europe. These men were shot or knifed to death in Vienna, Paris, Geneva, and elsewhere. Some observers attributed the killings to radical groups within the ruling coalition, rather than to the government itself. If so, then at the very least, the Iranian government acquiesced in and condoned these assassinations. The likely explanation, however, is that the assassinations were carried out by Iranian state security organizations.

Severe repression, the use of bully boys and violence as an instrument of state policy, coexisting alongside a seemingly vigorous political give-and-take, is not difficult to explain. Iran has a politics of the ruling elite. Within the inner circle of the clerics and laymen in power—in the government, the revolutionary organizations, the *majlis*, the mosque network, and the informal organizations of the Islamic Republic—a degree of politics take place. Factions compete over policies, financial reward, and control over the institutions of the state. But outside this inner circle, little dissent is tolerated.

Moreover, the politically active population remains small. There are clerics and political leaders with constituencies within the larger society. Asghar-zadeh's "unity" committees are an example of one type of loose organization, with radical tendencies. The thousands of members of the revolutionary organizations, such as the Revolutionary Guards, the revolutionary commit-tees, and the Crusade for Reconstruction, can be mobilized for political action if they believe their interests are at stake. But these groups still form a narrow sector of the electorate.

Among the middle classes and the large mass of urban population, however, cynicism and political apathy is widespread. There is a huge gap between the government's revolutionary rhetoric and its actions, between the claims made on behalf of the "disinherited" classes and the economic realities the working and poorer classes face in difficult economic conditions. The salaries of white collar workers and middle and lower-rank civil servants have stagnated while businessmen, importers, distributors and contractors with links to influential clerics and officials have amassed immense wealth. The regime faces no organized opposition, and for many, Rafsanjani's brand of prag-matism represents relief from the revolutionary turmoil, ideological radicalism, and sense of personal insecurity of previous years.

But the government must nevertheless contend with a widespread discontent that derives from official corruption, bureaucratic inefficiency and red tape, gross mismanagement of the economy, shortages, lack of political freedoms, controls on social behavior, and an endless barrage of empty official rhetoric. According to the government's own statistics, per capita income in 1991 was 50 percent of its pre-revolution figure, and both the white-collar and salaried middle class and the working class have suffered. The dissatisfied elements—the professional and middle classes, parts of the bazaar, the intelligentsia, dissenting clerics, even the urban working class—tolerate rather than actively support the government.

Among the huge population of recent rural migrants in major urban centers discontent appears deep and widespread. In the summer of 1992, attempts by the municipal authorities to raze ramshackle housing built by squatters led to severe riots in Arak, an industrial center in Western Iran, and other Iranian cities. The disturbances were especially serious in the shrine city of Mashad, where banks, government buildings, a police station as well as shops and cars, were stormed and torched. In Shiraz, riots broke out when the authorities sought to prevent a demonstration over benefits demanded by those disabled in the war and their families. Four of the alleged perpetrators were hanged in Mashed, another four in Shiraz—yet another indication of the government's propensity to react violently to any perceived threat to its authority.

Not surprisingly, members of the government and the factions of radicals, conservatives and pragmatists in the ruling coalition either actively oppose or remain unenthusiastic about opening up the political system. There is little guarantee the present ruling group would survive genuinely free elections or public scrutiny of the corruption, mismanagement, and repression of the first decade of the revolution.

Succession

At Khomeini's death in 1989, it was my prediction that, contrary to expectation, the post-Khomeini period was likely to be characterized neither by total breakdown, as many predicted, nor by radical change.[15] Much more likely was continued muddle. That forecast has proven largely correct. Iran has settled down to a typical pattern of post-revolution malaise, characterized by relative stability and massive, seemingly intractable problems. Under Rafsanjani, the government has been seeking to come to terms with past mistakes. But officials are discovering that state takeover of private industries and government controls over the economy, once in place, are difficult to roll back. Industrial and economic assets lost through war, revolutionary turmoil, and general mismanagement cannot be easily recovered. A swollen bureaucracy which provides jobs to hundreds of thousands of upwardly mobile young men and women is difficult to shrink back to efficient size. Corruption cannot be easily rooted out when it involves the men in power. Bureaucratic fiefdoms are difficult to control. Professionals—doctors, scientists, engineers, economists, bankers, managers, entrepreneurs—who have chosen to emigrate are not easily replaced. The habit of rule through repression, prison, and the security organizations is difficult to overcome. Severe political controls, once established, cannot be eased without threats to the ruling group.

In addition, the Islamic Republic faces a succession problem particular to the constitutional system established after the revolution. Legitimacy under the Iranian system derives from the authority of the *faqih*, as heir to the mantle of the Prophet. The principle of government under the supreme authority of the *faqih* assumes that in each age, the most learned, most respected, most pious, most able Islamic jurist of his generation will assume the supreme leadership and that his pronouncements on matters of Islamic law, government, matters of peace and war, social justice and the like will carry weight by virtue of his great learning and grace. But under Khomeini's successor, as might have been predicted, the standing of the office has already been much diminished, and this process of the declining importance of the office of *faqih* could continue. Khamene'i, though only middle-aged, is not in good health, and there is no apparent successor who would satisfy the religious credentials for the office and also be acceptable to the key groups in the ruling coalition. This does not mean that the succession cannot be successfully managed; the succession from Khomeini to Khamene'i took place entirely peacefully and with no disruption. The mechanisms for choosing the next *faqih* are in place and have been shown to work. But it does suggest that, given the founding principles of the Islamic Republic, the problem of legitimacy could emerge to haunt Khomeini's successors.

Notes

1. For some typical formulations of the Iranian position regarding the Gulf crisis and postwar Persian Gulf security see, for example, Foreign Minister Ali-Akbar Velayati's interview with the Islamic Republic's News Agency (IRNA), reported in *Foreign Broadcasting and Information Service-Near East and South Asia (FBIS)*, January 2, 1991; Velayati's remarks to the Third Persian Gulf Conference in Tehran, reported in *FBIS*, January 22, 1991; Rafsanjani's Friday sermon of January 25, 1991, reported in *FBIS*, January 28, 1991; Rafsanjani's Friday sermon of March 8, 1991, reported in *FBIS*, March 12, 1991; and Velayati's wide-ranging interview with the Tehran newspaper *Jomhuri-ye Islami*, reported in *FBIS*, September 6, 1991.

2. In an interview with *Der Speigel* at the height of the Shi'ite uprising in March 1991, Rafsanjani not only denied Iran was giving any military assistance to the Shi'ites, but he was firm in rejecting any Iranian intention to get involved, even when the interviewer asked whether Iran "would tolerate your brothers in faith in Iraq being slaughtered by Saddam Husayn's Republican Guards." See translation of the interview in *FBIS*, March 26, 1991.

3. For the text of Saddam Hussein's August 14 letter to Rafsanjani, see *FBIS*, August 15, 1990.

4. An English text of the five-year development plan was published as a supplement to *Iran Focus* (Bonn), March 1990. A good summary of the salient points of the plan can be found in *Iran Focus*, December 1989 and February 1990.

5. Iran's National Security Council criticized the basing agreement for facilitating the deployment of foreign forces in the region, and Iran asked the Kuwaiti government for an "explanation" of the implications of the basing agreement. However, officials refrained from direct criticism of Kuwait. See reports in *FBIS*, September 23, 1991. The opposition press showed no such restraint, however.

6. Anti-American rhetoric during the Gulf crisis by members of the radical faction in the Majlis was harsh. See, for example, the January 20, 1991 speech by Ali-Akbar Mohtashami, reported in *FBIS*, January 22, 1991. Mohtashami called on Iran to join Iraq in a *jihad,* or holy war, against the United States. The Friday prayer leader of the shrine city of Qom, Ayatollah Ali Meshgini, prayed that American and British soldiers in the Gulf would be killed. See *FBIS*, January 22, 1991. Government leaders engaged in such rhetoric as well. The supreme leader, Ali Khamene'i, compared the depredations the United States was visiting on the Persian Gulf region to those visited on the Islamic world by the Mongol conquerors Genghis Khan and Hulagu and by Tamerlane. See *FBIS*, March 4, 1991.

Official criticism of the Arab-Israeli peace initiative began as soon as news of the proposals for direct talks became public in the summer and grew especially harsh when the Madrid talks convened. For examples, see Rafsanjani's depiction of the U.S. proposals for peace negotiations as "prejudiced against Islam and Muslims ... and the rights of the Palestinian people" and Khamene'i's description of the Madrid talks as "treason," reported in *FBIS*, July 25 and October 31, 1991, respectively.

7. Iran and Iraq also traded charges of cross border violations. For examples, see reports cited in *FBIS*, April 2, 4, and 11, 1991. For examples of Iranian attacks on the Ba'th and Saddam Hussein, see remarks by the head of the judiciary, Muhammad Yazdi, reported in *FBIS*, April 1, 1991. Iran's clerics were especially incensed at the forcible transfer to Baghdad, humiliating television appearance, and subsequent house arrest of Ayatollah Abol-Qasem Kho'i in March. Kho'i was over 90 years old and the most senior of Shi'ite leaders in Iraq, with a wide following among Shi'ites throughout the Middle East. He died in August 1992.

8. This was clearly the import of remarks by one of the leaders of the radical faction, Muhammad Musavi-Khoeniha, in an interview with *Ettelaat,* August 20, 1990, reported in *FBIS,* September 13, 1990.

9. For examples of some of these statements of support, see reports cited in *FBIS,* October 4 and 9, 1990.

10. In November 1990, Hosain Hashemian, the deputy speaker of the *majlis,* travelled to Qom with a number of deputies to enlist the support of senior clerics against the U.S.-sponsored Arab-Israeli peace initiative. They also called on Ayatollah Montazeri. Hashemian was subsequently summoned before a special clerical court, reportedly for actions violating principles laid down by Ayatollah Khomeini. This followed an incident in October, when another cleric, Abol-Fazl Musavian, editor of the Mashad newspaper *Khorasan,* was ordered by the clerical court to leave Mashad and take up exile in Qom. *Khorasan* had published remarks deemed supportive of Montazeri. The summons against Hashemian caused a sensation in Tehran, and in the ensuing debate, parliamentarian Morteza Alviri claimed that eighty to one hundred deputies continued to follow Montazeri, at least in religious matters, and to regard him as their source of emulation.

11. See Rafsanjani's remarks to the seventh ministerial conference of the United Nations Commission on Trade and Development, reported in *FBIS,* November 22, 1991.

12. See Human Rights Watch, *World Report 1990* (New York: Human Rights Watch, 1991), pp. 437-38.

13. For example, *Kayhan* newspaper reported in December that a magistrate of the "Special Court for Dealing with Forbidden Acts" (*Dadsara-ye vizheh-ye jara'em-e monkerat*) despatched officials of the "Office for Fighting Social Corruption" to a party in a private house in the northern part of Tehran. Sixty teenagers, both boys and girls, were arrested. The owner of the house and his wife were sentenced to flogging and the payment of twenty million rials in fines. The teenagers were released after paying monetary fines. See *Kayhan,* 1 Dey, 1370/December 22, 1991.

14. See "Iran: Over 900 Executions Announced in Five Months," Amnesty International report, June 1989. Human Rights Watch reported that the government admitted to executing 113 persons between March and October, 1990, including seventy-one on drug-smuggling charges. See Human Rights Watch, *World Report 1990,* p. 430.

15. "What Khomeini Did," *New York Review of Books,* July 20, 1989, p. 19.

4

The Nine Lives of Hashemite Jordan

Adam Garfinkle

For many decades, foreign observers of Hashemite Jordan have predicted its instability, decline, and even its imminent destruction. Particularly in the heyday of American liberalism, many analysts confidently asserted that the days of the Arab monarchies were drawing to a close, the future bequeathed to "progressive" socialist regimes of secular inclination.[1] But those few outsiders who really knew Jordan saw the considerable hidden strengths of the Hashemite regime: its loyal core East Bank constituency; the support of the Western powers and, tacitly, Israel; and the very considerable skill of its kings in maneuvering through social tensions within the country and regional threats without.

Because of these basic strengths, Hashemite Jordan has managed to weather some very tough times since formal independence in 1946. But now the regime faces a systemic crisis unlike any it has faced in the past. The monarchy as it has existed, in its form of one-man rule, cannot continue beyond the reign of the present monarch, Hussein ibn Talal. The key question is: Will the monarchy be able to lead and manage the transition process to a more broadly based polity or will it lose control of the regime altogether? Put differently, will it give a little and survive to rule another day, or will it find itself forced, in effect, to give up? Related questions revolve around what fundamental political change inside Jordan will mean for Jordan's neighbors and for the United States. Will a carefully devolved monarchy change Jordanian foreign policies in important ways? If the country collapses in violence, who will pick up the pieces, and how would the new overlords see the world around them?

The hour of decision might well coincide with the next political succession in Jordan. This adds yet another element of uncertainty to the equation, because, with a single exception, none of Jordan's major crises over the years has coincided with disarray at the top. There has never been a regime transition in Jordan; it has been a Hashemite emirate/monarchy from its inception in 1921 and so it remains. Nor has there been a political succession within the basic regime structure since 1953, when Hussein took the throne from his ailing father, Talal.

The 1953 transition, too, was complicated by the fact that it involved the deposition of Talal on grounds of mental illness after just eleven months on the throne, followed by a period of regency owing to King Hussein's tender age. The only other transition, from King Abdullah to Talal in 1951, was somewhat unconventional, too. It was occasioned by Abdullah's murder and never fully executed because of the new king's illness. In short, there are no normal models of political succession in Jordanian history upon which to base an analysis of the next one.

Watersheds of Jordanian History

The Jordanian monarchy has survived eight major challenges to its stability and longevity, and today it faces a ninth. Two main characteristics define Jordan's situation in all eight of its previous historical turning points: first, as noted above, with the exception of Abdullah's assassination, none coincided with governmental crisis at the top; and second, every one of these crises, Abdullah's assassination included, has had its origins in developments that began outside the kingdom and that were largely beyond its control. The first datum is testimony to the strength and flexibility of the monarchy as an institution and to King Hussein's talent for survival, and the second is testimony to Jordan's pervasive regional political weakness.

These eight historical watersheds are as follows:

1. 1946: formal independence from Britain.

2. 1948-1949: the Palestine War, which resulted in Jordan's annexation of the West Bank and its Palestinian population, including those Palestinians who continued to reside on the West Bank and those who fled to the East Bank.

3. 1951-1953: monarchical transition, extending from Abdullah's assassination in July 1951 through the brief interregnum of Talal's rule, to the regency that followed Talal's deposition and the formal assumption of the young Hussein's constitutional powers as king in May 1953.

What is potentially significant for future successions in Jordan was the role of oligarchical figures around Talal. These former Abdullah courtiers left little chance for serious policy discontinuity to develop under Talal, as they jealously guarded the main pillars of government lest the inexperienced and unpredictable king err in excess. The intercession of the oligarchy contributed continuity at the price of diffusing and, in a sense, really subverting royal prerogatives. As Talal's psychological grip on reality loosened, he spent much time abroad seeking medical treatment. A regency, dubbed a Crown Council, was culled from the oligarchical families of Abdullah's rule to protect the kingdom—and the elite—from any accumulated consequences of bad judgment. When Talal was deposed on August 11, 1952, therefore, there was already a functioning regency to govern Jordan until Hussein reached eighteen by the Muslim calendar, there to advise, protect, and tutor him. It continued its formal duties until May 2, 1953, when Hussein returned from schooling in Britain to be crowned. Informally, it continued to advise, protect, and tutor the young monarch for some years thereafter, as well.[2]

Unlike Talal, Hussein did shift his advisors, gingerly at first, with more confidence as time passed. Hussein preferred his generational peers, and this new royal entourage held different attitudes toward political life. In time, Hussein turned to friends like Zaid al-Rifa'i and Hussein's younger cousin Abd al-Hamid Sharaf, as well as Mudar Badran and Marwan al-Qasim. But early on, he preferred the company of more nationalist officers like Ali Abu Nuwar, the Jordanian military attache and Ba'thist sympathizer whom the king befriended after a few wild nights in Paris. Together, the two engineered the dismissal of Sir John Bagot Glubb (Glubb Pasha) from the Arab Legion, for which Hussein was praised throughout the Arab world. Within months, though, Abu Nuwar (elevated from lieutenant colonel to chief-of-staff) and his officer cohorts turned on the king and helped provoke the political crisis between the palace, the army and the elected government of Sulayman al-Nabulsi in 1957. When Hussein was forced to dismiss that dangerously anti-monarchical government, a coup attempt—in which Abu Nuwar was implicated—almost cost the young king his throne and life.[3]

Taken together, Hussein's youth and the company he kept partly explain the erratic Jordanian policy that led first to the anti-traditionalist tilt of 1956-1957 and to the sharp *volte-face* thereafter. Clearly, this seminal period left a deep impression on the king, as his 1962 memoir attests.[4] In retrospect, too, the al-Nabulsi period is important because it was the first time that the king and the government stood on opposite sides of an ideological and policy line, a development that is likely to arise again sooner than later.

Assuming that King Hussein recalls his own formative period as king, he has doubtlessly given thought to his own successor. The idea of a protective regency made up of experienced members of the oligopoly and selected Hashemite family members surely figures in his thinking. Current plans are for the present crown prince—Hussein's youngest brother, Hasan—to become king next, and for Hussein's eldest son by an Arab Muslim wife, Ali (b. 1975) to then become crown prince. But if, for any reason, Ali becomes king at a relatively young age, an informal crown council will likely be formed to protect him from the errors of youth, just as Abdullah's men tried to protect Hussein in the early 1950s.

4. 1956-1958: a volcanic period in Arab politics which witnessed the Suez crisis, the al-Nabulsi episode, the Lebanese crisis, and the Iraqi Revolution of 1958—all of which, taken together, taught Hussein important lessons about the dangers of Arab politics; the fragility of the monarchy in the face of pan-Arabist or Nasserist appeal; and the increasing vulnerability of the country to external influences.[5]

5. 1964-1967: a period marked by the "Arab Cold War"[6] and the "Palestini-zation" of regional politics, that ranged from the founding of the Palestine Liberation Organization in Cairo in 1964, to the Syrian coup of February 1966, to the June 1967 war. Though Jordan was not involved as a primary actor in the events that led up to the war, it was nevertheless the biggest and most immediate loser from it. Egypt lost Sinai and Gaza, and Syria lost the Golan Heights, but neither loss can be compared to Jordan's loss of the West Bank and East Jerusalem—whether in economic, demographic, or symbolic terms.

6. 1970-1971: civil war, pitting the Hashemites against their mortal enemy, the PLO, in perhaps the most seminal political event in the lives of living Jordanians. The civil war proved the general success of the process of "Jordanization," given that most Palestinians in Jordan either stayed neutral in the fighting or supported the regime. But the battle to extirpate Palestinian organizations from Jordan also showed that Jordan could not afford to absent itself entirely from Arab-Israeli politics; too many interests, domestic and regional, would suffer from so doing. The emergence of a Palestinian national movement that is romantic, armed, and active in Jordan has, since 1970, been the Hashemites' greatest fear. Israel's containment of the movement has, therefore, been of objective benefit to Hashemite Jordan, even though, of course, harsh Israeli policies in the territories also feed the radicalism that threatens Hashemite rule.

7. 1973-1979: the era of "oil boom, peace bust," from the October War to Camp David and the Iranian Revolution. This was a period of great ambivalence in Jordan. The money that poured into the country, particularly after the start of the Lebanese civil war in 1975, was a golden opportunity. Jordan had never been able to survive without external subventions, first from Britain, then the United States. The arrival of the Arab oil age promised undreamed sums of money for indigenous development, but the price to be paid would be greater vulnerability to the vicissitudes of inter-Arab politics. Such vulnerability eventually proved disastrous after the decline of the oil market in the mid-1980s. Arab subventions and worker remittances carried Jordan's economy up as if on a bubble, but when the flow of money fell (for both political and economic reasons) even as consumer appetites rose, the bubble burst and the economy nearly collapsed.

The peace process, on the other hand, held out the appealing prospect of normalization with Israel, a country with which Jordan has shared a long but discreet diplomatic relationship.[7] But to join the peace train in the Camp David era, 1977-1979, risked being pushed off the oil wagon. At the same time, after the 1974 Arab League summit meeting in Rabat, it was not clear that Jordan could control the Palestinian issue, at home or in the region, well enough to risk a public peace process with Israel. In the end, Hussein elected not to take the risk, perhaps the greatest error of his long rule.[8]

8. 1982: Israel's Lebanon war and the extended period of regional dislocation it produced was a time full of initial danger and subsequent opportunity for Jordan; both the kingdom and its king survived without succumbing to the former or taking full advantage of the latter.[9] The danger was that the Israeli government under Menachem Begin and Ariel Sharon would win its way in Lebanon and turn its attentions to the Palestinization of Jordan; the opportunity was that the simultaneous weaknesses of the PLO and Syria, combined with the return of a Labor prime minister in Israel in 1984, would open the way to a reassertion of Jordanian activism in the peace process. As it happened, neither Sharon's plans nor those of Shimon Peres proceeded very far. In the fullness of time, the crucible of Lebanon has also come to illustrate what can become of Arab countries hemmed in by stronger and more avaricious neighbors. Jordan is not disadvantaged by the raging sectarian heterogeneity of Lebanon, but it has other weaknesses—and other neighbors—that leave the example of Lebanon hanging over the country like a mean-spirited jinn.

Jordan's Systemic Crisis and the Next Transition

A ninth watershed confronts Jordan today. It describes a gradually deepening crisis composed of acute and structural economic weaknesses, a new political activism based partly on spillover effects of the Palestinian uprising (*intifada*) but also for other reasons, and questions about the well-being of King Hussein. Even before the Kuwait crisis, Jordan's regime was in jeopardy, but the crisis accelerated and deepened Jordan's dilemma in most respects. As a cat is said in folkloric legend to have but nine lives, this ninth watershed in Jordanian history stands forth as the one that the Hashemite monarchy, at least as it has been known it since 1946, may very well not survive.

Jordan's crisis of the late 1980s and early 1990s accumulated from the many regional and domestic political changes of the last thirty years, punctuated with some bad luck and an occasional, rare lapse of royal skill. Ultimately, as suggested above, it will become a crisis of political succession. It has been composed of three interlocking parts: economic problems, political pressure, and the fallout from regional politics centered on the Palestinian problem.

The Economic Dimension

By the end of 1986, if not earlier, it was clear that the Arab oil boom had ended and was unlikely to recur. Ending with it was the largesse of Arab oil money given to Jordan. Pledges made to Jordan at the Arab League's 1978 summit meeting in Baghdad were never completely fulfilled, and each year saw less money arriving in Amman. The decline was particularly sharp between 1988 and 1989, when, according to World Bank figures, aid fell about one-third, from $536 million to $377 million. In addition, remittances from Jordanian workers in the Gulf were affected negatively by the softness in the oil market, although Jordan's relatively skilled work force suffered proportionally less than other national contingents of unskilled laborers. Meanwhile, rising expectations and increased consumer consumption had bred a frenzy of imports that the government was reluctant to curtail, fueling a foreign trade gap that increased five-fold between 1976 and 1982.[10] The trappings of prosperity in Jordan facilitated relative social amity and political calm, and a growing economic pie worked doubly as a general palliative to soften the reality of sharply uneven income distribution and as a means to get Palestinians out of refugee camps and into the mainstream economy.

Lean times, of course, had the opposite affect. When the economy worsened, the government temporized, powerless to change the regional economic environment but afraid to announce and act upon the bad news. In the event, Jordan suffered a sudden and acute financial crisis, demonstrated dramatically by a plunge of foreign currency reserves to nearly zero.[11] A two-sided reaction to the economic crisis developed: the government introduced stringent austerity measures to protect Jordan's capacity to borrow from international institutions until matters could be put right, and Jordan's non-government intelligentsia and growing middle class developed a sharpened look-out for parvenu corruption by business "fat cats" and government officials.

King Hussein's declaration of July 31, 1988, in which he announced Jordan's "disengagement" from the West Bank, had negative results for the kingdom's economy, as well. It contributed to the collapse of the value of the Jordanian dinar, further worsening the economic crisis, and in turn undermined the status of the regime's supportive oligopoly and the patience of East Bankers. In reality, Jordan's economic trouble, whatever the recent catalysts have been, does not stem from episodic bad luck or particularly bad management and corruption. It is structural. An ongoing population explosion (including an annual increase ranging between 3.5 percent and 4.3 percent) in a country bereft of many natural resources and too small to support the infrastructure of a modern economy is driving the country to ruin. Indeed, that the mismatch of population with the natural carrying capacity of the land did not send Jordan spiraling into disaster earlier testifies to King Hussein's talent as royal mendicant. But the reality of the kingdom's limits is finally catching up with it and, unfortunately for the monarchy, it is happening after one of the most affluent and economically optimistic eras in the country's history.

The Kuwait crisis, of course, made things even worse. Though the most dire of early projections were not realized, Jordan still suffered a 8.5 percent decrease in 1990 gross national product (GNP, measured at market prices) and a further gross decline of about 13 percent in 1991.[12] The years 1991-1992 did witness an economic boomlet inspired by Gulf returnees spending their savings on a construction binge in and around Amman, but drawing down savings can only be a short-term stimulant to the economy. In the longer run, the added social and economic burden of the 300,000 Palestinian returnees, combined with the continued shutoff of Saudi subsidies, the lockout from most Gulf trade, and the absence of future remittances, may mean that the worst is yet to come.[13]

Political and Social Pressures

Beyond economic matters, a desire has been brewing on the part of Jordan's new, well-educated, and growing middle class to have a greater role in running the country. That Jordan's population as a whole has become more educated and politically aware represents a success of government policy but, as was the case in Iran in the 1960s and 1970s, opportunities to participate in public life failed to keep pace with the desire and capacity of new constituencies. King Hussein has been aware of this restlessness but anxious about giving it loose rein. In the early 1980s, he created "National Consultative Councils" that had no real power, and he hinted at reconvening parliament, which had been suspended since just after the 1967 war. He also used his brand of personal monarchical populism to convey the impression that even without democracy or pluralism, Jordan's government cared about and listened to its people.

But in reality, little changed. The king remained unchallenged at the pinnacle of power; next came the army and the *mukhabarat,* the control of both vouchsafed to loyal East Bank supporters; followed by a group of business-government oligarchs, some of whom were, very importantly, Palestinian in origin. All aspects of public administration, from customs personnel to education ministry functionaries, were staffed through the tribes and the oligarchs. The same groups virtually controlled the print and electronic media, which never criticized the king or any important aspect of government policy. The Muslim Brotherhood was cautiously tolerated and modestly patronized from time to time; troublemakers were occasionally jailed but the leadership was mostly co-opted. It was a typical patronage system, with typical advantages and typical drawbacks.

Withal, the demand to participate grew in intensity, and the groups making demands became more diverse. In addition to Palestinian merchants and East Bank technocrats were professional groups, which, in lieu of political parties, became an organizational focus of the new middle class political thinking and activism.[14] Also, ominously, Islamic fundamentalists, some far more militant than the Muslim Brotherhood had ever been, arose in the wake of the Iranian Revolution. When the demand for political participation converged with the economic crisis, a sense of generalized discontent emerged and pressure for change reached the political elite. The monarchy bent; it reconvened parliament and then promised elections in an effort to appease popular demands and, no doubt, deflect the unpopularity of present and planned austerity measures.

Most important of all, and perhaps most surprising to the king, epochal changes had been brewing in the kingdom's East Bank constituency. That group, the most crucial to the maintenance of the monarchy, has experienced the greatest change in educational levels, technical and managerial experience, and overall economic success.[15] Similarly, because of these changes, the likelihood that educated people will be unemployed or underemployed—always a recipe for trouble—is now relatively higher among East Bankers than before. Though, as a group, East Bankers are probably only marginally less loyal to the monarchy today than they were three decades ago, their capacity to be effectively critical and loyal simultaneously is a new phenomenon.

Younger generations, in particular, are susceptible to new forms of politicization. As one, young East Banker, resentful of what he saw as a patronizing attitude by the government, said:

> We are not goats and sheep out in the desert, and we do not wish to be treated that way. We respect and honor the king, and he is a good man. But when he is doing wrong we will not say he is doing right.[16]

Changes among East Bankers imply the relative politicization of the army and the intelligence services, too. Although a new social environment for them does not call into question the army's fundamental loyalty, it does suggest that the traditional, paternalistic nature of the relationship between the military and the monarchy is changing rapidly and profoundly. Insofar as the upper ranks of the army and the security apparatus evolve different attitudes from those of the royal court, they are likely to be to the king's right when it comes to the central domestic political issue: controlling the effects of Palestinian nationalism in Jordan. This development was first foreshadowed by the 1970-1971 civil war, when high-ranking army officers pleaded with the king not to back down before the insulting hubris of Palestinian *fedayeen* (guerrilla) groups; Hussein ultimately found that he had to listen to them. The independent tendencies of East Bankers have become more pronounced ever since.

Related changes in Jordan have to do with general trends toward urbanization and secularization.[17] In conjunction, one of the most important developments in Jordanian society over the past two generations has been the relative decline in the cohesiveness and importance of tribal affiliation.[18] This is not to say that clan and family do not matter—far from it. But tribalism is much less significant today than a generation or two ago, a process accelerated by the settling of the tribes and their recruitment first into the army and then into the civil service.[19]

While specific tribal affiliations and primordial ties are likely to matter less to an increasingly urbanized, secularized, and culturally perforated society, this does not mean that East Bank society has lost its sense of exclusivity. Instead, a new trans-tribal East Bank political personality profile is emerging and is potentially anti-Palestinian in net effect. Younger East Bankers feel more antagonism toward those they consider aliens and interlopers, particularly as those of bedouin origin migrate to Jordan's cities only to find themselves far worse off than many Palestinians. Indeed, one cause of April 1989 price riots was East Bankers' resentment that, as they saw it, Jordan's middleman-oriented, oil-boom economy enriched urban Palestinians and government oligarchs at their expense.

In Jordan today, two socio-political paradigms thus coexist, although not always harmoniously: the Palestinian and the East Banker. But for the integrating factor of Islamist thinking, they would be growing even farther apart. Among Palestinians, status is increasingly determined by criteria more or less familiar to Westerners: wealth, education, talent, and experience. But, as one of their own noted, that is not the case among East Bankers:

> The family name, and not the position of the father, has the say. People of similar backgrounds move together in groups. And here [in East Bank society], privilege [belongs to] a son of a known family rather than of a merchant clan. I do know of people of well-known families who look down at elite-son students. [The] elite in Jordan ... is not only ministers and high bureaucrats ... Family background, not [one's] father's position, was always considered first.[20]

In other words, to many East Bankers, status still flows from primordial associations. Merchants and landlords are mainly Palestinian, and while such positions may be laden with social status in Palestinian sub-culture, the same is not the case for tribesmen just one or two generations removed from the bedouin tent. Thus, the longstanding distinction between bedouin and *hadari* (townspeople) that exists throughout Arab society is telescoped in Jordan. Though not rejecting urban and sedentary life as such, many East Bankers still disdain the values and traditional occupations associated with it, thereby generating cultural gaps between East Bankers and Palestinians.[21]

Regional Factors

These were not the only issues on the public agenda, however, in the late 1980s; the *intifada* clearly had a major impact on Jordanian politics as well as on politics in Israel. The outbreak of the uprising immediately raised the worry that a romantic and violent form of Palestinian nationalism would again spread to the East Bank, as it had in the late 1960s. There was specific reason to worry, given that some of the early leaflets of the Unified National Leadership of the Uprising targeted Jordanian institutions (e.g., Jerusalem's pro-Amman *al-Nahar* newspaper) and personalities (e.g., Palestinian members of the Jordanian parliament). But after the first full year of the uprising, no real spreading of the *intifada* to Jordan occurred. This was a function of bitter memories of the civil war, of the authorities' skill in suppressing the first sparks of a rising, and also of the fact that enough Palestinians in the East Bank had been sufficiently Jordanized that they feared risking what they had for their brethren across the river.

This was in part the motivation, or at least a facilitating factor, in King Hussein's July 1988 declaration severing "legal and administrative links" with the West Bank. To say in the midst of the *intifada* that Jordan was not Palestine and that it had a prior and separate agenda of its own was testimony to the king's confidence that his Palestinian problem was manageable, even if Israel's was not. Better to be farther away than closer to the havoc on the West Bank, and it did not require the army to "explain" the decision to the Palestinians in the kingdom, however uncomfortable many of them felt about it.

Over time, however, the *intifada* undeniably affected Palestinians in Jordan, although not all of them in the same way. The reactions compose a paradox. On the rhetorical level, the *intifada* united Palestinian society in Jordan, but on every other level it sharpened differences among the layers of Palestinian demography in the East Bank. Those most firmly established in Jordan, mainly from the generation of 1947-1949 (and even earlier) that never saw the inside of a refugee camp, are the most cautious; those more newly arrived (post-1967) have the least to lose and are more prone to impatience and activism, often in recent years under the banner of militant Islam.[22] On balance, as control over the Jordanian status quo moved away from the king—partly by design, partly not—one of the new currents flowing was a revived Palestinian nationalism, as the initial support of Jordan's "street" for Saddam Hussein after the invasion of Kuwait clearly showed.

Before the Deluge

The marginal recession of royal authority, hard economic times, the heady symbolism of the uprising, and the catalyst of the Kuwait crisis all contributed to the rise of a parochial and oppositional Palestinian self-consciousness in Jordan, a reverse of what the 1988 disengagement decision sought to produce. Initially, the disengagement confronted Palestinians and Palestinian organizations with a question: to what extent and in which ways should Palestinians in Jordan participate in a new era of Jordanian politics? Implicitly anyway, if not more directly, the disengagement was Hussein's way of saying to the PLO: "You take the West Bank (if you can), but you have to leave me alone on the East Bank."[23]

If the disengagement was designed to make East Bank Palestinians choose, knowing that they would choose to protect their concrete stake in Jordan, then the period of Jordanian *glasnost* that came after redefined what "choosing Jordan" meant in practical terms. Palestinian political activities and parties flourished in Jordan after July 1988, and there seemed to be little or no price to pay for it. In late 1988, Palestinian activists pondered whether PLO constituent organizations should set up Jordanian affiliates when political parties were finally legalized, wondering at the same time whether the regime would find a way to use these parties to weaken and co-opt the PLO. Such questions were no longer as compelling during the heady period of the Kuwait crisis, simply because the regime had suspended use of so much of its leverage over the country's political processes.

The disengagement was most likely a sign of the king's determination to put the Jordanian government on a more secure and institutionalized political footing, focusing on the monarchy's core East Bank constituency.[24] The king, however, seemed to have underestimated how much this core constituency, like the Palestinian one, had changed. Riots in April 1989 in the southern part of the country, centered near Ma'an, in that region traditionally most loyal to the monarchy and most passively long-suffering in hard times, brought home the point with alacrity. The riots quickened the plan to hold parliamentary elections, which occurred in November 1989. The riots clearly shook Hussein, and while the government of Zaid al-Rifa'i was made the scapegoat, Hussein was under no illusion that merely sacking the prime minister would mollify angry citizens. To pin Jordan's long term hopes more heavily on East Bankers required dealing with them in new ways; the idea of an extra-constitutional National Charter that would legalize political parties and broaden participation in government fit well with this intent.

In preparation for the elections, the regime resorted to old-fashioned district gerrymandering to ensure that Palestinian representation would be shaved in favor of East Bankers, and it largely succeeded. But what the king and his court did not anticipate was how well Islamic fundamentalists would do, nor did they guess that fundamentalism and Palestinian activism would merge and reinforce each other's strength to such an unprecedented degree. A large protest vote looking for new faces on the ballot added to Islamist success because fundamentalist candidates alone were not associated with the patronage system of the past. The surprising election results, which awarded the fundamentalists a parliamentary plurality and spelled defeat for a score of establishment luminaries, clearly gave the ruling elite pause.

The Jordanian constitution is drawn so that the king retains the power to select his cabinet regardless of who wins the largest parliamentary bloc. Following the 1989 election, the king appointed as prime minister a political veteran and close confidant, Mudar Badran, but he made a concerted effort to introduce new faces into the cabinet, too.[25] This, however, could not undo the damage. On balance, the election was a gamble that may well have backfired. The king had clearly intended that it produce a parliament to absorb discontent from unpopular economic measures to come; in other words, the election was supposed to siphon off pressure. Perhaps, too, the king believed he had to set things up that an orderly, if very partial, devolution of monarchical authority could eventually proceed therefrom as well.

Whatever Hussein thought, the election results and the reported coincidental deterioration of his health produced a rogue element in the political status quo. Parliament took on a life of its own and the king either chose not to rein it in or found that he could not. Increasingly in 1989 and early 1990, a new and more open public life evolved faster than the regime's capacity to control it. If parliament was intended as a tool of the regime to weather tough times, it turned instead into political juggernaut. Press freedoms and periodic scandals, like those concerning corrupt bankers, fed the beast. Political parties arose before they were chartered legally.[26] Parliament called for a new "eastern front" against Israel, and unauthorized border incursions into Israel increased in frequency.[27] When public figures dared question the motive of the king's National Charter idea, it provided a stunning example of one public relations control mechanism (Jordanian *glasnost*) doubling back to attack a second (the National Charter).[28]

The momentum of the new parliament confronted the king with a serious problem. The non-Islamist elements of parliament, although an absolute majority, were too divided to offset the power of the Islamists, and the

Jordanian regime had never succeeded in creating a front political organization for itself to use in co-opting and outflanking such problems.[29] Therefore, the king allowed and even encouraged leftist elements, long banned from the public realm in Jordan, to emerge as a counterpoise.[30] He also cozied up to Yasser Arafat, and the world saw the remarkable spectre of two establishment politicians teaming up to oppose the Islamists in their respective ranks.

The only other option open to the king was for the regime to confront the Islamists directly through use of the army. But this was too dangerous, particularly since Islam had become so entangled with Palestinian activism that doing so might provoke a much larger conflagration. Hussein acted calculatingly in 1988 and early 1989, but not boldly or quickly enough to prevent upheaval in 1990 and 1991. Thus, much of the turbulence of the pre-Kuwait crisis period in Jordan had a simple source: royal misjudgment.

Jordan and the Kuwait Crisis

Even had King Hussein been in perfect health before August 2, 1990, it still might have made sense to let parliament find its way to that sense of responsibility that generally comes with real political experience. Then, royal thinking may have gone, if the Israelis poured across the border, as most Jordanians believed they would in the summer of 1990, the country would unite behind the army to save the monarchy. More importantly, if Jordan were to evolve into a more stable polity with a diminished monarchy in the future, it would sooner or later have to pass through a form of political adolescence. So, the king might have reasoned, why not now?

The answer to that question came on August 2, when an invasion did indeed occur, but not the one Jordanians expected; Hussein got caught beneath the falcon's wing. By then, the king had given the "street" in Jordan such a wide swath of self-expression and organizing energy that opposing its spontaneous support for Iraq was almost out of the question. The only way to have done so unequivocally was to call out the army to shoot demonstrators. Had the king done that, even assuming the army's fealty in such heady times, all he had been trying to build in the event of his abdication or death would have been for naught.

The Kuwait crisis also worsened Jordan's economic situation. Aqaba was brought to a near standstill, income from tourism plunged to near zero, remittances were severely reduced, oil from Saudi Arabia was cut off, and Jordanian products were prevented from reaching the Gulf by Saudi diktat.[31] In addition, Jordan's Saudi subsidy was eliminated and special privileges formerly enjoyed in Saudi Arabia by Palestinians with Jordanian passports (as well as by Yemenis), such as being able to work without having a specific Saudi sponsor, were rescinded. As bad luck had it, too, the phosphate market was depressed, phosphates being Jordan's main physical export. Unemployment, hovering at around 15 percent before 1990, reached nearly 40 percent by spring 1991.[32] Most ironically of all, because of the crisis, Iraq had a good excuse not to repay what it owed to Jordan, a sizeable sum which stood at about $835 million in autumn 1989.[33]

Moreover, the crisis furnished precisely what Jordan's Islamists needed in order to take the modest political space opened up by the November 1989 election and turn it into a wider playing field. Until 1990, the Jordanian regime had been adept at co-opting and accommodating religious forces. This was made easier by the fact that it is not noteworthy to be an orthodox Muslim in a traditional monarchy, and the general religious atmosphere undercut fundamentalist criticisms. Although there was a logic for religious sensibilities to translate into political mobilization against the regime in the period from 1979 to 1985—rampant materialism, conspicuous consumption, the open sale of alcohol, and the presence of scantily-clad women not far from Third Circle mosques—a catalyst was lacking.[34] With the invasion of Kuwait, the catalyst arrived.

Jordan's troubles notwithstanding, radical scenarios were hard to credit before the Kuwait crisis, because a thoroughgoing overturning of the status quo would have required four improbable things to happen simultaneously or in near sequence. First of these was a deep economic unravelling, with little help from the outside when it happened. Second, the regional environment would have had to be particularly crisis-prone, either because of sudden regime transitions in nearby countries, war, or other equally serious dislocations. Third, there would have had to be a new cadre of alternative and reasonably united radical leadership. Fourth, the king would have had to die or fall ill and abdicate. The Kuwait crisis furnished the first three conditions in total or in part, and for all anyone knew, biology or a bullet may have provided the fourth before the war ended.

The question of an opposition leadership underwent the most dramatic change. Before 1989, it was hard to identify an incipient Palestinian leadership cadre to challenge the regime; indeed, political activism and violence was at a twenty-five-year low. Nor was it easy to find an East Bank cadre devoted to an Islamic revolution. Aside from Layth Shubaylat, a maverick Islamic legislator, little was known about the new generation of politically minded Islamic activists.[35] But after the election and the Kuwait crisis, this new elite became more visible, and the rise of the Arab "street" propelled it forward with great speed. A united political front, led by Islamists, formed in August 1990, and it effectively operated not as a Jordanian government as such, but as a power that challenged strongly the palace's prerogatives.[36]

By not reasserting royal control in August 1990, the regime courted further challenges. In October, the parliament, led by Shubaylat, demanded that the regime arm the people, which neither the king nor Prime Minister Badran wanted to do. In response, the regime hit upon a compromise: Palestinians would be given People's Army uniforms and trained by the regular army, but they would not be allowed to take their weapons out of secured training areas.[37]

Then, on November 17, 1990, Jordan's lower house elected a fundamentalist as speaker against the opposition of secular leftists and liberals. This spelled trouble to come between parliament and palace, but by the end of 1990, the trouble was still just latent. As long as regime and street moved in the same general direction, a tense internal peace endured.

Thus, one can discount the hagiographic mumbo-jumbo about Saddam Hussein that came from the Jordanian regime after the outbreak of the Kuwait crisis, and one can even de-emphasize the importance of Jordan's economic links to Baghdad. To understand the Jordanian reaction in the Kuwait crisis, one need not look further than the exigencies of domestic politics as the king likely understood them.

Some Bush administration principals did not seem to grasp this situation very well. Before long, however, the U.S. administration came ineluctably to the conclusion that, as nasty as Jordanian policy had been during the war, all the alternatives to the king and his court were worse. This realization was focused for the administration with the aid of Congress, which tried in March 1991 to cut Jordan's $55 million aid package in a fit of pique. While there was also support in the Executive Branch for punishing the king for siding with Iraq in the war—for example, Secretary of State James Baker's March 1991 trip to the Middle East pointedly omitted a stopover in Amman—cooler heads realized that hurting Jordan would only spite long-term U.S. interests.[38]

This debate came amid unmistakable signs in spring 1991 that Hussein was trying to climb back from the diplomatic and financial abyss. In late February, the king stated a willingness to reactivate the February 1985 Jordanian-PLO political agreement—not, to be sure, to save the PLO from oblivion, but to subsume it beneath Jordanian interests.[39] He also reportedly informed Israeli Labor party leader Shimon Peres that he was ready to reinstate the abortive London Agreement of April 1987.[40] Moreover, the king coyly told the *New*

York Times that Jordan had a major role to play in a peace process, but that he would not substitute for the PLO unless Palestinians asked him to; at the same time, the royal court was quietly pressing Palestinians friendly to Jordan to do just that.[41] Iraq's defeat, said the king, "opened a new window" for the peace process.[42] Jordan's interpretation, however, resembled far more closely old formulas designed to take advantage of the PLO's nadir in the wake of the Gulf War. The king pursued this tack until he succeeded in hosting Secretary Baker in Aqaba on April 21, thereby gaining formal re-entry into the peace process.

Hussein had five likely reasons for wanting to partake in peace diplomacy. First and most important, while Jordan was weak, the PLO was even weaker; the chance to kick Arafat while the PLO was down must have seemed irresistible, especially given the two decades of sparring between them. Second, with Syria and Israel likely to become the focus of post-Gulf War diplomacy, Jordan did not want to be left out on the off-chance that a new peace process achieved success. Third, even if it did not, Syria was Jordan's once and perhaps future adversary after Saddam Hussein had been reduced, and, as always, the king wanted to head off trouble at the pass. In accord with the Arabic proverb "kiss the hand you cannot bite," Hussein has always preferred to deal with danger by snuggling up to it rather than by confronting it. Fourth, Hussein had to appear active diplomatically in order to gain the good graces of Americans, Europeans, and Japanese that might reward the peacemakers. Fifth, the king hoped that a helpful diplomacy would buy protection from Washington against future Israeli predations directed at Jordan; the specter of "transfer"—a euphemism for the expulsion of Palestinians from the West Bank and Gaza into Jordan—was foremost among Jordanian fears, albeit exaggerated.

Jordan's gambit forced the question of how Washington should respond to Hussein's hints at diplomacy. Nearly everyone (outside of Congress, that is) understood the common sense of helping the Hashemites if only because every alternative to the monarchy—East Bank-led military government, Palestinian rule, fundamentalist Islamic upheaval, chronic instability, civil war—was worse for U.S. interests. But it only made sense to allow the king to participate in a future peace process if he waived his previous demands to join the process only with the direct participation of the PLO and with prior Israeli agreement to the concept of territorial compromise, either of which would have broken Israeli "red lines" and torpedoed the diplomatic effort. In the end, the king agreed to waive both preconditions. It was not without some meaning that he began making sharply anti-PLO remarks:

> A real Palestinian nationalist in my book is someone ... who has been enduring hardship for years and years, much more so than someone who is sitting outside the territories pontificating about nationalist matters from a position of comfort ... People who have lived far from hardship that has lasted all these many years have no right to offer advice on what must or must not be done.[43]

Hussein even suggested that once liberation was achieved, there would be no need for the PLO at all.

The New Limbo

King Hussein survived the Kuwait crisis because he bent skillfully with the national mood—a feat described by one writer as being "never so popular, never so precarious."[44] This the king succeeded in doing despite rationing, despite cutting back the work week to five days to save energy, and despite what seemed to be the galloping devastation of the economy. Indeed, in some respects, Jordan's general circumstances a year after the end of the Gulf War were better than they were a year before it.

First, the economy was recovering. Returnees to Jordan were slowly but surely finding work, and the population seemed resigned to a lower set of expectations. Foreign workers were being sent home as Jordanians began to accept lower-paying, lower-status jobs that they used to reject out of hand.

Second, the king's nationalist credentials, even among Palestinians, never shined more brightly, whereas Arafat's position had never been worse. Even former close PLO associates started to call for his ouster.[45]

Third, thanks to the Palestinian issue and the energies swirling around the U.S.-sponsored peace process, relations with the United States improved, even as Jordan remained Iraq's only window to the wider world.

Fourth, the radical threat to the monarchy, and especially the fundamentalist challenge, receded. Islamic fundamentalism may wax or wane in Jordan over the longer run; it is not clear which is more likely. But there is no question that with Saddam's defeat, Jordanian Islamists were sent scrambling. Although superficially united with secular forces in late 1990, deep differences between fundamentalists and secularists surfaced soon after Iraq's withdrawal from Kuwait. Also, Islamists unwisely pushed their parliamentary power, by ordering such socially divisive changes as gender segregation in some government ministries and by introducing legislation banning all co-educational schools.[46] Needless to say, the more Westernized strata of Jordanian society were appalled, and said so. One example of many was journalist Rami Khouri, who—in the pro-democratic parlance of the hour—worried that Jordan would "make political history by making the transition from autocracy to democracy to theocracy in one smooth motion."[47]

The social backlash against the Muslim Brotherhood was strong, and together with the depression caused by Iraqi defeat, doomed their parliamentary power, at least temporarily. In July 1991, the king appointed Nablus-born Tahir al-Masri as prime minister, with no Islamists or prominent leftists in the cabinet.[48] The Brotherhood tried—and failed—to lead a no-confidence motion to defeat the government's accession. Meanwhile, the monarchy took advantage of the decline of Islamists, leftist factions, and exclusionary Palestinian political forces in the country by promulgating a political parties law that poses explicit constraints on any sectarian or externally-connected political organization that would function in the kingdom.[49] Both the National Charter and the political parties law are designed to protect the regime against an Islamic version of Sulayman al-Nabulsi, and while no guarantee is foolproof, these are well crafted to the purpose and are likely to work as long as political willpower at the center holds fast.

On balance, the comeback staged by the Jordanian regime under the guiding hand of King Hussein has been little short of breathtaking. Before the Kuwait crisis, the essential question was whether the king would still be on the throne when the social changes accumulating in Jordan eventually exploded in crisis. If so, the country had a better chance of weathering any storm. In 1990-1991, the question evolved into whether the Kuwait crisis would provoke that explosion before its time. Clearly, the process of transformation, begun initially at Hussein's instigation, was for a while cast to the mercy of forces largely beyond his control. Now, as Jordan's skies seem to lighten, some are asking whether there was any reason to worry in the first place.

The answer is "yes" and the worry remains justified. The dangers of the Kuwait crisis on the regime were exaggerated, mainly by those who did not know much about Jordan. But the longer-term dangers were underappreciated before the Kuwait crisis, and despite the king's masterful performance since, they are liable to be underappreciated again. The regime survived the Kuwait crisis and has managed to land on its feet thanks in part to U.S. American peace diplomacy and the weakness of the PLO. But it remains to be seen how much control the king will be able to regain, or will wish to regain, over the top-down approach to constitutional devolution he began some years ago. And if the peace process fails, as well it might, the king could find himself back in the hot-seat once again for having made public concessions to Israel—such as the detailed agenda for a future peace treaty announced in November 1992—and gained nothing to show for it.

What Next? The King, His Choices, and His Successors

Whatever the uncertainties of the present moment, the longer-term alternatives in the Jordanian case can be stated with some confidence. The regime's control over national politics will either diminish in a more or less orderly manner from the top-down; or it will do so more haphazardly from the bottom-up; or it will alternate between the two modes. The first possibility implies a process designed to spread political participation and authority from the monarchy to some division of labor and spoils among the tribes and the oligarchy. The second implies, at its extreme, chaos, civil war, and either revolutionary reassertion or national dismemberment and destruction. The third suggests that top-down and bottom-up possibilities are not mutually exclusive, that the pressure of the street may push the reform process from on high, and the reform process from on high may either feed or diminish the pressure in the street, depending on how it is carried out and on what Jordan's neighbors may do, as well.

One thing is clear, however: the Hashemite regime as it has been known it over the decades—a centralized and nearly absolute monarchy—is unlikely to survive a transition from Hussein to either his brother or son. Secularism has undermined Hashemite sherifian legitimacy and, in a different way, Islamic fundamentalism has invalidated old verities connecting king and Islam. Also, King Hussein has reigned securely because he has been able to transcend the narrow basis of authority inherent in the monarchy through the power of his personality, the force of time and habit, and good luck. But the king is mortal, and without him, all bets are off. It makes sense at this juncture to focus on the king, whose prospective longevity is perhaps the crucial ingredient in Jordan's future.

King Hussein's significance in Jordanian political life is hard to exaggerate. Not only has he been effective head of state longer than anyone on earth (save North Korea's Kim Il Sung), but he has managed to reformulate the basis upon which the monarchy rests. In the beginning of Hashemite rule, Abdullah's sherifian status was instrumental in winning the loyalty of the bedouin tribes that became his key constituency. Sherifian status helped Hussein, too, but he recognized early on that it meant little to most Palestinians and might be of waning significance in the rest of the kingdom over time. So Hussein cultivated what, for want of a better phrase, might be called a populist monarchy. He was regal but humble. He made the decisions but touched base with a wide stratum of society. He never hid his affection and admiration for things Western, including in his wives, but he constantly affirmed his Arabism, too, with sincerity and conviction. In short, the tone of the monarchy has been so dramatically associated with Hussein that it is very hard to imagine anyone else as king of Jordan.

Hussein not only redefined the monarchy, but he and fate together redefined Jordanian society. The influx of Palestinians that came with the capture of the West Bank in 1948 and then with its loss in 1967 presented the Hashemites with a unique problem. Unlike other Arab states, which could and did exclude Palestinians from mainstream social and political life, Jordan could not, for the Palestinians' demographic and economic weight was too large. Instead, Jordan made them citizens, hoping to develop a hybrid national identity compatible with Hashemite sovereignty. To do this, however, required reliance on externally financed integrative economic policies, rhetorical pan-Arabism, and a crack internal security force as insurance against setbacks. Such integrative policies and rhetoric did not always sit well with East Bankers, however, many of whom resented Jordan's being sucked into the Arab-Israeli maelstrom. Many socially conservative East Bankers would have preferred that the country stay away from all debilitating pan-Arab commitments, too.

Such tensions never got out of hand, with the partial exception of the 1970-1971 civil war,[50] because the king managed to function as a sort of mediative filter between the two halves of Jordanian society. So, Palestinians might complain that East Bankers hampered Jordan's contribution to the struggle against Israel, and East Bankers might complain that Palestinians were taking too many jobs and dragging Jordan into matters that were little its affair, and yet the monarchy possessed enough real and symbolic patronage to appease both camps. But the prospect of a Jordan without Hussein, and with Palestinian nationalism and a trans-tribal East Bank political consciousness both growing, shrouds the country's basic social comity in doubt. If monarchical power continues to ebb as Hussein grows older or weaker—particularly in harsher economic times and amid pervasive regional turbulence—old constants cannot be counted upon to endure.

While observers have longed speculated on "Jordan after Hussein," the king's public admission of his fight with cancer lent an urgency and reality to such discussions. In August 1992, King Hussein underwent surgery in the United States; his doctors acknowledged the king's urinary tract cancer but declared him cured. After convalescence, the king returned to a hero's welcome in Amman, with nearly one million Jordanians lining the capital's streets. In November 1992, however, the king announced to his people plans to return to the United States for periodic examinations. The heavily fatalistic tone of that speech suggested that the king had indeed reconciled himself to his own mortality and was in the midst of preparing himself and his kingdom for what may lie ahead.

For these reasons and perhaps others, as suggested above, it is likely that since early 1988 the king has planned a transition to put Jordan's government on a footing ultimately independent of him as a person and much less dependent on near-absolute monarchical authority. The July 1988 disengagement, the political opening represented by the November 1989 election, the National Charter, and the king's willingness before August 1990 to allow parliament an independent (and disruptive) influence over important policy questions can together be seen to fit such an intent. Indeed, Hussein said as much in a May 1990 interview, in which he explicitly linked the disengagement and the National Charter to his own mortality:

> It is time we resumed the march after the disengagement with the West Bank. This is the truth and the freedom which we followed before others in the world. We hope that the royal commission ... will succeed in formulating the National Charter. I believe that no person will last forever; we all perish. But this people and this nation will remain. In my personal opinion, we as leaders should do the impossible to unite the people and make them agree among themselves. We should provide them with the wherewithal to learn about everything and to take part in shouldering their responsibilities. This is the real guarantee for the continuation of the democratic option.[51]

But why did Hussein do all this? Perhaps he became convinced from events in Eastern Europe that the days of one-man rule were over. Perhaps he came to believe that Jordan's longer-term situation was untenable and that change would be forced in very unpleasant ways if he did not take the initiative himself. Perhaps he lost interest and energy in the kingship, as he sometimes intimated, and perhaps he lacked confidence that either Crown Prince Hasan or his eldest son from an Arab Muslim wife, Ali (b. 1975), can carry on successfully should he soon pass from the scene. This last element might be the key.

There appears to be in Hashemite Jordan an established procedure for royal succession. Hussein is son of the last king and grandson of the one before that. In truth, the succession process is murkier, mirroring troubles in other Islamic lands throughout history. In European history, the right of succession through eldest male (or even female) child was well established. In Islamic history, the line of royal descent to son, uncle, or brother was far less clear, a consensus (*ijma*) of the royal court traditionally playing a larger role. So in Jordan today.

Hussein's eldest son, Abdullah, was named crown prince after his birth in 1962, replacing the king's brother Muhammad, but pressure soon mounted to strip Abdullah of the crown princeship, partially because his mother, an Englishwoman, was neither Muslim nor Arab. In the event, Abdullah was replaced as crown prince in 1965 by the king's youngest brother, Hasan, with Muhammad having been judged temperamentally unfit to hold the post. A decade later, Hussein's only Muslim Arab wife, Alia, had a male child, Ali. (Alia subsequently died in a helicopter crash.) In 1977, Hussein named the infant Ali to be Hasan's eventual successor; Ali has since reached the age of majority and could, theoretically, be named crown prince himself. Meanwhile, Hasan, the current incumbent, is married to a Pakistani woman—Muslim but not Arab—and has a son of his own.

Matters are murkier still on account of Hasan's personality, which is widely thought to lack his brother's populist touch. But whatever Hasan's character and talents, his main difficulty is simply that he is not Hussein. True, there was less obvious panic in Jordan when the king entered hospital in June 1991 with heart fibulations than there was in the United States over the possible accession of Vice President Dan Quayle when President Bush fell ill. Nevertheless, Hasan lacks his brother's stature and suffers from a confidence gap among much of the elite.

As a result, there has been speculation that Hussein would in time ensure that Ali, not Hasan, succeeds him. There appears to be no foundation for this, but whoever does become king after Hussein—assuming a monarchy remains in place—is sure to inherit much less than an absolute monarchy. The succession question, however important, is probably less important than the question of what kind of political institution a new king will inherit. That is still in its definitional stage.

Constitutional Devolution: Top-Down

It is possible—and even likely—that the monarchy, upon the king's abdication or demise (or even earlier), could become a constitutional or limited monarchy, with the current parliament coming to hold more genuine and lawful power than it does now. This, it seems, is what the king has had in mind as the best path and, clearly, what the National Charter and political parties law seem designed to encourage.

If this proceeds, then the same elite classes that run society just below the palace today—the tribes and the military, the East Bankers and the Jordanized Palestinians in the civil service bureaucracy and business sector—will fill these new political spaces as best they can. The army would retain the upper hand against excessive inter-elite competition, and in time an adjusted social *modus vivendi* could emerge. This process of devolution downward could trigger a protracted struggle for relative leverage among political families, bureaucrats, Islamists, businessmen, and possibly the military. In such a scenario, the monarchy could remain a crucial power broker, depending on the skill of the monarch and the condition of the rest of civil society. One would, in effect, have a reconstituted monarchy, with either a little less power than before or very much less power than before.

It is possible, however, that new political competition could lead to political violence and social breakdown, especially if the country were subject to possibly strong outside pressures from Syria, a rebuilt Iraq, or a radical, right-wing Israel bent on turning Hashemite Jordan into Palestine. If this were to happen, and if the monarchy failed to control the fray, then the possibility of a military government would rise in proportion. Even with such a government, it is not clear that a new status quo could be worked out without concessions offered to new claimants to social power, including the Islamists.

One could even see a more attenuated devolution of the monarchy in the safekeeping of the army. Jordan's army and intelligence services are skillful, but they are not set up to run the country. They are, however, the natural constituency of the oligopoly to whom most social power would initially fall, and this oligopoly knows how to circle the wagons if need be. A military government made up mainly of a frightened and re-mobilized tribal confederacy, with fewer rather than more Palestinian establishment allies, might also at some point "elect" a new monarch from their own midst if future Hashemites prove themselves unable to rise to the occasion. But it would be a monarch with far less power and status than the current one.

Social Revolution: Bottom-Up

Even if constitutional devolution were to succeed and social revolution from the bottom up is avoided, new and potentially destabilizing forces could still arise or be coaxed into existence. The success of constitutional devolution might then only delay, not prevent, a more encompassing social upheaval. Differences between Palestinians and East Bankers might become too bitter to keep a compromise power-sharing arrangement together. Moreover, if the army factionalized, parts of it supporting different leadership clusters along tribal, ethnic or ideological lines, the country could court civil chaos and, with it, foreign intervention and possibly even dismemberment or dissolution.

If no equipoise can be established over a protracted period in a post-Hussein scramble for power, then a social upheaval from below could develop, probably accelerated by Islamist political ambitions. Should that happen, the degree of social comity between younger East Bankers and Palestinians could deteriorate sharply. In this regard, the pent-up hostility toward Palestinians by the new generation of East Bankers, who see a world of opportunity before them usurped by Palestinian interlopers, is especially critical. The words of one East Banker sum up the attitude that has come to be known as that of the "Jordanian Likud":

All Jordanian native people are more or less bedouins even if they dwell in cities and towns. Bedouins by nature have gloomy prospects and work hard to keep their families cohesive. Even we, this generation, still share with our fathers the same views—we really don't think with all the intruders in Jordan that this is no more required ... Jordanian-Palestinian relations was [sic] never good since the 1949 annexation and despite Hussein-Arafat hugging and kissing it would never be. Palestinians always consider themselves Palestinians first and Jordanian only when the Jordanian citizenship benefits them more. Otherwise, they are anti-Jordanian, regime and people. Those among them who support the regime could co-exist with us are either oligarchs or merchants who had emigrated to Jordan on or before the 1948 war. Beside that, I don't think any one of them nurture good feelings toward the Jordanian people or regime. I, however, do hope that with the severance of ties with the West Bank it will be easier to live with them. From now on, Palestinian would remember [sic] that Jordan is a host country, love it or leave it ... Jordan is better off without the West Bank and the Palestinians and I think it is high time for them, along with their supporters, to take the responsibility which Jordan shouldered for the past forty years.[52]

Because this is an increasingly popular attitude among young East Bankers, the easing of communal divisions that has progressed steadily over the years may not be the wave of the future. With the passage of time, most (but not all) Palestinians have become increasingly inured to being Jordanian, but East Bankers have been increasingly resentful of Palestinians at so being. In a way, the Palestinians in Jordan cannot win: if they integrate and try to become Jordanian, they are resented for usurpation, but if they do not integrate, they are resented for being ungrateful.

If authority broke down into social chaos, a civil war much deeper than 1970 could result. Memories of 1970 are growing dimmer; indeed, with a mean population age of fifteen, a civil war in Jordan would pit many people born after 1970 against each other. It is a war that East Bankers would probably win, and afterwards the attitudes of the victors would look much like the attitudes of many young East Bankers today, only more hostile and flush with military success.

A social upheaval in post-Hussein Jordan, were one to come, would not develop in a vacuum. Just as Jordan's eight historical watersheds had their origins outside the kingdom, so would at least the later stages of a ninth. A Palestinian upheaval in Jordan might be either aided or abetted by an irredentist mini-state or entity on the West Bank and/or by a right-wing Israel bent on "transferring" its Arab population to Jordan. But for a self-described Palestinian rising to succeed, there would have to be a virtually total unraveling of the Jordanization process and the congealing of what is a divided Palestinian society in Jordan into a single political community. Neither was likely before the Kuwait crisis; if economic trouble worsens sharply in the future, however, this is less far-fetched than before. Inept or weak royal leadership could be crucial here, too. Radical opposition cadres would have a better chance to seize power after the demise or collapse of the monarchy amid an intra-elite fight so debilitating that a wide political vacuum was created in its wake.

But far more likely than an anti-regime upheaval describing itself as Palestinian is one describing itself as Islamist, having a Palestinian core with East Bank allies. Thus, if Palestinians in Jordan ever attain a majority share of real political power to match their demographic weight, they may not turn the East Bank over to Arafat and company. Instead, Palestinian Islamism, as foreshadowed by the November 1989 election, is more likely.

Certainly, the Palestinian uprising, the declaration of a Palestinian state, and the role of Islamic elements in that whole process make the conjunction of Palestinian frustration and the new Islamic political paradigm specifically for Palestinians much less remote than had been thought in the early 1980s. There is a compelling inner logic for such a development. Palestinians in Jordan are still relatively marginal in Jordanian society, and they are more likely to protest the main object of their frustration—Israel—through combinate forms of political identification. They are more likely, for example, to confront the government on occupational lines, Palestinians protesting as, say, unemployed engineers rather than as ethnic "Palestinians." But Islam is a more powerful and sustaining rubric, particularly in times of general political unrest. A Palestinian who redefines his antipathy for Israel in religious terms, terms that already carry an important and a growing resonance in Jordan, has found a way to be radically anti-Israel and at the same time express himself such that it does not compromise his Jordanian experience and alienate potential East Bank allies. Indeed, the failure of every other approach—Marxism, conventional nationalism, revolution by committee (i.e., the PLO)—leaves Islam as the one, major untried way to turn in the minds of many. Islam is thus a means to transcend the divisions in Jordanian society and, in an age of increasing activism, the growing merger of Palestinian nationalism and Islam is not hard to understand.[53]

Moreover, insofar as fundamentalism is uncompromising, it is useful for a Palestinian in Jordan who does not wish to live in a hypothetical Palestinian mini-state or autonomous region in the West Bank and Gaza, it being understood that a mini-state is far more likely than the complete destruction of Israel. In this formulation, religious radicalism would allow the rejection of partial solutions as inadequate; at the same time, it would eliminate the need to choose whether to stay in Jordan with family and the security of known quantities or cross the river to unknown prospects.

Whether Islamist power waxes or wanes over time—and this may depend in part on how well Islamic fundamentalists in the occupied territories fair in the future—Jordan's growing educated population is up against structural limits to growth such that whichever political forces inherit Jordan over the next decade, they shall find themselves with a powder-keg on their hands and contending demands in their ears.

Which of these alternative futures is most likely? Before the Kuwait crisis, an orderly devolution of monarchical authority, however tricky in practice, seemed the most likely outcome so long as King Hussein was around to manage the process. Such a development is still the best bet; after all, no modern Arab government has ever fallen to a revolution from below. Certainly, nothing like what happened in Iran in 1978-1979 has ever happened in the Arab world, where so-called revolutions are usually little more than inter-elite fratricides or military takeovers.

But this does not mean that it cannot happen in the future, and now that Islam is so much more a part of the political equation in Amman, Jordan could be the first Arab society to suffer an accelerated and violent social revolution in modern times. If Jordanian society starts to break apart, it will depend largely on the skill and resources of the monarchy to prevent total disaster, for social chaos is more likely to invite foreign intervention into Jordan than into any other country in the region (including even what is left of Lebanon). The present monarch sees the old way of rule as making things worse in the future if not already in the present. He seems to believe that only in a more open environment can Jordanian society work out its problems—and he is probably right. If it takes time, however, as it surely will, he can only hope that when the process is finished there will be a place left for a Hashemite successor.

Foreign Policy Fallout

A final question remains: what might alternative future Jordanian leaderships think and believe about its neighbors (including Israel), about the United States, and about the Arab-Israeli peace process?

If Jordan's future leadership is composed of the present oligopoly in expanded form, changes would probably not be dramatic. Greater weakness, however, would yield more diplomatic meekness. If it were a more conservative East Bank elite, then Jordanian interest and activism in peace process affairs would be reduced, ironically opening up broader opportunities for Palestinian politics both in Jordan and outside of it. Such an East Bank state might get on well with the United States and maintain, or even expand, functional cooperation with Israel. But it would be less likely to be an active part of the solution to the core of the Arab-Israeli conflict; it would probably not make a public, formal peace with Israel, at least not unless Syria did so first.

Jordan's broader orientation in international relations and regional politics would not change dramatically either. It would still have enemies, it would still need money, and as long as it remained opposed to radicalism, it would have at least minimal support from the United States. After all, as with the current situation, all alternatives would be worse.

But if the regime turns Palestinian—either secular, Islamist, or some combination thereof—it would surely destroy most or all of the *modus vivendi* built up over the years between Israel and Jordan. This, in turn, would undermine such political forces as exist in Israel favoring territorial compromise over the West Bank and Gaza; indeed, any protracted political instability in Jordan would redound to the general political advantage of those Israelis who believe the occupied territories should never be returned to Arab sovereignty in any form. It is even quite possible that political instability in

Jordan could cause the disintegration of Israeli-Palestinian agreements on Palestinian self-rule, should these be worked out beforehand.

Worse, a rump Palestinian entity on the East Bank would be both irredentist and weak. It would probably be impelled toward conflict not only with Israel, but also with stronger Arab states nearby jockeying for influence in and over it. This is a formula, ultimately, for war, destabilization, multipartite foreign intervention, partition, and the destruction of Jordan in its current frontiers.[54] Except for the interests of Greater Syrian nationalism, no party would be well-served by such a development. But it might happen anyway, and it is more likely to the extent that Israel's dilemma over the West Bank remains unsolved.

As far as the United States is concerned, virtually every imaginable outcome, likely and not, represents a less favorable situation than the Hashemite status quo it has known for more than forty years.[55] A Palestinian-Islamic regime would be anti-American, and while the U.S. government might find ways to limit the damage that such a regime would do to its interests, such ways would be few. Ironically, the more democratic Jordan is, at least in the sense of having a government that appeals to the sentiments of the majority, the poorer U.S.-Jordanian relations are likely to be.[56] Even while King Hussein sits on his throne, this much is already clear.

Notes

1. One example of a left-of-center writer erroneously projecting his politics onto the Middle East is Michael Hudson, *Arab Politics* (New Haven: Yale University Press, 1977), p. 30 in particular.

2. For details of Abdullah's early shifts in preference for succession, from Talal to second-son Nayif and back again, see Mary C. Wilson, *King Abdallah, Britain and the Making of Jordan* (New York: Cambridge University Press, 1987), pp. 132, 149-50.

3. For the best account of this period, see P. J. Vatikiotis, *Politics and the Military in Jordan* (London: Frank Cass, 1967).

4. King Hussein, *Uneasy Lies the Head* (New York: Bernard Geis, 1962), chapter 10.

5. This period is particularly important to an understanding of the past few years because the Jordanian *glasnost* of 1988-1989 resembles that of the Nabulsi period in some ways, and the king has spoken of the former in the

reflected light of the latter. See the king's remarks about having gone "through harder times in the past" with political openings. King Hussein interviewed in *al-Ra'y*, (Amman), July 17, 1989, as reported in *Foreign Broadcast Information Service-Near East and South Asia (FBIS)*, July 19, 1989.

6. Malcolm Kerr, *The Arab Cold War*, second edition (New York: Oxford University Press, 1970).

7. See Adam Garfinkle, *Israel and Jordan in the Shadow of War: Functional Ties and Futile Diplomacy in a Small Space* (New York: St. Martin's, 1992).

8. Common wisdom has it that Hussein's entry into the 1967 war was his greatest error, but that is wrong. Hussein worried, rightly in my view, that not joining Nasser in May 1967 would have led to civil war with Syrian and Iraqi intervention to overthrow him. (Recall: the West Bank was in upheaval, and both Syrian and Iraqi armor were already on Jordanian soil.) Given the choices, joining a doomed war coalition with Nasser was the lesser evil.

9. See Adam Garfinkle, "The Importance of Being Hussein: Jordanian Foreign Policy and Peace in the Middle East," in Robert O. Freedman, ed., *The Middle East from the Iran-Contra Affair to the Intifada* (Syracuse: Syracuse University Press, 1990).

10. This is derived from the Central Bank's *Monthly Statistical Bulletin*.

11. See the charts in Valerie Yorke, *Domestic Politics and Regional Security: Jordan, Syria, and Israel* (Aldershot, England: Gower, 1988), pp. 64-66.

12. Tony Walker, "Jordan on the Rebound after Gulf Conflict," *Financial Times*, May 31, 1991. For 1991 estimates of gross national product, see "Less guns and butter," *The Jerusalem Report*, March 12, 1992.

13. Some Jordanian economists agree. See Fahd al-Fanik, "Economic Damage Has Yet to Come," *Jordan Times*, July 21, 1991.

14. Note, for example, the role of Dr. Mamduh al-Abbadi, president of the Jordan Medical Association and of the Council of Jordanian Professional Associations, in organizing the April 1990 march to support the *intifada*. See Maryam M. Shabin, "Unionist Planning March to King Husayn Bridge," *Jordan Times*, April 12-13, 1990.

15. See Mahbub Ahmad and Siham Muhammad Mahmud Hosain, "Length of School Life in Jordan," in *Aspects of Population Change and Development in Some African and Asian Countries* (Cairo: Cairo Demographic Center, Research Monograph Series No. 9, 1984), pp. 657-66.

16. Personal communication, May 1989.

17. The rise in religiosity after 1978 is not to be denied; but it is partly a response to broad trends toward secularization over the preceding thirty years. As a result, Jordanian society is more polarized today between the religious and the not-so-religious than ever before. See Fahmi Ghazwi and Steven L. Nock, "Religion as a Mediating Force in the Effects of Modernization on Parent-Child Relations in Jordan," *Middle Eastern Studies,* vol. 25, no. 3 (July 1989), pp. 363-369.

18. See Paul Jureidini and Robert McLaurin, *Jordan: The Impact of Social Change on the Role of the Tribes* (Washington: Center for Strategic and International Studies and Praeger, 1984).

19. See Peter Gubser, *Politics and Change in Al-Karak* (Boulder: Westview, 1985); and Yorke, pp. 24-29.

20. Private interview, Amman.

21. This does not mean that bedouin disdain commerce as such. On the contrary, many (if not most) bedouin tribes have sought involvement in commerce and transportation.

22. Although the leadership of Jordanian fundamentalists is not Palestinian, up to 75 percent of its rank-and-file is. Generally, the leadership is evolutionist, the Palestinian rank-and-file militant.

23. Chances are that this understanding was private but explicit. This is because the matter was addressed publicly in considerable detail, as if it had been thought through and discussed. See Mustafa Abu-Lubdah, "Minister Says PLO Ties Reaching 'New Stage'," *al-Siyasah* (Kuwait) reported in *FBIS,* March 30, 1990, and "PFLP Official Comments on Jordan Ties, U.S.," *al-Dustour* (Amman), May 22, 1990, as reported in *FBIS,* May 24, 1990.

24. A similar argument is put by Valerie Yorke, "A New Era for Jordan?" *The World Today,* February 1990.

25. Of the twenty-three cabinet members, thirteen were new from the previous cabinet; but only a few were new altogether. "New Cabinet Named in Jordan," *New York Times,* December 7, 1989.

26. One even had the temerity to decry "nepotism"—this is a hereditary monarchy! See "Democratic Unity and Justice Party Established," *al-Dustour,* August 27, 1990, as reported in *FBIS,* August 28, 1990.

27. Mirmin Murad, "Lower House Calls for Reviving 'Eastern Front'," *Jordan Times,* February 11, 1990.

28. Badr 'Abd al-Haq, "Deputies, Notables Question National Charter," *al-Yawm al-Sabi',* April 30, 1990, as reported in *FBIS,* May 7, 1990. *al-Yawm al-Sabi'* is published in Paris, but the session took place in Amman and the transcript was widely available there.

29. The point is made in Robert Satloff, "Islam Ascendant: Jordan, the West Bank and Gaza," in Robert Blecher, ed., *Islamic Fundamentalism in the Levant* (Washington: The Washington Institute for Near East Policy, 1990), p. 15.

30. See Maryam Shahin, "King Meets with Members of Leftist Parties," *Jordan Times,* April 26-27, 1990, and Lamis Andoni, "King Husayn Meets JCP Leadership 15 April," *Jordan Times,* April 17, 1990.

31. For a brief survey, see Judith Miller, "Jordan Economy Devastated by Effects of the Gulf Crisis," *New York Times,* October 21, 1990.

32. *Middle East Economic Digest,* November 2, 1990, p. 15.

33. This figure is used in Joe Stork, "The Gulf War and the Arab World," *World Policy Journal,* vol. 8., no. 2 (Spring 1991), p. 369.

34. See the discussion in Robert B. Satloff, *Troubles on the East Bank: Challenges to the Domestic Stability of Jordan* (Washington: Center for Strategic and International Studies and Praeger, 1986), chapter two.

35. Robert B. Satloff's *They Cannot Stop Our Tongues: Islamic Activism in Jordan,* (Washington: The Washington Institute for Near East Policy, 1988), the result of fieldwork in Jordan, was virtually the only important exception.

36. "Islamists, Leftists Form 'National Front'," *Jordan Times,* August 20, 1990.

37. See Lamis Andoni, "Jordanians Clamor for Giving Weapons to People," *Christian Science Monitor,* October 18, 1990; for a pithy description and some color photographs of this training, see Joel Brinkley, "Divided Loyalties," *New York Times Magazine,* December 15, 1990.

38. I have drawn the story in more detail in "Allies of Diminishing Returns: The Hashemite Question," *The National Interest,* 25 (Fall 1991).

39. See "King Husayn's *Le Point* Interview Reported," *Jordan Times,* June 4, 1991.

40. For background to that agreement, see *Israel and Jordan in the Shadow of War,* pp. 121-123.

41. See Jim Hoagland, "Palestinians: Starting from Zero," *Washington Post,* March 19, 1991.

42. See William Drozdiak, "Jordan Revives Proposal for Confederation," *Washington Post,* March 30, 1991.

43. See Ehud Ya'ari, "Hussein's Game Plan," *The Jerusalem Report,* August 22, 1991, p. 38; and "News Analysis: Signs of New Tensions in Jordanian-Palestinian Relations; King Husayn's Criticism of PLO Arouses Questions in Cairo," *al-Sharq al-Awsat* (London), August 7, 1991, as reported in *FBIS,* August 15, 1991.

44. *Middle East Economic Digest,* September 14, 1990, p. 4.

45. "Fatah's al-Hasan Calls for Arafat's Removal," Kuwait News Agency, August 10, 1991, as reported in *FBIS,* August 12, 1991.

46. *Middle East Economic Digest,* April 12, 1991, p. 14.

47. Rami Khouri, "Thank Heaven for Little Girls (in shorts)," *Jordan Times,* May 7, 1991.

48. Joel Brinkley, "Jordanian King Moves to Isolate Islamic Militants," *New York Times,* June 19, 1991.

49. For text of the draft law, see *Sawt al-Sha'b* (Amman), July 6, 1991, translated in *FBIS,* July 9, 1991.

50. Partial, because even the civil war was not simply an East Banker versus Palestinian affair. Most Palestinians in the kingdom were either neutral or supported the regime.

51. My emphasis. The interview with the Bahraini paper *Akhbar al-Khalij* was published in the Jordanian *al-Ra'y* on May 12, 1990, translated in *FBIS,* May 15, 1990.

52. Private interview, Amman.

53. This is also, to some extent, true in the West Bank and Gaza, where frustration with another kind of weakening establishment leadership, i.e., the PLO, is also well advanced.

54. Partition could, hypothetically, involve Syria, Iraq, Israel, and even Saudi Arabia. Many of Jordan's tribes summoned the courage to side with Riyadh against the "street" in Amman during the crisis, and they might choose to join with the al-Saud if they could.

55. Some Israelis, anyway, are already preparing for this. See Sheila Hattis Rolef, "Nostalgia and Reality," *Davar,* September 30, 1990, reported in *FBIS,* October 1, 1990; Joshua Brilliant, "'Very senior' source: 'Hussein's days are numbered'," *Jerusalem Post,* September 15, 1990.

56. See Robert Satloff, "When the Friendly Tyrants Debate Doesn't Matter: The Hashemite Kingdom of Jordan," in Daniel Pipes and Adam Garfinkle, eds., *Friendly Tyrants: An American Dilemma* (New York: St. Martin's, 1991).

5

Regime Stability and Change in the Gulf: The Case of Saudi Arabia

Emile A. Nakhleh

The 1990-1991 Gulf crisis not only generated profound political and security challenges for Gulf Arab states, but it also provoked deep concern in the Arab "street" and among Arab intellectuals. For the states, their inability—individually and collectively through the Arab League—to thwart Iraqi aggression and reestablish Kuwaiti sovereignty, combined with their reliance on foreign forces to restore the peace, raised serious questions regarding the ultimate defense and security of the Gulf region. For the peoples and elites of the Gulf, the crisis sowed widespread confusion about the continuing relevance of concepts like Arab unity, Arab nationalism, and pan-Arabism.

The challenges facing the Gulf states as a consequence of the Gulf War are both internal and external. It is somewhat ironic that many of these challenges were brought forth by Saddam Hussein's "public diplomacy" message justifying his aggression against Kuwait. Regardless of the veracity of Saddam's message, several of his claims found resonance in the Arab street. These included his calls for democratization, political participation, and redistribution of wealth; his condemnation of the artificiality of state boundaries and the presence of foreign forces on Arab soil; and his appeal to universal human rights, the Palestinian-Israeli conflict, and Islam.

The internal challenges focus principally on the relationship between the individual and the regime and the Arab peoples' desire to participate in the political and economic national policies of their countries. Though mostly

119

centralized, Arab regimes—monarchies and single-party autocracies—are responding to these demands by promising some kind of a *shura* (consultation) system of limited participation in governance. Not surprising, no ruler has come forth with a promise for a true democracy. However, even a trend toward "shuracracy" is sure to generate some upheaval in the region. In this regard, the disturbances in Algeria are a precursor of further confrontations.

Demands for democratization have generated a range of important question for the ruling regimes: Can regimes survive without greater popular participation? Can they survive *with* greater participation? Does greater political participation mean more stability—internally and regionally—or less? Will pluralism work in an Islamic context? Can the Islamic concepts of *shura*, *ijtihad* (reasoning), and *ijma* (consensus) be the basis for political participation in Muslim polities?

While the challenges facing the Arab state system cover the entire region, from the Western Sahara to the Arabian Peninsula, this chapter addresses the challenges that apply to the Gulf Arab states, particularly Saudi Arabia. While many of these challenges predated the Gulf crisis, others were brought into sharp focus by the war. Although one is tempted to identify regional security as the most important short-run challenge resulting from the Gulf crisis, in the long term, internal stability looms as the largest challenge. In this context, internal stability of the family-ruled Gulf states, including Saudi Arabia, cannot endure unless a functional partnership is established between the ruling family and the citizenry.

A precondition for that to occur will be acceptance by the ruling elites of the principle of popular political participation in decision-making as well as the underlying assumption that such participation can enhance the legitimacy of the regime. Indeed, some elite groups in Gulf states—i.e., academics, businessmen, professionals, journalists, and high-level officials—have been vocal in their demands for greater participation in governance. They have based their case on the argument that participation undergirds stability and that internal stability is inexorably linked to regional security.

Prior to the Gulf crisis, Gulf ruling families had, for the most part, rejected such ideas on the grounds that their oil wealth permits them to provide their citizens with free health, education, and welfare services without collecting any taxes. No representation is granted, beyond the Islamic principle of *shura*, because no taxation is required. The lubricant of abundant wealth allowed them to make the transition from classical tribalism into urban tribalism. However, as the rentier state's ability to provide such largesse is reduced, the demands for accountability increase. Consequently, the traditional tribal basis of accommodation between the ruler and the ruled becomes less acceptable to those who are provided less. The tribal state begins, therefore, to apply other methods to enforce allegiance, thereby making it more urban and less tribal; the rentier state is slowly and surely being replaced by the *mukhabarat* (security forces) state. As a result, the ruling family becomes a "regime," not much different from other authoritarian regimes in the region. The Gulf crisis accelerated this process throughout the Gulf Cooperation Council; Saudi Arabia is no exception.[*]

The Saudi Political System: Stability and Change

On June 13, 1992, Fahd ibn Abd al-Aziz al-Saud celebrated his tenth anniversary as king of Saudi Arabia. He succeeded his late brother Khalid a decade earlier, after serving as prime minister and crown prince. The succession went smoothly, both within the inner council of the House of Saud and in the country as a whole. Fahd received the allegiance (*bay'a*) of the major tribes of the kingdom and of the influential religious scholars (*ulama*).

Saudi Arabia, like the other states of the GCC, has shown a remarkable degree of stability. Yet, in spite of this stability, all these states will face several serious challenges in the next decade. The most formidable among these is the need to respond to demands for power-sharing.

In building their political societies, leaders of the Gulf Arab states began to face new challenges and demands for political reform. The transformation of these societies into modern, viable political entities has centered around the single question of how to maintain political development at an evolutionary, not a revolutionary, pace. In other words, governments were forced to grapple with the dilemma of reconciling the tribal/Islamic principle of *shura,* the basis of family rule in the shaykhdoms for centuries, to the introduction of new partners into the decision-making process—all without undermining the heretofore unquestioned authority of the ruler. At least rhetorically, the rulers of the Gulf Arab states have answered these questions in the affirmative. The fact that these regimes have survived, one might argue, is a confirmation of their ability to establish modern functioning polities in the context of tribal traditionalism. Yet only after the Gulf crisis do those

---

[*] This six-nation grouping includes Saudi Arabia, Kuwait, Bahrain, Oman, Qatar, and the United Arab Emirates.

regimes face rising demands for political participation that do not appear willing to settle for platitudes and rhetoric.

Saudi Arabia is a conservative Muslim monarchy ruled by a powerful king whose authority derives from a large, closely knit royal family (Al Saud), an influential group of religious scholars (*ulama*), wealthy merchants, senior government officials, and tribal support as expressed by the allegiance of powerful tribal shaykhs throughout the land. The constitutional basis of government is lodged in *shari'a* (Islamic law). The two primary supports of the *shari'a* are the *sunna* (traditions) and the *hadith* (the sayings and actions of the Prophet Muhammad). Saudi religious conservatism and support for a strict adherence to the faith are based on the Wahhabi movement, founded in the heart of the Arabian Peninsula by the eighteenth-century religious reformer Muhammad Abd al-Wahhab.

The jolting transformation in the 1970s from a *terra incognita,* as far as the international community was concerned, to world prominence has placed Saudi society, with all of its traditions and institutions, under a close and uncomfortable international scrutiny. It is a situation which Saudi rulers cannot wish away but to which they have adjusted more or less successfully. As a result of this international prominence, the connection between Saudi Arabia's internal political system and the country's regional and international foreign policy has come into sharp focus. There is also the pressure brought to bear by systemic social change, occasioned by new wealth and a growing middle class, and most specifically by the post-Gulf crisis petitions by various elements of Saudi society demanding some sort of political participation.

Over the last half-century, the Saudi monarchy—unfettered with an elected legislature—has shown a remarkable ability to survive. This includes weathering four monarchical successions since the 1950s, suggesting that the centralized political system itself has transcended the personality of the leader. (See Table 5.1) The record indicates that regardless of the occasion of succession—natural death, deposition, assassination—family and other influential actors in the polity (civil servants, military officers, business families, and the intelligentsia) have shown deep commitment to preserving the state. In the formative decade of the 1960s, the Saudi leadership, particularly the late King Faisal, laid the broad outlines and philosophical/ideological underpinnings of the modern Saudi state. The booming 1970s brought about the establishment of a technocratic public administration which embraced a comprehensive public policy of growth. The sober 1980s witnessed adaptation and readjustment. Perhaps the most basic characteristic of the Saudi system, at least through the late 1980s, has been its remarkable stability—a result of consciously balanced and carefully supported tribal traditions, religious influence, family power, and, of course, oil wealth. This combination is the heart of traditional political dynamics in Saudi Arabia. Over the past decade, several factors have particularly contributed to this stability. These include: enormous oil-generated wealth and the widespread distribution of this wealth in the society; the size and ubiquity of the royal family; large expenditures on the armed forces and the corresponding rise of a satisfied cadre of military officers; the presence of a massive infrastructure in commerce, industry, agriculture, transportation, communication, and other public services; the ability of the Saudi polity to adapt to changing social, economic, and political conditions and demands; the rise of Saudi Arabia as an influential actor in the Gulf, in the Arab/Islamic world, and in the world community; the relatively small indigenous population and the dispersal of the population throughout Saudi territory; the Iran-Iraq War and the Saudis' determination to maintain national unity in the face of the perceived Iranian threat; and Iran's failure to win the war militarily and the consequently receding tide of Iranian-supported, Shi'ite-oriented Islamic fundamentalism.

TABLE 5.1   Accessions to the Throne in Saudi Arabia

King	Reign	Comment
Abd al-Aziz al-Saud	1932-1953	Died
Saud ibn Abd al-Aziz	1953-1964	Deposed
Faisal ibn Abd al-Aziz	1964-1975	Assassinated
Khalid ibn Abd al-Aziz	1975-1982	Died
Fahd ibn Abd al-Aziz	1982-	

Since the early 1990s, new factors have begun to disturb this equilibrium. On the social level, the growth of cities and rural-to-urban migration has upset traditional patterns of settlement; modernization in culture, education, and technology has fueled the development of a well-educated, politically conscious middle class. This has had ripple effects in government and the army, where a technocratic elite has filled the ranks of an expanded government and military bureaucracy. At the highest level of power, a second generation of princes—uniquely wealthy and foreign-educated—have shown signs of emerging as a powerful political class; they should be viewed as distinct from the current ruling group of princes that is comprised of sons of the kingdom's founder, Abd al-Aziz al-Saud, popularly known as Ibn Saud. These elements, which have begun to challenge the country's political traditionalism, have been sharpened dramatically since the Gulf crisis. Their growing significance underscores the emerging dichotomies that will be the prime source of pressure for Saudi rulers in the near future: traditionalism versus modernity; tribalism versus urbanism; Islamic Wahhabi social rigidity versus secular mobility; family autocracy versus participatory government; and customary tribal rules of conduct versus written legal regulations. The durability of the Saudi political system will be determined by the reconciliation of these dichotomies.

As Gulf states in general, and Saudi Arabia in particular, head into the mid-1990s, demands for democratization will be fueled by the shrinkage of oil revenues, the competition for government contracts and jobs, and the return of thousands of indigenous university graduates from abroad, all of which will stretch existing domestic political structures. New challenges will emerge, which, if not addressed adequately, might increase the fragility of Gulf Arab polities and threaten their existence. The following specific challenges facing Saudi Arabia and the other GCC states may be identified.

Role of the Ruling Family

Despite great economic and social advancement, political authority in Gulf states has remained vested in the person of the ruler and his family; the founding of modern polities has not eliminated the tribal source of legitimacy. Although each one of the constitutions promulgated in Kuwait, Qatar, Bahrain, and the United Arab Emirates claims to be "democratic," popular elections have been held in only two: Kuwait and Bahrain. In no state is accession to power subject to popular decision; that choice is the restricted preserve of the inner councils of the ruling family, whose members normally occupy the most important cabinet posts and other high government positions.

In Saudi Arabia, the regime has not even gone so far as other Gulf states in accepting a written constitution and in labelling itself, at least rhetorically, as a "democracy." The Saudi family reigns supreme in name as well as in fact. The Saudi king himself serves in four separate roles simultaneously: head of state, supreme religious leader, supreme tribal chief, and custodian of the holy places (*khadim al-haramayn*). It is a monarchy with several peculiar and unique characteristics, most notable of which may be the high degree of loyalty, cohesiveness, and political acumen among a ruling family that numbers in the thousands. This is perhaps because the group that actually governs the country is limited to just a handful of brothers and half-brothers, all of whom are the sons of Ibn Saud.

The most powerful of the brothers in recent years have been nine: seven full brothers (the "Seven Sudayris") and two half-brothers. Among themselves, the brothers control the entire country. Two of the nine have died, King Faisal (assassinated in 1975) and King Khalid (died in 1982). In recent years, the influential brothers and their sons have occupied the highest government positions (see Table 5.2); other children of the late Ibn Saud, who are not "Sudayris," occupy different appointed positions throughout the kingdom—both in the government and in the private sector—with varying degrees of influence.

TABLE 5.2   Saudi Royal Family and Government Positions

Name	Position
Fahd ibn Abd al-Aziz	King and Prime Minister
Abdullah ibn Abd al-Aziz	First Deputy Prime Minister, Crown Prince, Commander of the National Guard
Sultan ibn Abd al-Aziz	Second Deputy Prime Minister and Minister of Defense and Aviation
Nayif ibn Abd al-Aziz	Minister of the Interior
Mut'ib ibn Abd al-Aziz	Minister of Public Works and Housing
Saud al-Faisal ibn Abd al-Aziz	Minister of Foreign Affairs
Majid ibn Abd al-Aziz	Governor of Mecca *
Abd al-Majid ibn Abd al-Aziz	Governor of Medina
Salman ibn Abd al-Aziz	Governor of Riyadh
Muhammad ibn Fahd ibn Abd al-Aziz	Governor of Eastern Province
Faisal ibn Fahd ibn Abd al-Aziz	President of Youth Welfare
Ahmad ibn Abd al-Aziz	Deputy Minister of the Interior

* Governors have ministerial rank

In recent years, a group of young, foreign-educated (mostly in the West) and well-traveled Saudi princes has entered the ranks of influential policy-makers. They are the sons and nephews of the brothers and uncles who have ruled Saudi Arabia for two generations, and though they are all members of the ruling class, they share a secular orientation and perceptions of nation-building that have made them more attuned to the hopes and aspirations of the new, technocratic middle class. These princes find themselves in the unique position of being able to exercise influence through three channels simultaneously: the royal family, the formal bureaucracy, and the new middle class. As a special and a unique elite within the new generation of Saudis, this group will likely have a strong impact on the future course of Saudi politics.

The absence of organized political activity in Saudi Arabia, its sparsely distributed population, and the nature of the country's terrain make it extremely difficult, at least in the foreseeable future, for any major political upheaval or revolution to occur. Any political changes or socio-political reforms will likely originate with the royal family. It is in the planning and execution of social and political reforms that the new group of princes, and through them the new middle class, will play a crucial role.

Role of the New Middle Class

Whether it is called the "middle class," a "new middle class," or a "technocratic elite," a new sort of social stratum is developing in Saudi Arabia. Recent studies have attributed the rise of this new group to education, wealth, urban entrepreneurship, technocracy, managerial bureaucracy, and, of course, the armed services officer corps. The nature, composition, training, background, and demands of the class will have a significant impact on the future direction of Saudi Arabia as a political community. It is safe to assume that the traditional nature of Saudi society and the stable relationship between the monarchy and its subjects will be affected by the influence of this new class within the Saudi polity.

Oil revenues and the expanding educational base have combined to create a new and diverse stratum of professionals, managers, administrators, adequately trained teachers, lawyers, army officers, pilots, skilled workers, electronics engineers and technicians, planners, corporate managers, and systems analysts. The common characteristic of this class is its occupational foundation. It perceives itself and is perceived by others in terms of the functions it performs and the unquestioned need for these functions in the building of a modern state.

The specialized training which members of this class have acquired bestows upon them special privileges; influence flows naturally from this privileged position and is based solely on the functions performed—an unprecedented phenomenon in a traditional society. Familial and other contacts, traditional prerequisites for acquiring an influential position, are less important for this class; training, expertise, and competence, not family background or tribal extraction, are the source of its influence. This can be a shattering experience in a traditional society that is thrown, almost unwittingly, into the massive complexities of modernization.

The new middle class exercises its power through the ministerial positions and other high bureaucratic offices its members hold. Since no political parties exist in Saudi Arabia and since politics still remains the prerogative of the royal family, the new middle class wields influence more in economic policy-making than in the political sphere. There are no tangible indications that the middle class has acted as a cohesive pressure group on political issues; the submissions of petitions to the king are the first and only evidence of a joint action on the part of the Saudi middle class in the political realm.

Role of Religious and Traditionalist Leadership

Religious influence is yet another powerful characteristic of the Saudi socio-political system and has played a particularly significant role during monarchical successions. During the power struggle between King Saud and his brother Faisal in March 1964, the grand *mufti,* head of the *ulama,* issued an Islamic legal proclamation (*fatwa*) siding with Faisal, essentially endorsed the transfer of power from Saud to him. Eleven years later, in 1975, the *ulama* again played a decisive role in their support of King Khalid's accession to the throne following Faisal's assassination. Fahd also enlisted the support of the *ulama* when he became king after Khalid's death in 1982. Also, during the 1979 Grand Mosque crisis, the *ulama* again played a major role by issuing a *fatwa* in support of the government's actions.

The rise of Islamic fundamentalism—whether Sunni, as in the case of Egypt and Jordan, or Shi'ite, as in the case of Iran—has indirectly increased the power of religious-traditionalist leaders in Saudi Arabia. Indeed, the Saudi monarchy's response to the fundamentalist trend has been to highlight the role of the Saudi king as the protector or guardian of the Islam's two holiest shrines and, in recent years, *khadim al-haramayn* has become the king's most prominent title. Other Gulf states have also responded to the rise of Islamic fundamentalism by adopting overtly pro-Islamic policies, such as promoting the construction of "state" mosques and imposing new restrictions on social behavior.

The influence and boldness of the Islamists in Saudi Arabia has increased since the Gulf crisis, evidenced by the public submission in spring 1991 of a petition to King Fahd calling for government accountability and the establishment of a *majlis shura.* The strictly conservative groups in the kingdom, as represented by the *mutawwa'in* (morals police), have also become more vocal in their attempt to enforce Islamic practices in society. They believe that the presence in Saudi Arabia of thousands of American and other Western troops—men and women—during the Gulf crisis made the Saudi society more lax. Since then, the challenge facing the Saudi king of balancing the influence of the radical Islamists against the more moderate pro-Western, secular elites has only grown more difficult.

Fluctuations in the Price of Oil

Oil dominates the economic life of Saudi Arabia; revenues from its sale have made it possible for the kingdom to construct a modern state with a highly advanced infrastructure offering comprehensive public and social services. They have also provided the principal underpinning of Saudi foreign policy, making Saudi Arabia a state to be reckoned with in commerce, economics, and diplomacy.

Saudi Arabia's proved oil reserves total approximately 20 percent of the world's total share, larger than any other country, both in quantity and in percentage. Saudi oil is expected to last more than one hundred years. By comparison, the United States' proved oil reserves are less than 4 percent of the world's total.

Saudi Arabia has relied on its oil revenues in attempts to diversify its economy, build a broad industrial base, improve the quality of life for its citizens, educate and train its nationals, and defend itself. But the late 1970s and early 1980s have shown that oil can be a mixed blessing. For example, for Saudi Arabia to continue to benefit from its oil revenues, certain conditions must prevail. First, a stable market must exist at prices high enough to guarantee sufficient revenues for the anticipated expenditures in the budget. Second, international trade and shipping operations must remain relatively stable. Third, an atmosphere of cooperation must exist between oil producers and oil consumers.

In late 1985 and early 1986, when the price of oil dropped significantly, Saudi Arabia and other oil-producing countries experienced a financial crisis. Most observers agreed then that an oil-generated crisis would extend beyond economics into the social and political spheres. Though this did not happen then, the prospect for such a crisis occurring in the 1990s is as strong, if not stronger. On the economic level, such a crisis would be felt in the following specific areas: a slowing of national manufacturing; an increase in the balance of trade deficit; a drop in official reserves; and an increase in the budget deficit.

If the oil market (price, production, and shipping) is subjected to serious shocks in the future, a social and political crisis might then engulf Saudi Arabia and the rest of the GCC states. Three possible scenarios could occur: These states might ride out the storm; they might experience a change in the palace guard; or they might witness a violent overthrow of the regimes in power. The magnitude, severity, and duration of any potential economic recession would determine which scenario would prevail at any given time. The worst-case scenario would, of course, have the most serious repercussions for long-term stability. Severe economic dislocations brought on by a sustained oil-related crisis inevitably would lead to political instability. Specifically, those groups which heretofore had benefited from the tribal power structure would, in desperation, form coalitions to oppose this power structure openly and try to destroy it. This process would be inflamed by racial animosities, religious rivalries, and nationalistic conflicts. A *wealthy* urban tribal government could be tolerated in the 1970s and 1980s; a *poor* urban tribal government would be intolerable in the 1990s and beyond.

Demands for Power Sharing

The rise of the new middle class and the changing educational level of the Saudi population have increased demands for power-sharing. The Saudi royal family will find it increasingly difficult to remain at the apex of power without bringing the middle class into the decision-making process.

The gradual evolution of Saudi Arabia into a modern state with a functioning government was first given significant impetus in the social and economic spheres in November 1962. It was then that Faisal, serving as prime minister, issued his ten-point program for the modernization of the country, calling for many of the basic elements of modern government. Most notable among those projected elements were the promulgation of a "Basic Law" based on the *shari'a* and the Qur'an; the creation of a Supreme Judicial Council and a ministry of justice; the reorganization of the Committee for Public Morality; social legislation to improve the average standard of living; and the abolition of slavery.

While most of the social and economic provisions of the ten-point program have been implemented, there has been little change in the political sphere. No constitution has been written, and the king's authority has not been diminished. Nevertheless, the kingdom's organizational structure has been formalized, new ministries have been created, and the central bureaucracy has grown in size.

Saudi demands for political reform in one form or another began to appear on the Saudi scene early in the 1980s. Indeed, a government statement in spring 1980 promising the promulgation of a constitution was believed to be a response to these rising demands. In March 1980, the Saudi government announced the appointment of an eight-member committee under the chairmanship of Prince Nayif ibn Abd al-Aziz, minister of the interior, to draw up a "basic system of rule" guided by Islamic principles. However, throughout the next decade, nothing came of it, presumably because of the Iraq-Iran War. At the time, Gulf regimes argued that the perceived threat from an aggressive Iran rendered it an inappropriate time for them to consider implementing political liberalization at home.

Since the beginning of the 1990s, demands for political participation (*musharaka*) in the Gulf Arab states have become more vocal, more open and more persistent. Although some of these demands preceded the Gulf crisis, the crisis itself was a watershed in the process of political participation in the Gulf states, including Saudi Arabia. Such calls for political participation by Gulf elites have been expressed in at least four avenues: regional organizations or societies; regional symposia; newspaper articles and analyses; and direct petitions to the rulers (especially those submitted to the amir of Qatar, the amir of Bahrain, and the king of Saudi Arabia). In order to place the Saudi case in its proper regional context, brief discussions of these four paths would be useful.

Regional Societies

Two forums of indigenous Gulf elites were founded in the last decade and a half to promote social, economic, and political development in GCC states. They are *Muntada al-tanmiya* (Development Panel), founded in December 1980 (under the name *Nadwat al-tanmiya,* Development Club), and *al-Multaqa al-watani al-khaliji* (Gulf National Forum), founded in May 1992.[1]

Although it has a relatively small membership, *Muntada al-tanmiya* is a significant regional forum because it brings together some of the most widely respected, moderate, and pragmatic members of upper-middle class, the professions, and the senior bureaucracy, up to the rank of minister and deputy minister.[2] Meeting annually, the *Muntada* discusses studies written by members on aspects of GCC political, economic, social, informational, commercial, regional, and international problems. Such studies have focused on themes of traditionalism and change; family rule and political participation; tribalism and the building of the modern state; religion and the need for a secular administrative infrastructure; the domination of the oil sector and the need to plan for a post-oil economy; and parochial interests and regional concerns. In attempting to plan for the post-oil era, *Muntada* studies are critical of centralized family rule in the GCC states, but their views are reformist, not revolutionary or subversive. Their prescriptions tend to advocate power sharing and individual freedoms.

A 1986 study by one of the group's founding members, Usama Abd al-Rahman, classified into four groups the attitudes of Gulf elites toward the ideas of change and development in the GCC states over the last two decades.[3] The first group views change as a positive achievement accomplished in record time and believes that such an accomplishment has been made possible by the vast oil revenues. This view, which generally reflects the official government positions in GCC countries, is supported by the enormous strides which these countries have made in education, the standards of living, health and welfare, and public services.

The second group believes that economic growth does not necessarily constitute economic development in the true meaning of the term, because it only developed haphazardly in response to the influx of enormous oil revenues and because it lacked comparable development in the cultural, social, and political lives of GCC societies. This group also believes that some order may be brought into the process of economic development by the creation of a functional public administration system which would involve competent representatives from the private sector.

The third group, which Abd al-Rahman believes is the largest, concurs with the second but goes one step further. It believes that economic growth in the GCC states neither reflects genuine economic development nor is based on a productive base. According to this view, economic development can be influenced by the political leadership; however, the bureaucracy shares a major part of the responsibility for economic development. High level government intervention is a prerequisite for genuine economic development.[4]

The last and most radical group believes that economic development must be part of a comprehensive process of social, economic, and political development and that the political decision-making process is the primary force which enhances or impedes "correct" economic development. According to this view, "incorrect," "harmful," or "superficial" economic development is the responsibility of the government and the political leadership. No genuine economic development will occur unless the political leadership is changed.[5]

Meetings in the early and mid-1980s revealed that the crisis of development has several salient characteristics. First, a general consensus emerged in those meetings that the political dimension, which was invariably represented by family rule, was clearly an impediment to real development.[6] Second, consensus emerged that senior government bureaucrats in charge of development also share in the blame for the lack of genuine developmental strategies. Although political authority remains in the hands of the ruling family, the bureaucracy can, and often does, act as a major source in the "allocation of values."[7] And third, the group concluded that "extravagant consumerism" and "conspicuous consumption" have permeated both the citizenry and the political leadership, leading to a cycle of dependency that has left typical citizens alienated from the political process.[8]

When, in January 1986, the organization reformulated itself as a "panel" *muntada*, rather than a "club" (*nadwa*), it did so in order to expand its membership, reach more intellectuals, and discuss far-reaching developmental strategies among wider segments of society. Today, the broad objective of the *Muntada* is to help create an intellectual atmosphere which would establish an interactive link among concerned individuals in the region regarding developmental issues, to study the realities of development, to analyze its impediments, and to offer solutions.[9] To help guide members, the *Muntada* has also adopted a list of principles that critique the present political direction of GCC states and underscore the need to emphasize individual rights as an essential element of national security. Furthermore, *Muntada* supports the idea of open debate of national issues and is wary of the negative impact of pseudo-religiosity and the damage which might be caused by the use of religion as a disguise for parochial interest.[10]

The intellectual activities of the *Muntada* were overshadowed by the Gulf crisis, and once the Iraqi invasion of Kuwait was reversed and Kuwaiti sovereignty restored, several Gulf and other Arab elite groups began to discuss democratization and the role democracy can play in preventing acts of political adventurism. Thus was established, on May 7, 1992, a new group called *al-Multaqa al-watani al-khaliji* (Gulf National Forum). Consisting of sixty GCC nationals headed by an eleven-man steering committed under the coordination of Ahmad Bishara, *al-Multaqa* aims at achieving five goals:[11]

- To defend the national unity of each Gulf state and to work for the creation of an open atmosphere which would foster free debate and exchange of views.
- To expand the foundations of civil institutions in order to promote individual endeavors among GCC citizens on the local as well as the regional levels.
- To call for genuine participation in government in order to build a true and effective citizenship.

- To promote collaborative Gulf action on the official and popular levels.
- To emphasize the Arab and Islamic identities of Gulf action.

One of the *Multaqa*'s most fundamental objectives is to emphasize the need for democratic values, political participation, and the establishment of a civil society. The group's members—academics, politicians, and businessmen—have also voiced their support for social justice, civil liberties, political freedoms, human rights, and the creation of an atmosphere which would foster tolerance, dialogue, and a pluralism of views.[12] Most specifically, the organization supports free elections and advocates the democratization of Gulf regimes—notions that would have been unthinkable for any group to endorse prior to the Gulf crisis without fear of government retaliation.

Regional Symposia

Since the end of Operation Desert Storm, several regional meetings have been held by Arab elite groups to discuss the future of the Arab world and the nature of political systems in Arab countries. Using the Iraqi aggression to argue that a direct link exists between autocracy and adventurism, Arab elite groups have begun to openly advocate political reform and liberalization; indeed, the terms "democratization" and "participation in decision-making" have now taken up a prominent role in the lexicon of Middle Eastern political debate. Of the numerous symposia held on the subject, two should be singled out for their political significance.

In May 1991, the Center for Arab Unity Studies held a symposium in Amman, Jordan, which was attended by academics from throughout the Arab world.[13] Participants agreed that Arab political leaders had begun to recognize the need to search for a new political identity to replace old ideologies and the need to reform authoritarian systems so as to restore unity to the larger Arab region. Moreover, the group collectively viewed the general absence of political freedom as a major contributing factor to Iraq's occupation of Kuwait and the subsequent armed intervention in the Gulf. In this regard, conference participants agreed that the most promising models for democratic transformation were Jordan and, at the time, Algeria. Most importantly, conference participants concluded that democracy should not be sacrificed for any value or cause, including Arab unity.

The Amman conference represented a turning point in Arab political thinking. In the past, priority had always been given by Arab intellectuals to sovereignty and political unity *over* democracy. Since the Gulf War, the reverse trend has taken hold. While on the surface, many Arab regimes and leaders seem to have reverted to pre-war behavior, the crisis has caused subtle and more far-reaching changes among all segments in the Arab world—from philosophers to the man-in-the-street.

Demands for participation in Gulf Arab states have been the focus of discussion among Gulf intellectuals and other elite groups in a series of symposia held under the sponsorship of the Gulf Arab Studies Center and *al-Khalij* newspaper in Sharja. Of the four symposia held in autumn 1991, the third, which brought together academics, journalists, researchers, and business people from the United Arab Emirates, Qatar, and Kuwait to discuss the future prospects of Gulf security, is of particular significance.[14] After debating vital questions about the relationship between oil, regime stability, authoritarian regimes (*anzima sultawiyya*), and the absence of popular participation throughout the region, the participants reached five major conclusions:

1. That regional security cannot be separated from internal stability, and as a result, the Gulf remains politically unstable;
2. That Gulf security will always reflect the interest of industrial states in Gulf oil and will therefore remain tenuous;
3. That to promote Gulf security, the GCC states must resolve their outstanding boundary disputes and establish a common oil policy (production and pricing);
4. That internal stability can only be safeguarded through political participation in decision-making, democratic reforms, and respect for human rights;
5. That long-term security would be enhanced through the establishment of a confederated structure for GCC states.

Given the heretofore quiescent nature of political debate among Gulf elites, these conclusions marked a clear departure into serious discussion of Gulf security concerns and especially the role that internal political development can play in safeguarding national and regional security.

Gulf Media and Participation

These themes have been taken up with vigor by the Gulf media in the post-crisis atmosphere. In fact, media coverage is only the tip of the iceberg, especially in light of the extensive coverage of this topic at private gatherings throughout the Gulf. One newspaper article even stated that "not one private gathering [*majlis*] in Ramadan escaped a discussion of the question of democracy."[15]

al-Khalij (UAE) and *al-Ayyam* (Bahrain) newspapers have led the discussion of democratization, in terms of interviews, editorials, and reports on symposia. *al-Khalij* also houses at its headquarters the Gulf Arab Studies Center, which in turn frequently sponsors conferences, meetings, and symposia on Gulf social, political, and economic issues. Both *al-Khalij* and the Center act indirectly as a coordinating medium for Gulf intellectuals and other elites to express their views and reflect on the future of their society.[16] Moreover, *al-Shuruq*, a sister weekly magazine of *al-Khalij* which started publication in April 1992, initiated a series of interviews and articles on "Democracy in the Gulf" that generated great interest and a plethora of views and opinions.[17] Responses by those interviewed agreed on several common points, including that democracy is the single most important issue facing the Gulf today; that "shuracracy" will be an inadequate substitute for formal political participation; and that democracy requires parliamentary government based on free elections, human rights, and the guarantee of political pluralism. At the same time, most respondents recognized that the future of democracy in the Gulf is not especially bright.

As a result of the symposia and articles of *al-Khalij* and *al-Shuruq*, many elite groups in the Gulf began, as one Reuters news report noted, "to come off the fence to call publicly for political reform and greater democracy."[18] Indeed, the banding together of sixty Gulf personalities in the Gulf National Forum in May 1992 represented "an unprecedented move by liberals to organize themselves across Gulf borders."[19] In spite of the differences among Gulf elite groups regarding the most efficacious route to participation, a consensus is emerging that, as one of them said, "democracy is our guarantee and safety-valve."[20]

Another example of the demands for political participation was a public lecture given by a Bahraini professor of Islamic studies in Kuwait in December 1991. In discussing the role of popular participation in decision-making, Professor Abd al-Latif Mahmud al-Mahmud argued that true popular participation in Gulf Arab states involves four specific assumptions: that legislative assemblies be established through direct popular election; that they be legislative, not merely consultative; that their role be similar to that of parliaments in advanced societies; and that the media be given the freedom to discuss all kinds of public issues and to scrutinize the behavior of high public officials.[21] A Sunni Muslim fundamentalist, al-Mahmud was detained by Bahraini authorities at the airport upon his return from the Kuwait conference. According to press reports, he was accused by Bahraini authorities of making remarks critical of the GCC's ruling families.[22] After a short detention, al-Mahmud was eventually released once the country's ruler and government had received a large number of telegrams protesting his arrest.

Petitions

Since the Gulf War, public demands for political participation in Gulf Arab states have extended beyond symposia, lectures, and newspaper articles to include direct petitions to the rulers of some of these states. Four important petitions were submitted since the winter of 1991 demanding the establishment of a *majlis shura*. The first was submitted in December 1991 to the ruler of Qatar, Shaykh Khalifa bin Hamad al-Thani. Signed by fifty well-known Qatari personalities from academia, business, and government, the petition decried the poor conduct of high government officials and the absence of any sort of government accountability. The petitioners, including many middle to upper-class Sunni liberals from Qatar's recognized families, urged the ruler to establish an elected *majlis shura* with broad legislative, regulatory, and investigative powers. Such a *majlis,* they argued, should be charged with drafting a permanent constitution to guarantee a democratic system of government with clearly defined checks and balances.[23] So far, Qatar's ruler has yet to respond to the petition. Indeed, according to press reports, some of the signatories have since been questioned by the authorities regarding their political activities.

The second petition was submitted to the ruler of Bahrain, Shaykh Isa bin Salman al-Khalifa, on November 15, 1992. Signed by over two hundred people, this petition called for the election of a national assembly, in accordance with Article 65 of the Bahraini constitution. The ruling family's response was expressed in an announcement by the shaykh to the press that same month promising to establish an appointed, thirty-member consultative council (*majlis istishari*). It was widely expected that the council would be established by Bahrain's Independence Day, December 16, 1992.

An unprecedented and even more publicized development was the submission of two separate petitions to Saudi King Fahd in the spring of 1992, each of which asked for a restructuring of the Saudi political system according to Islamic law. One was signed by forty-three well-recognized, mostly liberal and reform-oriented Saudi personalities; the other, by hundreds of the kingdom's more renowned religious leaders, scholars, teachers, judges, and *ulama.*

While the two petitions differ in orientation and ideology, both agree on the demand for a *majlis shura,* accountability in government, a restructuring of the political system, a return to the "true" teachings of Islam, honesty and integrity in public life, and social and economic equality. But there the similarities ended. The "secular" petition demanded that Saudi women be integrated in Saudi life, hinted at curbing the role of the religious police (*mutawwa'in*), and included ten specific areas to be targeted for fundamental reform, ranging from the judiciary to education.[24]

In contrast, the "Islamist" petition was based squarely on Hanafi Islamic teachings and principles and on the *shari'a*.[25] Its twelve demands included the following:

- A *majlis shura* should be established to decide on domestic and foreign matters and to consist of honest, loyal, independent people who are also recognized specialists in their respective fields.
- All current laws, and political, economic, and administrative procedures should be reviewed in light of *shari'a*, and any that contradict *shari'a* should be discarded.
- Government officials and diplomatic representatives should display good behavior and should be appointed on the basis of honesty, integrity, and expertise.
- Justice, equality, and civil rights should be guaranteed for all citizens without any privileges for the powerful or discrimination against the weak.
- An effective system of accountability should be established for all government officials. Those convicted of corruption or malfeasance in office should be punished.
- Public wealth should be distributed on a just basis among all citizens in society, and all forms of monopoly should be prohibited.
- A strong, well-integrated army should be established whose responsibility would be to protect the country and its holy places.
- The media should be restructured according to a well-defined and integrated policy of information which serves Islam and reflects the morality of society.
- The kingdom's foreign policy should serve the interests of the community and the world of Islam and should refrain from joining alliances that are inimical to the teachings of Islam.
- Religious and doctrinal institutions in the country should be strengthened and supported financially.
- The judiciary should be unified and granted total autonomy.

• Individual and community rights should be guaranteed, and human dignity should be protected according to accepted laws and practices.

The Monarchy Responds. Demands for political liberalization in Saudi Arabia preceded the submission of the two petitions and were heard with ever-greater strength before and during Iraq's occupation of Kuwait. Such demands were expressed at informal gatherings, in newspaper articles, and in recorded cassettes surreptitiously circulated throughout the kingdom.

The first official response to these demands was announced by King Fahd in November 9, 1990, when he promised to liberalize the Saudi political system and fulfill a longstanding commitment to establish a *majlis shura*. The king's announcement caused a reaction of surprise and promise, though many questioned the timing and motives of the king's statement. Indeed, some viewed the king's statements as more of a response to Western demands for democratization, at a time of Western defense of the Gulf, rather than a response to indigenous demands for change. Others believed they marked an implicit bargain between government and citizenry, promising political reform after the crisis had passed in return for loyalty during the time of the crisis itself. More generally, observers concluded that recognition of popular political demands was only natural at a time of economic recession following the end of the oil boom.

The most dramatic Saudi response to demands for political reform came on March 1, 1992, about eighteen months after the king's earlier promise to establish a *majlis shura* and almost a decade since Fahd's earlier promise to create such a council. In a major address to the nation, the Saudi monarch issued three royal decrees that constituted a three-part plan for restructuring the Saudi political system. Together, the plan aimed at "remodeling the Kingdom with a touch of democracy"[26] and called for reorganizing the Saudi system of government, establishing a *majlis shura,* and redefining the governorates and the authority of regional governors.[27]

The first decree, which consists of nine parts and eighty-three articles, established *inter alia* three branches of government and defined the general policies and principles of the Saudi state. In skeletal form, it is outlined as follows:

Part 1: General principles—Saudi Arabia is an Arab, Muslim state; the state constitution is based on the Qur'an

Part 2: System of government—hereditary monarchy in the House of Saud; legitimacy emanates from the Qur'an; rule is based on justice, *shura*, and equality, according to the *shari'a*

Part 3: Foundations of Saudi society—the family; national unity; and Islam

Part 4: Economic principles—natural resources belong to the state; private ownership and capital are fundamental; right to private property is protected by law; *zakat* will be collected and distributed according to law

Part 5: Rights and duties—The state protects Islam and guards the *shari'a;* protects the two holy shrines; facilitates the *hajj;* protects human rights according to *shari'a;* and provides for health, education, and welfare

Part 6: Branches of government—judicial, executive, organizational[28]; the Qur'an is the source of all legislation, arbitration and judicial decisions; independent judiciary; a Supreme Judiciary Council to be established and headed by the king; the king serves as prime minister and commander-in-chief of the armed forces; *majlis shura* to be established

Part 7: Financial affairs—to be determined by law

Part 8: Regulatory agencies—State revenues and expenditures subject to oversight of regulatory agencies

Part 9: General rules—amendment only by royal decree.

According to the royal decree, the *majlis shura* will consist of sixty members, all of whom to be chosen by the king. Ostensibly, the council should have been established within six months of the royal decree—i.e., by September 1, 1992—but only the prospective council speaker was named by the end of that month. The *majlis shura*'s specific duties are threefold: to review and recommend general plans for economic and social development; to study and advise on laws, agreements, alliances, international accords, and concessions; and to debate annual reports submitted by ministries and other government organizations.[29]

The third royal decree defines the administration of governorates, stating that each governorate will be administered by an amir with ministerial rank who shall rule in conjunction with the local citizenry. The specific powers of the amirs will be delineated by the minister of the interior, to whom the amirs will report annually.[30]

A review of the three royal decrees leads to several observations. First, the anticipated reform reflects what the king believes to be the realities of Saudi Arabia and the traditional religious conservatism of Saudi society. Second, the decrees assert beyond any doubt the kingdom's Islamic and Arab identities and its commitment to the Qur'an and the *shari'a*. Third, the decrees also

commit the state to protect the citizen's basic rights and to provide the citizen
with all necessary services in health, education, and welfare. Finally, the three
decrees together emphasize the continuity of society while still offering
something new. Change will not be attempted or pursued at the expense of
tradition, embedded in the Qur'an, the *sunna,* and the *shari'a.*[31] The state,
headed by the House of Saud, is the protector and enforcer of the Qur'anic
tradition and the guardian of Islam.

So far Gulf elite groups are taking a cautious wait-and-see attitude toward
the Saudi reform plan. This, however, has not stopped some Gulf intellectuals
from questioning the adequacy of the "shuracracy" approach to political
participation. Other than Kuwait, which supports national elections, the other
GCC states seem to have decided on the *majlis shura* as a vehicle for
participation. This vehicle is seen by some Gulf elites as a means to preserve
monarchical family rule with the most minimal introduction of democracy.

Change and Stability: How to Meet the Challenge

The invasion, occupation, and liberation of Kuwait were traumatic for Saudi
Arabia and forced the Saudi monarchy to reassess most, if not all, of its
earlier assumptions about the nature of the monarchy, the stability of family
rule, the security of the region, and the reliance on foreign forces for survival.
While the crisis demonstrated the monarchy's ability to make tough decisions
regarding its own survival and the security of the region, it also forced the
Saudi ruling family to recognize two unpleasant realities: first, that the long-
term stability of family rule in the Gulf is dependent on foreign support and
second, that the people of the GCC play an important role in maintaining
internal unity in the face of external threats.

By exalting the bravery of the Kuwaitis who stayed in Kuwait and who
resisted the Iraqi occupation when Kuwait's ruling family sought refuge on
Saudi soil, the Gulf Arab regimes grudgingly accepted what their elites had
told them for years: that a partnership between the rulers and the ruled is
fundamental to regime stability. They were forced to recognize that in spite
of their military arsenals, Gulf ruling families cannot rely on themselves to
guarantee their own survival. The *samidoon* (those who stayed behind) of
Kuwait proved to the al-Sabah ruling family that the people are essential for
national legitimacy and sovereignty. The *hariboon* (those who fled the
country), including the ruling family, could not claim any sort of national
legitimacy apart from the Kuwaiti people who endured the Iraqi occupation.
This development brought home to Gulf ruling families the need to bring
their people into the political process. The results of the Kuwaiti parlia-

mentary elections on October 5, 1992, in which about two-thirds of seats were won by regime critics, suggest that such a new relationship will not be easy.

Indeed, while there is consensus among Gulf regimes regarding the unavoidable need for popular input, there is no unanimous agreement among them regarding the nature and modality of participation. Most ruling families seem to agree that the *majlis shura* is the most appropriate approach to political participation at this time. Indeed, some of them have begun to implement the *shura* approach. In Oman, for example, a *majlis shura* has been established based on special elections and appointments, and in Qatar, an appointed *majlis shura* which has been functioning since 1972. In the United Arab Emirates, there is increasing talk among the elites about the need for participation, but there is no tangible evidence that the federal government is ready to embark on a participatory system of government. Indeed, in Bahrain, the formula for opening up the political base only envisions the National Assembly, dissolved in 1975, being replaced by a limited consultative council—a *majlis istishari,* not even a *majlis shura.*

While the Saudi monarchy is closely following the evolution of the Kuwaiti move toward an elected parliament, observers do not expect the kingdom to introduce any form of national elections. A more immediate challenge for King Fahd in establishing the *majlis shura* is to maintain a balance among four Saudi groups: the moderate Islamists, the radical Islamists, the opposition moderate nationalists, and the powerful members of the ruling family. Such a balance will require Fahd to display a high degree of political acumen as well as to gain the support of the inner council of the ruling family and the endorsement of the Saudi elites—Islamists and secularists alike.

The composition of the *majlis shura* will likely be affected by regional developments as well. In this regard, the Kuwaiti experience will be watched closely by other GCC leaders. If the Kuwaiti opposition groups, now emboldened by electoral victories, successfully press their case for parliamentary inquiries into sensitive matters of state, elites throughout the GCC states—including Saudi Arabia—would likely become more vocal in their own demands for participation. It is also probable that these elites would view the *shura* approach as an inadequate model for popular participation. In such a situation, King Fahd could face two possible scenarios, both of which are potentially troublesome. Either the Saudi elites might refuse to cooperate with the king's appointed *majlis shura* and demand an elected body instead or Fahd might find himself simply unable to strike any functional balance among the kingdom's different political and religious groups. Saudi elites are awaiting the establishment of the *majlis shura* with anticipation, in as much as its composition would be an ideological barometer of the king's leanings.

Any sign of the king's failure in his attempts at liberalization will likely weaken his stature in the eyes of the ruling family and the Saudi elites. It would be somewhat ironic but not unthinkable that Fahd's brush with liberalization might bring about his downfall. Any perceived delay or failure of his plan to restructure the Saudi political system in accordance with the three royal decrees would increase the demands for more liberalization and government accountability. It is also likely that communal conflict might erupt between the moderates and the Muslim fundamentalists in Saudi Arabia.

Should King Fahd abdicate for whatever reason, the future king, presumably Abdullah, the current crown prince and Fahd's half-brother, would find it difficult to receive the allegiance of the Saudi tribes, the *ulama,* and other elites without accepting certain unpalatable conditions. In that light, Abdullah's succession to the throne would not likely be as smooth as the previous two successions. Whereas successions in 1975 and 1982 were merely changes in the "palace guard," the next royal succession could very well involve the whole regime. Such a development would not necessarily mean instability, but it would point to a process of regime change that would strike at the heart of the Saudi monarchy.

In order to meet the challenge of participation, the Saudi leadership, together with the rest of the GCC ruling families, must realize that the Gulf crisis has created at least two fundamental realities. The first of these is that demands for participation have been made by *indigenous* Gulf elites—not Palestinians, Egyptians, or Iraqis—and cannot be dismissed as "foreign" or "alien" ideas. The second reality is that Gulf states do not have the luxury of maintaining their security in obscurity, given that they will continue to be in the limelight of international energy policy. Despite the passage of the Cold War, Gulf states will continue to find themselves for the foreseeable future entangled in some facet of a three-pronged "cold war": Arab-American; Arab-Arab; and Arab-Israeli. For Saudi Arabia, it is possible to reconcile change and stability if the ruling family accepts the argument of Saudi and other Gulf elites that political participation in decision-making is the most important challenge ahead.

Notes

1. *Muntada al-tanmiya* is a new name given in January 1986 to a group known as *Nadwat al-tanmiya li duwal al-jazira al-arabiyya al-muntija li al-naft* (Development Panel for the Oil-Producing Countries of the Arabian Peninsula).

See Usama Abd al-Rahman, *Intellectuals and the Search for a Path: Development Role of Intellectuals in the Gulf Arab Countries* [Arabic] (Beirut: Center for Arab Unity Studies, 1987), pp. 213-221.

2. By 1985, the membership included nine corporate directors; four university administrators; three editors, writers, or publishers; two bankers; seven businessmen; two government ministers or deputy ministers; five teachers or professors; four other government officials; three directors of regional organizations, and one judge. By 1987 the membership had risen to fifty-six.

3. Usama Abd al-Rahman, *Challenges of Development and the Role of Nadwat al-Tanmiya* [Arabic] (unpublished manuscript obtained by the author), pp. 15-19.

4. Ibid., p. 18.

5. Ibid., p. 19.

6. Ibid., p. 86.

7. Ibid., p. 92.

8. Ibid., p. 95.

9. Ibid., p. 206.

10. Ibid., pp. 222-227.

11. *al-Khalij* (Sharjah, UAE), May 15, 1992.

12. *al-Khalij*, May 12, 1992.

13. Lamis Andoni, *Christian Science Monitor*, June 19, 1991.

14. The proceedings of the symposium were published in *al-Khaleej*, September 15-18, 1991. The other three symposia dealt with Gulf-Arab relations, development, and lessons from the Gulf crisis.

15. *al-Khalij*, March 28, 1992.

16. An example of such coordination is a symposium on inter-Gulf relations held at the Gulf Arab Studies Center in June 1992. For a review of the symposium proceedings, see *al-Khalij*, June 15-17, 1992.

17. *al-Shuruq* (Sharja, UAE), May 11-15 and May 21-25, 1992.

18. Yousef Azmeh, "Democracy Debate Rages in Conservative Gulf," Reuter report, June 18, 1992.

19. Ibid.

20. Ibid.

21. An unpublished manuscript of the speech is in the author's possession.

22. Reuter report from Manama, Bahrain, December 15, 1992.

23. A copy of the petition and a list of the signers are in the author's possession. It should be noted that an appointed *majlis shura* has functioned in Qatar since 1972, and that Qatar still operates under a *provisional* constitution adopted by the present ruler in February 1972.

24. This petition was first published in *al-Ahali* (Egypt), March 20, 1991.

25. A copy of the petition is in the author's possession.

26. *New York Times*, March 2, 1992.

27. For a complete reading of these decrees, see *al-Khalij*, March 2, 1992; for an unofficial English translation of the *majlis shura* decree, see *New York Times*, March 2, 1992.

28. It is important to note that this third branch of government is organizational (*tanzimiyya*) not legislative (*tashri'iyya*).

29. *The New York Times*, March 2, 1992.

30. *al-Khalij*, March 2, 1992.

31. *al-Ayyam* (Bahrain), May 21, 1992.

6

The PLO and the Palestinians:
A Revolution Institutionalized

Barry Rubin

The Palestine Liberation Organization has been both a national liberation and a terrorist movement, one nation's hope and another's would-be executioner. Simultaneously populist and repressive, it saw itself equally as a revolutionary group and as a state-in-the-making. The PLO "is not one of many Palestinian institutions," Yasser Arafat has said. "It is the all-embracing Palestinian institution that comprises all the institutions of the Palestinian people." As such, Arafat claimed, it had given Palestinians pride and recognition, transforming them "from a refugee people waiting in queues for charity and alms into a people fighting for freedom."[1]

But the very characteristics preserving the PLO as an institution have also led to its paralysis and frequent defeat. A quarter-century of armed struggle and a mass uprising failed to bring tangible material gains for Palestinians or pry Israel from the territories. Egypt had made peace with Israel, Iraq derailed the Palestinian issue by invading first Iran and then Kuwait, Arab rulers in the Gulf worried more about Iran or Iraq than about Israel. Syria and Libya supported anti-Arafat groups.

For the PLO, the *intifada* (uprising) came out of the blue and forced the organization for the first time to consider seriously, albeit hesitantly and inconsistently, recognizing Israel, rejecting terrorism, and accepting a two-state solution. But Arafat has followed his least-common-denominator technique, avoiding any step that might cause factions to split or even vote against the program. The PLO had already long lost any chance of destroying Israel. By the time the *intifada* had started in December 1987, the PLO seemed deadlocked and at a dead end. The hope of eliminating Israel and ruling all Palestine, no matter how unrealistic, was the source of PLO legitimacy among Muslims, Arabs, and Palestinians. Any serious peace initiative risked dependence on some Arab states (Jordan and Egypt) and antagonism with others (Syria and Iraq). Harder-line factions and groups would probably walk out. Consequently, the PLO's intransigence was a response to its internal and regional politics. As Hani al-Hasan, an advisor to Arafat, admitted shortly before the Kuwait crisis, "It took us a hell of a long time to come unambiguously to terms with reality."[2]

Yet even then, this adjustment was hardly unambiguous. Now, as a result of its handling of the Kuwait crisis and Gulf War, the PLO seems to have also forfeited any chance of establishing a Palestinian state. These failures, in turn, could jeopardize both its continued unity and its hegemony over Palestinians frustrated at the PLO's inability to achieve material gains or end Israel's occupation.

The same events, however, also contributed to other important developments, opening up the peace process and making Arab states more willing to talk with Israel. U.S. power and influence in the Arab world increased while U.S.-Soviet (and then U.S.-Russian) cooperation and Israel's diplomatic standing in the world improved. The *intifada* continued but obviously lacked the strength to force Israeli concessions, and hundreds of thousands of Jewish immigrants continued to arrive, strengthening Israel and posing—in Arab minds—a point of no return on Israel ever leaving the territories. In short, the PLO lost its veto in the diplomacy over the Arab-Israeli conflict at a time when negotiations seemed more likely than ever.

Not only did these factors affect the PLO's position, they also shook up PLO policy and internal politics directly. Two points were especially important. First, the relative power of Palestinians from the territories had been growing since they staged an uprising of their own. In general, this group demanded more action to end the occupation and a greater willingness to negotiate with Israel. Second, while the influence of Arab states had often pushed the PLO to be intransigent, the majority of these governments— including Egypt, Syria, Jordan, and Saudi Arabia—now demanded that the organization make concessions in order to allow talks. The regimes cut off aid and hinted that they would go forward even without PLO participation.

The result was a loose alignment between the United States, the Soviet Union (then Russia), most Arab regimes, more moderate Palestinians in the territories, and Israel for talks in which West Bank and Gaza Palestinians participated. While the PLO hoped that this pressure would go away, Arafat could not ignore it, at least until the situation changed once again. While working with the Arab states and trying to direct the West Bank and Gaza activists, Arafat feared and mistrusted both as potential rivals.

The activation of the Palestinian masses in the territories was not wholly the PLO's doing, and their attitude toward it could not be taken for granted. While the overwhelming majority saw the PLO as their leader, it did not necessarily see the PLO as a good or competent one. The outcome of diplomatic processes will determine whether the majority accepts the PLO as a revolutionary vanguard in a continuing struggle; a government; an ethnic, interest group representative under a non-Palestinian regime; or an outdated organization which no longer serves a purpose.

Traditional PLO Politics

The PLO's goal for most of its history was Israel's destruction and its replacement by a PLO-ruled Palestinian Arab state. By the late 1970s, there was a line of argument—embodied in some official positions—that this should be achieved in two stages, with the first step being a PLO takeover of the West Bank and Gaza Strip. During the 1980s, there was increasing talk about having a Palestinian state in the West Bank and Gaza alongside Israel. The November 1988 meeting of the PLO's legislative arm, the Palestine National Council (PNC), and a December 1988 statement by Arafat implied moves toward a "two-state" solution. If we lose this historic chance, Arafat said, "we are criminals."[3]

But the PLO did fumble the opportunity and then supported Iraq, returning to a more radical position which seriously damaged its standing in international and inter-Arab politics. Trying to respond to this disastrous situation, the September 1991 PNC meeting accepted U.S. proposals for a regional conference to be attended by West Bank and Gaza representatives. For the first time, the PLO had delegated authority, and Palestinians were going to negotiate with Israel over their future.

To come even that far had been a long, hard process with many reverses along the way. The PLO achieved hegemony among Palestinian refugees in Lebanon, Syria, and Kuwait in the post-1967 era. The PLO also drew strong support from Palestinians in Jordan but could not mobilize that support in the wake of the PLO's expulsion in 1970 and Jordanian suppression thereafter. In the 1970s and 1980s, it overcame competition from Jordan and local notables to become the main political force in the West Bank and Gaza Strip.

While having many well-wishers among Palestinians in Israel itself, though, the PLO failed to turn them into active followers, let alone an effective pressure-group.

It is difficult to measure Palestinian popular support for the PLO. Public criticism of the organization among Palestinians has always been limited; opinion polls are unreliable. There is much private criticism about its shortcomings, incompetence, and corruption. Yet these attitudes do not negate the fact that most Palestinians think the PLO has been their only independent political option. They think the PLO represents them but that it also does not incorporate them into actual participation. Moreover, Palestinian citizens in Jordan and Israel also accept, to some degree, the governments they live under.

In discussing the PLO's relationship with the Palestinians and its claim to be their sole, legitimate representative, two of the organization's core myths must also be kept in mind.

First, the PLO has portrayed itself as a democratic organization. The masses supposedly elected the PNC which, in turn, controlled a ruling Executive Committee. In fact, the PLO has been popular without being democratic, though it did permit a limited pluralism. Power passed from the top down and was held by a small group of strong men, not formal institutions, with Arafat first and foremost. Hence, the PLO had legitimacy because the great majority of Palestinians accepted it as their leader. But the people have had no actual control over the organization, nor have they necessarily approved of its specific tactics and policies. Loyalty has been motivated by a sense of solidarity, concern over the costs of disunity, hope that the PLO would triumph, and fear of violent retribution or a loss of their own position. The fact that the PLO has constantly failed, then, has not resulted in its loss of legitimacy, but rather it has had the effect of generating private criticism and some demoralization among Palestinians.

Second, the PLO has claimed to be united. In fact, it has generally preserved Palestinian unity while itself being badly divided and highly decentralized. The PLO, as such, had little or no influence over its constituent groups. And inasmuch as the "PLO" has any material strength at all, it has been due not to any independent existence, but to the role of cadre from Fatah—the largest group—wearing their "PLO" hats.

Arafat's legitimacy may have come from popular support, but his power has required the consent of PLO's constituent groups and the tolerance of Fatah's chiefs. The PLO's anarchic internal politics have made it hard to forge a consensus for compromise among the many leaders, groups, and constituencies. Fatah is the leading group, yet its domination has been far from complete; Arafat has been the unquestioned leader, but he has avoided decisions difficult to enforce. He has never brought the masses actively into the struggle, and he has done nothing to prepare his public for a shift toward moderation.

Ideology, too, restricted him. The PLO reflected popular Palestinian goals of reconquering all mandatory Palestine by any means necessary. As a pro-PLO writer has noted, the organization's "activists were only reflecting community feelings when they argued for the total 'liberation of Palestine' from its Israeli/Jewish colonists, as Algeria had been liberated from the *colons*, or China from the Japanese." The PLO saw itself as future ruler of a Palestine incorporating Israel, the West Bank, and Gaza. All the PLO's symbols showed a map of that projected country. In this context, both cadre and the masses believed, in the words of the late PLO and Fatah leader Salah Khalaf (a/k/a Abu Iyad), that "steadfastness and adherence to our land is our only card ... We would rather be frozen for ten more years than move toward treason."[4]

The PLO's misconceptions about Israel fed its inability to compromise. Rather than see Israel as a product of an authentic nationalism, it was perceived as literally demonic, intent on conquering everything between the Nile and Euphrates rivers. Thinking Israel a U.S. puppet, PLO leaders focused on Washington instead of persuading Israelis to compromise, expecting the United States would abandon Israel or order it to leave the West Bank and Gaza,. They thought the PLO's power, not moderation, would force a change in U.S. policy. This view made an alliance with Baghdad seem an acceptable substitute for dialogue with Washington in 1990.[5]

The PLO believed total victory inevitable: either through force; subversion; Israel's collapse (from internal dissension, economic feebleness, or the loss of U.S. support); or simply a higher Palestinian birthrate. Arafat said that while his was "the generation of suffering, of sacrifice," the next generation "will win the victory reaching the sea." Although the PLO's assessments became more pessimistic over time, its hopes and beliefs changed very slowly.[6] If time was on the PLO's side, there was no hurry to make a deal. Thus, the PLO has been willing to throw away apparent opportunities in order to keep open its options for total conquest in the future.

In this light, the PLO's tendency never to miss a chance to miss an opportunity was not altogether illogical. Sacrificing possibilities for progress was done to maintain unity in an umbrella organization of competing groups, ideologies, and constituencies. Verbal attacks on the United States, calls for

Israel's destruction, and terrorist operations were acceptable as serving a more essential political purpose of mobilizing Palestinian and Arab support while maintaining PLO unity and independence. What appeared to the West as opportunities were actually dangerous in the PLO's eyes, since compromise would have unacceptably diluted its program and long-term goals.

Therefore, in the early 1990s it threw away the public relations and diplomatic triumph of the West Bank/Gaza uprising and the U.S.-PLO dialogue. Arafat destroyed the latter in May 1990 by refusing to honor his pledge to condemn terrorism by a PLO group, then he cheered Iraq's seizure of Kuwait and war against a powerful American-Arab coalition.[7]

The Costs of the Gulf Crisis

Arafat's turn to Iraq was a strategic decision made at least a year before the invasion of Kuwait. In December 1988, he inaugurated a huge Palestine embassy in Baghdad. He visited Baghdad often in 1989, moving PLO offices from Tunis and holding many high-level PLO meetings there.

Arafat came increasingly under Saddam's wing in trying to escape Egypt's pressure for moderation. The PLO opposed the return of Arab League headquarters from Tunis to Cairo. A PLO leaflet issued the day before Iraq attacked Kuwait called Egypt an American "puppet" and "an obedient tool in the hands of the American administration." For Arafat, Cairo was too close to the Americans, pressing too strongly for PLO concessions toward Israel and acceptance of U.S. diplomatic initiatives. In contrast, Arafat saw Saddam as the region's new strongman, the champion who would replace lost Soviet superpower support for the PLO and the Arabs. When Saddam proclaimed himself leader of the Arab world and threatened to attack Israel in the spring of 1990, Arafat rallied to his side. Arafat's policy followed his constituents' preferences but also brought disaster on the PLO. Soviet support—already in rapid decline given Moscow's internal troubles and disillusion with the PLO—waned further. The opening to the United States—evinced in the U.S.-PLO dialogue—was destroyed. Most important of all, Arab states which had often been of help to the PLO—Egypt, Kuwait, Saudi Arabia, and Syria—were turned into enemies.

Nonetheless, Palestinians did not abandon the organization. Frustrated by the inability of the *intifada* or the PLO to gain territory either through militancy or negotiations, most Palestinians hailed Saddam as a liberator. They thereby repeated previous mistakes: making the fate of the West Bank and Gaza dependent on those outside the territories, subordinating their future to Arab leaders, and preferring a military to a diplomatic option. The

Palestinian adulation for Saddam implied that Arafat had failed. After all, if Palestinians needed Iraq to save them, it was because the PLO had not done so yet and was incapable of ever doing so. The pro-Iraq stand also once again presented Palestinians to the West as a radical, anti-American, and destabilizing force. As an Arab writer put it, "God save this nation from its heroes!"

When Iraq seized Kuwait in August 1990, the PLO tore up all its promises from the previous two years. Arafat called on Iraq to attack Israel, reverting with an audible sigh of relief to his traditional, radical stance. The crisis estranged the PLO from the United States and once again threw into question its reliability as party to a peace agreement. The PLO acted partly from pique at the failure of its 1988 initiative, yet this merely further injured the Palestinians. If, as Arafat often said, the PLO's peace initiative was strategic, then it was difficult to comprehend it being abandoned so easily. And if the PLO really wanted a historic compromise entailing acceptance of Israel, it would have realized that hoping Iraq would defeat Israel by chemical weapons would never bring it a homeland. Yet Arafat could not resist the revolutionary posture which had made him at once a fixture of Arab politics and a failure at solving the Palestinians' problems.

Arafat strongly supported Iraq at the Baghdad Arab League summit in May 1990, arguing that Saddam's missiles and chemical weapons gave the Arabs the strength "to achieve liberation from Baghdad to Jerusalem and from [southern Iraq] to Gaza." In reality, Iraq's aggression against Kuwait put the Palestinian issue on the back burner, as its war with Iran had done during the 1980s. If the PLO had backed Kuwait, it would have gained international support. Instead, PLO leaders attacked what they termed "aggression against Iraq"; urged a solution to Baghdad's advantage; and babbled about U.S. cruise missiles being fired from Israel, Israeli planes attacking Iraq from Turkey, and an impending Israeli invasion of Jordan.[8]

Arafat's support for Iraq antagonized or further alienated the Gulf states, his major source of money; Egypt, his Arab patron; the Soviet Union, his historic superpower patron; the United States, the conflict's mediator; and virtually all Israelis who might have agreed to talk with him.[9] By cheering Iraq and urging it to attack Israel, Palestinians disillusioned many Israeli doves. Arafat had abandoned Egypt, Washington's best Arab friend, for Iraq, its worst enemy. This phase ended any U.S. incentive to keep the PLO in the peace process.

Friction between Arab states and the PLO was more than verbal. Gulf Arabs pulled the financial rug from under the *intifada*. Kuwait, Saudi Arabia, and other Arab oil-producing states stopped their multi-million dollar subventions to the PLO, even suspending donations to West Bank schools and hospitals. Palestinians in Kuwait were thrown out of work, so there was no one from whom to collect the PLO's 5 percent "revolution tax," previously estimated at $120 million-$125 million annually, nor anyone to remit salaries back to the territories, a loss of a further $80 million per year. The sharp fall in Jordan's currency also hurt Palestinians there and in the West Bank. Most of the Palestinian community in Kuwait and many in the Persian Gulf were fired as potential fifth columnists.[10]

As chairman of the Palestine National Fund, Jawad al-Ghusayn saw Arab aid vanish and was the first to call Iraq's occupation "illegal." Abu Iyad agreed in opposing the invasion and annexation of Kuwait. But Arafat voiced no criticism of Baghdad and instead blamed the United States for the crisis. He accused Washington of trying to seize control of the world's sources of oil and predicted Saddam would win: "Iraq is not Panama or Grenada."[11]

Losing his temper, Arafat accused a friendly Egyptian editor who dared criticize PLO policy of being an Israeli agent. When an October 1990 Islamic conference in Iran excluded the PLO, Arafat claimed that some Islamic fundamentalists serve Israel. Once fighting began, the PLO accused the United States of "cowardly aggression" against Iraq and warned that "blood, catastrophe, and destruction" would sweep the world. A PLO statement declared: "We are all exposed to aggression when [Baghdad] is bombed." Two constituent groups of the PLO—George Habash's Popular Front for the Liberation of Palestine (PFLP) and Nayif Hawatmeh's wing of the Democratic Front for the Liberation of Palestine(PFLP)—urged revolution and anti-American terrorism.[12]

Even more than usual, the PLO seemed subject to paralysis and malaise. Lacking any strategy, it could only stall for time and hope for some dramatic development to restore its fortunes.

Structural Gridlock
In theory, the PLO's ruling body is the Palestine National Council (PNC) which appoints the organization's fifteen-member Executive Committee. Actually, the committee is the more powerful, seconded by a ninety-member Central Council. Arafat, Faruq Qaddumi, and Abu Mazin (Mahmud Abbas) represent Fatah on the Executive Committee. The other groups—the Marxist PFLP; both factions of the DFLP (Hawatmeh and Yasser Abd al-Rabbu); the pro-Iraq and the pro-Libya factions of the Palestine Liberation Front (PLF); the Iraq-controlled Arab Liberation Front (ALF); and the Communist

(now People's) Party—have one each. The rest are independents who owe Arafat their careers.[13]

About half the Executive Committee and PNC members are "independents"—technocrats, bureaucrats, and businessmen who ensure Arafat's control over the small groups. About one-fifth of the active PNC delegates come directly from member groups, others hold seats through jobs in the PLO bureaucracy and are also mostly Arafat's appointees. The top leadership has been very stable and is aging, proving relatively impervious to new faces.

While the PLO tries to present an image of nationalist unity, the rival appeals of Islam, pan-Arabism, and Marxism divide Palestinians. Although the PLO and Fatah are largely secular, Islam is central to their identity and doctrines. The PNC chairman is an Islamic cleric; Executive Committee meetings begin with a Muslim invocation; Arafat himself repeatedly stresses his own piety. The growing strength of Islamic fundamentalist groups, whose ideas appeal to many rank-and-file members of Fatah, also forces the PLO to show its loyalty to Islam. Still, such influences have been limited by the relatively secular orientation of the PLO elite's and its desire to avoid alienating the Palestinian community's Christian minority.[14]

Pan-Arab nationalism also influences and sometimes subverts Palestinian nationalism. As Palestinian nationalists working for the PLO's independent decision-making and an independent state, Palestinians are fighting for their own cause. But their pan-Arab rhetoric and demands for support from Arab states subsumes their struggle to the interests of a larger Arab nation. When Palestinians believed that Arab states would liberate them, this allowed Arab rulers to interfere in Palestinian affairs. As a result, this has led the majority of PLO member groups and factions to be clients of various Arab states.

Marxist influence was strongest among the smaller groups, especially the PFLP and DFLP. It had some effect on Fatah's thought and encouraged a PLO alliance with the Soviet Union. But Marxism's appeal was circumscribed even before the collapse of the Communist system, because the masses tended to view it as a divisive, alien, and anti-Islamic doctrine.

Palestinians know that the PLO's internal politics caused paralysis. As Hatim Abu Ghazala, a leading figure in Gaza, once asked, "Why we are the only nation in the world that has to govern itself by consensus and not majority rule. What is of paramount importance, the so-called unity of the PLO or Palestinian interests?"[15] Arafat has historically sought consensus, because he lacked authority over PLO constituent groups with competing loyalties, beliefs, and agendas. Fatah, Qaddumi commented, was "the backbone of the Palestinian revolution," but it could not "take exclusive control" and had to compromise with its "partners."[16] Arafat could not even always control Fatah's Central Committee which, for example, sabotaged his proposals to cooperate with Jordan in 1983 and 1985.

On top of Fatah's complex internal arrangements, the Damascus-based PFLP and DFLP and the Baghdad-headquartered PLF claimed Arafat made too many concessions, and they continued terrorist attacks on Israel which Arafat would neither punish nor condemn. As pan-Arab nationalists, they quickly rallied to Iraq's side in 1990. The DFLP saw itself as a Marxist-Leninist party; the PFLP has always been resolved to be the PLO's most militant element. Still, while threatening Arafat's hegemony, these and other small groups could never overthrow him, because their leftist orientation and disproportionately Christian leadership ran against the grain of general Palestinian politics. Moreover, most of these groups were viewed by many as clients of Arab regimes.[17]

The role of Muhammad Abbas (a/k/a Abu'l Abbas) and his tiny wing of the Palestine Liberation Front underscores the traditional leverage wielded by smaller groups inside the PLO. Despite numbering just a few hundred members, the PLF was able to use terrorism to gain world headlines and a seat on the PLO Executive Committee. Abu'l Abbas wrecked diplomacy first in 1985, by hijacking the *Achille Lauro,* and again in 1990, by launching a terrorist attack that Arafat refused to criticize or punish, thereby scuttling the U.S.-PLO dialogue. That episode highlighted Arafat's preference for preserving institutional unity and patronage from the PLF's Iraqi sponsor over diplomatic gain for the Palestinians.

Fundamentalist groups also constrained Arafat. Hamas, a Muslim Brotherhood front, is politically and theologically conservative but uncompromising in its demand for a Palestinian state from the Jordan River to the Mediterranean. It is not only close to the Brotherhood in Jordan and Egypt, which provide financial and material support, but it is developing increasingly warm ties with Iran, especially in the wake of the Madrid peace conference and Tehran's attempts to organize Hizbollah and Hamas into an Islamic opposition to the Arab-Israeli peace talks.

While conservative Arab states help Hamas, Islamic Jihad—actually several competing groups operating under the same name—appeals to revolutionaries and uses spectacular terrorist acts to achieve its goals. Its most important faction is the Beit al-Maqdis of Sheikh Asad Bayyud Tamimi, a deported cleric from Hebron now living in Amman. Tamimi looks to Iran for support but also praised Saddam. Arafat also courted him, making one of Tamimi's sons Fatah's deputy religious advisor. Other factions of Islamic Jihad are sponsored by Syria, Sudan, Iran, and even Fatah, which sponsored a group known as *Surayya al-islam* (Companies of Islam) to shore up its Islamic credentials.

All the fundamentalist groups accuse the PLO of being too secular and compromising. They reject negotiations with Israel and demand Arab control over all of mandatory Palestine. In addition, they insist that the movement must be based on Islam and openly declare their goal to be the creation of an Islamic state. Despite their successes and growth, however, the fundamentalists are likely to remain in the minority. That is because most Palestinians do see the PLO and the idea of secular nationalism as normative. Moreover, Palestinian leaders and activists seem too committed to the PLO to join rivals whose attacks on PLO authority and institutions are also seen as attacks on them.

None of the fundamentalist groups belongs to the PLO, PNC, or the Unified National Command coordinating the *intifada*. The PLO talked with Hamas and Tamimi about their entering the PNC, but could not agree on a division of seats. All sides benefit from this separation: fundamentalists do not want to be a minority in the PLO, and Arafat does not want to risk the possibility that fundamentalists would forge an alliance with smaller PLO member groups challenging Fatah's primacy. Divided, representing a minority ideology, and unable to spark an armed uprising, the fundamentalists appear able to undermine the PLO but not overthrow it.

In sum, it is clear that the PLO has been characterized by poor leadership, fractious internal politics, tumultuous relations with Arab states, inflexible ideology, contradictions between terrorism and diplomacy, and constituencies with conflicting interests. Arafat's balancing act has taken so much effort that it has left little energy for making material gains for Palestinians.[18] This sorry state was only worsened by the collapse of the Soviet Union. The PLO seemed trapped at the end of the Gulf War, having lost its Soviet ally, leverage in the Arab world, and armed presence in Jordan and Lebanon.[19] The dissolution of the Soviet Union cut the PLO's main source of political support, arms, and training, while permitting hundreds of thousands of Jews to emigrate to Israel. The new East European democracies stopped logistical aid to terrorism and became more friendly to Israel than to the PLO.

Together, these trends and events had important, though not irreversible, effects on internal PLO politics. With the great majority of outside forces pressing for a diplomatic solution to the Palestine question, an increasing number of PLO leaders began to move in that direction—some eagerly, most reluctantly. Conservatives linked to Saudi Arabia or Kuwait, notably Khalid al-Hasan, wanted the PLO to re-engage in the peace process so as to assure continued funding from Gulf oil producers. Some hardliners, such as Qaddumi, acquiesced when they saw Syria siding against rejectionism. Others, mostly Marxists, grew disillusioned and demoralized by the strategic loss of Soviet support. All these elements were also motivated by shock at the PLO's institutional decline and fear that the diplomatic train would leave the station without them on board. At this time, West Bank and Gaza Palestinians began to play a bigger role in PLO politics.

PLO Constituencies and the *Intifada*

While the *intifada* gave the Palestinian cause a great deal of international publicity and sympathy, its most significant effect was in activating the masses in the West Bank and Gaza. The "insiders"—i.e., those living in the territories—had been a second-class constituency in the PLO; they now became its vanguard. Potentially, they provided an alternative leadership. More immediately, they lobbied for the urgency of ending the occupation even at the price of historic concessions.

As significant as this was, the change should not be overstated. First, West Bank and Gaza Palestinians worked with the PLO, not against it. Second, they were not universally more moderate than the organization's leaders. Indeed, one effect of the *intifada* was to raise a new group of ultra-militant rivals for the PLO in the form of Islamic fundamentalists. Third, the PLO did not welcome this new assertiveness on the part of the "insiders," seeing them as possible rivals or traitors (i.e., willing to cut a deal with Israel, Jordan, and the United States) and resisting the hierarchy's policy proposals. Nonetheless, the emergence of the "insiders" as an interest group pressed the PLO toward diplomacy and pragmatism.

The existence of separate constituencies with conflicting interests has been as much of a problem for the PLO as maintaining unity among rival groups and independence among competing Arab states. The Palestinian people include refugees without citizenship living in Arab states (plus those in Europe and America); those under Israeli rule in the West Bank and Gaza; citizens of Jordan; and citizens of Israel.

Refugees

Palestinians living in Lebanon, Syria, and Iraq, often in refugee camps, would like to return to homes abandoned in 1948 by conquering Israel.[20] They have little special feeling for the West Bank or Gaza as the location of a Palestinian state. PLO leaders mostly come from this group: the late Khalid al-Wazir (a/k/a Abu Jihad) was born in Ramle; Abu Iyad in Jaffa; the al-Hasan brothers in Acre; Abu Mazin, Abd al-Hamid Hayil (a/k/a Abu al-Hul) and Nabil Sha'th in Safad; Shafiq al-Hut in Jaffa; Habash in Lod; Abdullah Franji in Beersheba; and Qaddumi, though born in Nablus, grew up in Jaffa. Because they lived their adult lives "outside," they are out of touch with the views and needs of those living in the territories occupied by Israel in 1967.[21]

"Insiders"

The PLO accorded West Bank and Gaza Palestinians "second-class" status as only one of several demographic constituencies represented by the organization. Despite the *intifada*, they had limited influence on PLO headquarters and never had more than one of their number on the PLO Executive Committee.[22] Moreover, none of the eighteen members of the Fatah Central Committee could claim to be a leader from the territories. The 1989 Fatah congress reserved just three seats for this group, but even those added were veteran "outsiders."[23]

In contrast to the PLO leadership, the majority of Palestinians in the West Bank have never been refugees. The territory of the West Bank has been their home for centuries, and their interest is to win sovereignty in the place where they already live. For them, a strong middle class and more deeply entrenched traditional society is a moderating force. With the most direct incentive to end the occupation, they are more willing to seek a West Bank/Gaza state in exchange for peace with Israel.

Refugees comprise a large minority in the West Bank. Most are poorer than indigenous residents, and many live under terrible conditions in refugee camps that have existed for decades. Having lost pre-1948 homes in what is now Israel, they have a greater incentive to destroy Israel in order to regain those villages and houses. With less to lose and more to demand, West Bank refugees tend to be more radical in theory and more militant in practice than the indigenous villagers and townspeople. Nonetheless, they have parallel interests to their fellow West Bankers in ending the occupation even at the price of concessions.

The great majority of Gazans are refugees. Living conditions are much worse, and the moderating power of a middle class far weaker. Since most Gazans come from pre-1967 Israel, they are more insistent on regaining it. Thus, the political norm in Gaza is more radical than in the West Bank. Historically, this has meant more support for Marxist PLO groups; in recent years, this has meant greater affinity to radical fundamentalists. An additional reason for the growth of religious extremism in Gaza was the contact between Gaza students and Islamic fundamentalists in Egyptian universities.

In general, Palestinians inside the West Bank and Gaza have a greater interest in ending Israel's occupation via political compromise that do Palestinians living outside. This is true of West Bankers more than Gazans, for the indigenous residents more than the refugees, and for the middle class more than the peasants. Despite these differences, all residents of the West Bank and Gaza would benefit more immediately and directly than would refugees in Jordan, Lebanon, or elsewhere.[24]

But despite their interest in a political deal with Israel, the traditional leaders of the "insider" Palestinians—the "notables"—believe themselves too weak in relation to the PLO hierarchy to act without the organization's support or to try to wrest control of it. At the same time, Arafat watches closely for signs of independence or autonomous decision-making on the part of the "insiders," lest Jordan, Israel, or the United States exploit them to bypass the PLO or they themselves challenge the exile leaders. However, that sort of challenge is unlikely. Many of the notables are western-educated intellectuals, a fact which may help them communicate well with Israelis and Americans but which does not make them better able to compete for power inside the organization. Moreover, most fear and hate Islamic fundamentalists and would be loath to confront the PLO hierarchy in a way that would open inroads for the religious radicals. The most significant of them is Faisal al-Husseini, heir of the leading Palestinian family, son of the most famous military commander in the 1948 war, nephew of that era's main political leader. Husseini's very credentials and charisma make the PLO nervous lest he threaten its power.[25]

Not only do the notables face "outside" Palestinian constituencies much less inclined toward compromise, they also cannot count on some of their neighbors inside the territories. The street revolutionaries of the *intifada* criticize the notables' privilege and relative moderation. They overestimate the *intifada*'s chance of victory and are unlikely to follow the notables in any independent diplomatic initiative. On the contrary, many of them see moderation as cowardice. As *New York Times* correspondent Thomas Friedman noted, "The fact is the West Bankers are too intimidated, divided, and politically suppressed to ever develop a coherent alternative leadership."[26]

Consequently, Arafat's interest is to keep the "inside" leaders weak. If its officials are not allowed to participate in negotiations, the PLO's next best choice are "insiders" more likely to be its puppets, i.e., those who are older or lack their own base. Of course, these same considerations made the United

States and Israel more eager to include independent-minded or more pro-Jordan figures.

Palestinians in Jordan

More Palestinians live in Jordan, where they constitute a majority, than in the West Bank and Gaza. Jordan and the PLO have long competed for the allegiance of Palestinian-Jordanians and for control of the West Bank, which Jordan ruled from 1948 to 1967. The rivalry led to war in 1970 and Jordan's subsequent expulsion of the PLO. In the 1970s, the PLO carried out anti-Jordan terrorism; Jordan periodically closed down PLO offices in Amman and arrested activists.

Mutual suspicion has remained high, despite the fact that the two sides have sometimes cooperated, notably in aiding the *intifada* after King Hussein severed "legal and administrative" ties to the West Bank in July 1988. Jordan distrusts the PLO because a PLO-ruled state could try to subvert Jordan's own Palestinian citizens. The PLO distrusts Jordan because it suspects that Amman wants to regain the West Bank, block an independent state, and subordinate the Palestinians. A particular problem for Arafat is the fact that much of the Palestinian elite in Jordan is loyal to the king and favors an Amman-dominated federation or confederation with the West Bank.[27]

Israeli Arabs

The Arab minority in Israel generally supports a Palestinian homeland on the West Bank and Gaza while also accepting Israel's existence. The PLO has tried to woo Israeli Arabs, calling them part of the Palestinian nation that should "shake the structure of the Zionist occupation off the land of Palestine."[28] Each group within the PLO adopted different clients within the Israeli political system: Fatah, the Progressive List for Peace and the Arab Democratic Party; the PFLP, the small Sons of the Village movement; the Palestine Communist Party cooperates with its Israeli counterpart. (For their part, the Muslim Brotherhood helps fundamentalists whose leaders often studied at Islamic schools in the West Bank.) Yet support for the PLO among Israeli Palestinians remains limited. It is viewed more as a way of providing help to brethren in the West Bank and Gaza than as a sign of allegiance to an outside leadership.

The PLO's Multiple Appeal

Arafat linked all these constituencies by a multi-faceted PLO program with a demand responding to each's needs and interests. The "right of return" was for the prime constituency, the refugees who want to go back to places of origin now in Israel and destroy that state even in its pre-1967 boundaries. "Self-determination" encouraged Israeli and Jordanian Palestinians to demand incorporation in a Palestinian state. "In no way," said Arafat in 1983, "do we accept as a price for the independent state the enslavement of our people who remain in the territories occupied in 1948." An often-voiced PLO slogan—displayed prominently, for example, at the 1988 PNC—says the organization represents "all our people in all places inside and outside their homeland."[29] Finally, the call for an independent Palestinian state especially appealed to indigenous West Bank and Gaza Palestinians, whose main objective is to be rid of occupation.

While "insider" support for Saddam was as great as that shown by PLO leaders, it was the latter who bore the political and diplomatic burden of those errors. The decline of a PLO military option also undermined Arafat's position. Thus, the effect of the Gulf War and post-crisis U.S., Soviet, Arab, and Israeli policies was to tilt the balance further toward the "inside" Palestinians, though they remained far from dominating the PLO or being able to exercise any independent initiative. Perhaps the best symbol of this trend in favor of the "insiders" was the appearance of Faisal al-Husseini and Hanan Mikhail Ashrawi at the September 1991 PNC. It was then that they won the acceptance of the "outsider" PNC delegates for conditions on Palestinian participation in the proposed Middle East peace conference that only allowed "insiders" to represent the Palestinians.

The Arab States and the PLO

The PLO has enjoyed the sponsorship of Arab states but has had to pay the price by suffering their interference and sometimes their attacks. Insistence on maintaining the PLO's independence, said Abu Iyad, was "the main reason we have been isolated." It had to compete with Jordan's claim to represent the Palestinians and rule the West Bank, as well as Syria's assertion that Palestine was "southern Syria" and its demand for a veto over PLO policy. Syria and other states have periodically sponsored radical and Islamic fundamentalist groups to criticize Arafat from outside the PLO as well as supported organizations and leaders to challenge Arafat from within the PLO and Fatah.[30]

When Arab states intervened in their affairs, the PLO and many Palestinians often welcomed them. They turned to Saddam, for example, as a savior when the *intifada* failed to achieve results. But Arab states never lived up to expectations, giving the struggle for Palestine only a small, declining portion of their resources. They feared Israel's power and were preoccupied by threats from Iran or Iraq, internal problems, and internecine quarrels. Arab states attacked the PLO in the name of the Palestinian cause, killed or imprisoned its leaders, helped anti-Arafat groups, and withheld aid. Jordan expelled it in 1970, Syria fought it in 1976, Iraqi assassins shot at it in 1977, Egypt abandoned it by making peace in 1978, Syria split it in 1983, Lebanese Christians and Shi'ite Muslims massacred its people in 1982 and 1985. Arafat found no consistent champion in any Arab leader or government.

The Kuwait crisis deepened all these trends. Arab coalition members were unimpressed with PLO claims of neutrality. A Saudi diplomat said the PLO stood by while "a giant murders a little child." Kuwaitis wrote Arafat an open letter: "Don't you remember how many years you spent in Kuwait and the continuous Kuwaiti contributions and support to the Palestinian revolution?" Feeling betrayed by the PLO, Arab coalition members no longer asked the United States to make any diplomatic concessions to Arafat. They were only interested in obtaining American help for their own defense.

The Arab states in the coalition rejected attempts to link the Gulf and Arab-Israeli conflicts, viewing this as an Iraqi ploy and stalling tactic. As the crisis wore on, their attacks on the PLO reached new heights. The PLO needed a new leadership, said a Saudi writer, which "can speak to the world in a more civilized way [to] oppose any kind of aggression and occupation, if it is by Israel, Iraqi, Palestinian terrorists, or others." The eight Arab coalition members at their March 1991 Cairo victory meeting ignored the PLO. In Kuwait, most of the prosperous Palestinian community fled or was expelled; hundreds were arrested as collaborators with Iraq. Other Gulf states also fired or deported them. Financial losses to Palestinians were enormous. The uprising against Israel was stalled and demoralized.[31]

Perhaps worst of all, the PLO could no longer play off Arab rivalries to its own advantage. Egypt, Saudi Arabia, Syria, and Jordan were all on the same side; Iraq was neutralized. Increasingly concerned with their own state interests, Arab states cared less about the Palestinians' concerns. Recognition that the United States was the world's sole superpower gave them a major reason to court Washington rather than please the PLO.

Another consequence of the Kuwait crisis, Syria's tightening domination in Lebanon, also damaged the PLO. The anti-Arafat Damascus regime and its Lebanese clients helped the reconstituted Lebanese government disarm PLO forces in the south, further reducing the organization's military option against Israel. The weakened PLO presence might also have further reduced the role of the Palestinian constituency there.

Having long been an enemy of the West and Israel, the PLO suddenly also became a foe of the Soviets and, at least temporarily, much of the Arab world. In the post-crisis diplomacy, the United States, the Soviet Union, and Arab states were uninterested in helping the PLO. No party demanded its inclusion in the Madrid peace conference. Indeed, Syria and Jordan agreed to participate even before the question of Palestinian representation was resolved. The PLO found itself friendless, pressured from all sides to permit Palestinians from the territories to attend in a joint Jordanian-Palestinian delegation. Egypt, Syria, Saudi Arabia, Kuwait, and Jordan had no vested interest in creating an independent Palestine to be ruled by a PLO which had done them no favors and over which they exercised no control.

Even given its weakened position, the PLO played its cards badly. Hoping the peace process would be derailed, its leaders cheered the short-lived, August 1991 anti-Gorbachev coup in the Soviet Union, a mistake which further undermined the PLO's standing with the victorious reformers in Moscow. More important, Arafat was slow to rebuild relations with Iraq's Arab rivals.

Why, then, did not the Arab states try to get rid of the PLO or overthrow Arafat? To some extent, of course, they had sought during the 1970s and 1980s to split or destroy the organization. Several Arab states had their own puppet groups outside or inside the PLO and friendly leaders within it through which they often exercised leverage. Arafat also reduced their incentive to take more drastic action by repeatedly bowing to pressure and skillfully giving Arab leaders the hope that he would bow to them in the future. The PLO, to Arab leaders, seemed a prize to be won, not something to be destroyed.

Arab leaders also had sound political reasons to tolerate the PLO's hegemony over Palestinians. The organization had achieved enough legitimacy among all Arabs to acquire some immunity. Arab states still worried that rivals might use an all-out attack on the PLO to isolate or subvert them. After all, Jordan and Egypt had so suffered after the 1970 civil war and the 1978 Camp David Accords, respectively. Lastly, Arab leaders wanted the PLO to exist as the address for Palestinian grievances so as to avoid being charged with that themselves. At the same time, the PLO relieved them of the need to struggle against Israel or to make Palestinian grievances the touchstone for their relations with the United States.

Developments from the Gulf Crisis

The Kuwait crisis did not transform the PLO, but it did further some existing trends, create new ones, and force certain adaptations. The most important alterations occurred in the balance of power among PLO constituencies and factions, the organization's sense of timing, and relations with the Arab states.

As noted above, internal political forces in Fatah previously resisting a policy change either shifted or were weakened by the war. Qaddumi was now urged by Syria to cooperate in the peace process. Friends of the late Abu Iyad were also on board. Those close to Saudi Arabia, notably Khalid al-Hasan, were encouraged to be more critical than ever of Arafat's inertia. The PFLP and DFLP no longer had Syrian support for rejectionism. The DFLP split between Hawatmeh and a pro-Arafat faction led by Executive Committee member Yasser Abd al-Rabbu. Abu al-Abbas was undermined by his Iraqi sponsor's defeat.

The Kuwait crisis and its aftermath certainly furnished some occasion for change, but the PLO resisted every step of the way. The new alignment of Arab states made them a force for moderation stand when they had previously most often been a factor for radicalism. In turn, this situation had an echo among the PLO's internal factions. A shifting balance of power among PLO constituencies begun by the *intifada* added to the power of the West Bank and Gaza Palestinians. Continuing failure to achieve material gains made compromise seem more attractive, though hardly inescapable.

Nor did the Kuwait crisis mark an end to Middle East history, making inevitable a strategic framework pushing in that direction. In fact, by shifting attention to tactical issues, the postwar situation allowed the PLO to avoid more difficult questions of principle. Thus, the 1991 PNC did not affirm the organization's willingness to recognize Israel, cease the use of terrorism, or accept even a West Bank/Gaza state as the PLO's final goal.

To achieve peace required Arafat to take a dramatic new approach, using his role as Palestinian nationalism's symbol to endorse an unambiguous two-state solution. He would have to pull Fatah into line; muster the masses and force, persuade, coopt, divide, isolate, or repress radicals and fundamentalists opposing a compromise peace with Israel. None of this had yet happened.

The PLO, of course, has never sought a negotiated solution as an end in itself. Its goal remains the creation of a PLO-run Palestinian state with its capital in East Jerusalem. The organization rejects the subordination of that state to any Arab state and also opposes any domination of the movement by competing forces from non-PLO groups or West Bank and Gaza Palestinians. It distrusts the United States, Israel, and Jordan as seeking to subvert all these goals.

The ongoing peace process involves considerable dangers for the PLO. Allowing "insiders" to represent the collective Palestinian will poses the possibility that the those representatives might adopt an independent stance which would reduce the PLO's power and prestige. More likely, the negotiators would be pressured by Arab states and the United States to make concessions beyond the PLO's minimum demands. Israel would offer less than the PLO sought. Jordan might, in some way, emerge as the master of the West Bank, an outcome which could forever end hopes of an independent, PLO-ruled state.

The shifts made by the PLO after the Gulf crisis were less surprising than the fact that they did not go further. "What more can we offer?" Abu Iyad once asked rhetorically. "Are we required to give up the PLO, the right to self-determination, a state, and all our national rights—while Israel gives up nothing?"[32] More accurately, the PLO's difficulty was in moving to pragmatism and compromise while radical ideas still dominated the minds of its leaders and followers.

Against this jeopardy was the fact that the PLO needed Arab state help, U.S. diplomatic acceptance, and Israeli willingness to make some kind of deal in order to change a status quo that was primarily hurting Palestinians. Supporting Saddam had caused a loss of ground with all these vital factors. Failing to act to correct this situation only made matters worse, especially if others were willing to negotiate without PLO sanction.

Still, even the PLO's inability to make gains does not mean it will split or disappear. Links will one day be rebuilt to at least some of the Arab states it has offended. The PLO's inability to offer Palestinians any immediate prospect to improve their situation may erode its authority in the long run but not overnight. Unity, steadfastness, and endurance have been more important factors in its political culture than an ability to deliver material successes.

Thus, international and regional changes in the aftermath of the Cold War and Gulf War undermined the PLO's interests. The PLO was too entrenched to disappear, but it also seemed to be too inflexible to achieve its goals. If the PLO were to be supplanted, it would be due to external forces. Otherwise, win or lose, it seemed likely to maintain control over Palestinian loyalty and fate, even at the cost of any gain for that long-suffering people.

Arafat and the Succession Issue

Arafat has been the only man to head the PLO in its current incarnation, and despite his errors and shortcomings, he has long been the organizations' only conceivable leader. Without him at the helm, the PLO would have splintered; without his charisma and wide acceptance, popular support would have fragmented. Yet Arafat also bears responsibility for the PLO's deadlock and paralysis. The same character traits that have served him well—political timidity, ambiguity, and a premium on consensus—have made him slow to take the bold decisions and difficult choices necessary to make progress. Throughout, Arafat has also known that his authority was limited. As one colleague put it, "He and we are partners. We are not his employees. [He] does not decide ... on his own personal whim."[33]

But surviving is not the same as succeeding. The West has long been frustrated by an Arafat unable to close the gap between his policies and the expectation created by his promises. Even Arab states tired of the game. "Every hero has his flaw," a Palestinian journalist commented. "Arafat's is indecisiveness."[34]

Arafat's inner circle was a group of Fatah founders who worked together from the 1960s, especially Abu Jihad, Abu Iyad, and Qaddumi. Abu Iyad called these personal links the main factor in the group's survival. But these men are either aging or dead and lack clear heirs. Arafat's most likely replacement, Abu Jihad, was assassinated by Israel in April 1988. Abu Iyad, the second most powerful man in the PLO, died at the hands of an Abu Nidal agent in January 1991. Arafat thus lost his two key supporters and potential successors.[35]

Of those left, only Qaddumi, head of the PLO Political Department since 1973, stands at the top rank. Born in 1930, he has worked with Arafat since the 1950s. Qaddumi is coldly austere but popular. He has often taken a hard and pro-Syrian line. These two positions have often been consistent, but the Kuwait crisis put Syria into the U.S.-led coalition, thereby inhibiting Qaddumi from backing Saddam. Once Syria accepted the basic U.S. proposal for peace negotiations with Israel, his opposition to the peace talks was defused.

Two other Fatah founders, Khalid al-Hasan (b. 1928), and younger brother Hani, have been key advisors to Arafat. They generally represent Saudi-Kuwaiti influence in the PLO. Khalid was a key author of the 1988 PLO policy shift in favor of the two-state solution, arguing that the PLO needed its own state to take advantage of the coming Israeli collapse from within and that the end of the Cold War meant that the United States could be pried away from its alliance with Israel.[36] Though the brothers backed Arafat's pro-Saddam policy during the crisis, Khalid became critical thereafter and urged cooperation with the U.S.-led peace process. But by personality—and, in Khalid's case, ill-health—these men are not potential heads of the organization.

Aside from the founders, leaders of Fatah's military-terrorist forces might take over, but two of the key candidates were also killed in 1991: Western Front commander Abd al-Hamid Hayil (Abu al-Hul) by an assassin in January, and Abdullah Abd al-Hamid Labib (Colonel Hawari), head of Fatah's Special Operations Group, reportedly in a May auto accident in Iraq. These deaths left Arafat's private terrorist group, Force 17, poorly led and deprived him of finding an obvious heir in the terrorist/guerrilla apparatus.[37]

If Arafat were to die—no other circumstance would be likely to remove him from leadership—the PLO is likely to face a major crisis. There is a high chance for a split within Fatah, on the one hand, and between Fatah and other constituent groups of the parent organization, on the other hand. Nevertheless, it is virtually assured that the next leader would come from within Fatah's hierarchy. No current or recent resident of the West Bank or Gaza is likely to have any chance. Nor were the "insiders" anywhere near to wanting to take over the organization.

Conclusion

Hani al-Hasan articulated the political contradiction among Palestinians when he stated they would "never abandon our hope and our dream that there will one day be a secular, democratic state of Palestine," but added that the "world will not give us more than" a West Bank/Gaza state. "For us Palestinians the brutal, heartbreaking truth is that if we want peace and an absolute minimum of justice, we have to pay for it with three-quarters of our homeland." To win part of Palestine requires giving up the claim on Israel, a psychological revolution requiring the PLO to "tell our people what they did not want to hear."[38]

But the reason why this had not yet happened was made clear by his brother, Khalid: "The very establishment of a Palestinian state alongside the Jewish one will be visible proof of the imminent collapse of Zionism, whose essence is territorial expansion. An Israeli withdrawal will totally undermine the basic foundations of Zionism" and that state will ultimately and peacefully disappear. "Thus will the democratic Palestinian state [encompassing all of Palestine] be born."[39] In short, the PLO could not fully transform itself. It has given minimal ground when necessary, always hoping to regain that terrain as quickly and completely as possible. Whether changing events or outside pressure could have a strategic, rather than merely a tactical, effect over time remained to be seen.

Notes

1. Interview, *Journal of Palestine Studies (JPS)*, vol. 11, no. 2 (Winter 1982), pp. 10 and 6.

2. Hani al-Hasan, Speech to Royal Commonwealth Society, December 11, 1989, published in *Middle East Mirror,* December 12, 1989.

3. Interview, "60 Minutes" program, February 19, 1989.

4. *al-Majalla* (London), March 10-16, 1984; *al-Watan al-Arabi* (Paris), January 13-19, 1984; *al-Jazira* (Riyadh), November 4, 1983. Helena Cobban, "The PLO in the mid-1980s: Between the gun and the olive branch," *International Journal,* vol. 38 (Autumn 1983), p. 642.

5. *JPS*, vol. 11, no. 2 (Winter 1982), pp. 4-5, 12-13. In a July 1989 interview with the author, Khalid al-Hasan repeated the old story that a map in Israel's parliament claimed a Jewish state of the same dimensions. Also, Jamal al-Surani in *al-Sharq al-Awsat* (London), February 8, 1990, reported in *Foreign Broadcast Information Service-Near East and South Asia (FBIS)*, February 9, 1990; "Yasir Arafat: An Interview," *Third World Quarterly,* vol. 8 (April 1986), pp. 399-410.

6. Arafat, January 1973, *JPS*, vol. 2, no. 3, (Spring 1973), p. 167. Matti Steinberg, "The Demographic Dimension of the Struggle With Israel—As Seen by the PLO," *Jerusalem Journal of International Relations,* vol. 11, no. 4 (December 1989), pp. 27-51; *al-Watan* (Kuwait), October 13, 1989, reported in *FBIS,* October 17, 1989. Indeed, the Vietnamese Communists first acquired the northern part of their country as a foothold, then used it as a base when conditions were ripe for conquering the rest of the country a quarter-century later.

7. *al-Ahram* (Cairo), February 21, 1985; *JPS*, vol. 14, no. 3 (Spring 1985), pp. 151-53; videotape address to International Center for Peace in the Middle East symposium, February 22, 1989; David Ottoway, "U.S. Again Says PLO Violating Vow," *Washington Post,* March 1, 1989; "PLO Says Not Responsible for Raids, Criticizes Europeans," Reuters, February 28, 1989.

8. *FBIS*, November 13, 1990.

9. Hazim Saghiya in *al-Hayat* (Beirut), August 21, 1990, cited in *Middle East Mirror*, August 21, 1990.

10. *The Economist*, September 22, 1990, p. 48.

11. *Le Quotidien de Paris*, November 9, 1990, reported in *FBIS*, November 14, 1990; *Sawt al-Sha'b* (Amman), November 15, 1990, reported in *FBIS*, November 16, 1990; Monte Carlo Radio November 20, reported in *FBIS*, November 21, 1990; Mahmud Darwish on Monte Carlo radio, December 12, 1990, reported in *FBIS*, December 13, 1990.

12. *Washington Post*, January 18, 1991; Karen Laub, "Palestinians Fearful of Attack, But Proud of Iraq for Targeting Israel," Reuter, January 18, 1991.

13. A formalist but useful discussion of PLO structure is in Sami Mussalam, *The PLO* (Brattleboro, VT: Amana Books, 1988).

14. Robert Satloff, "Islam in the Palestinian Uprising," *Policy Focus*, no. 7, The Washington Institute for Near East Policy, (October 1988); Daoud Kuttab, *al-Fajr* (East Jerusalem), September 27, 1987. An interesting case is Asad al-Siftawi, an UNRWA teacher and pro-Fatah activist in Gaza jailed between 1969 and 1974, who was close to the Muslim Brotherhood in the 1950s. His son, Imad, is active in Hamas.

15. Fouad Moughrabi, "The Palestinians After Lebanon," *Arab Studies Quarterly*, vol. 5, no. 3 (Summer 1983), p. 214; Thomas L. Friedman, "West Bank Grows Critical of Arafat, But It's More from Love than Anger," *New York Times*, November 20, 1984.

16. *al-Majalla*, August 30-September 5, 1989, reported in *FBIS*, September 7, 1989.

17. *al-Majalla*, April 5-11, 1989, reported in *FBIS*, April 7, 1989. The PFLP voted against key provisions of the November 1988 PNC resolution and opposed the September 1991 resolutions. All three groups rejected Arafat's December 1988 Geneva statements which made possible the dialogue with the United States. See, for example, *al-Anba* (Kuwait), February 1, 1989, reported in *FBIS*, February 15, 1989, pp. 13-15. For an al-Fatah critique of the DFLP, see Abu Mazin's open letter to Hawatmeh, *al-Anba*, March 2, 1989, reported in *FBIS*, March 10, 1989. See also Middle East News Agency

(Cairo), April 2, 1989, reported in *FBIS,* April 3, 1989; Voice of the PLO (Baghdad), April 5, 1989, reported in *FBIS,* April 6, 1989; and Khaled Abu Toameh, "Now We Don't Rely on Outsiders," *Jerusalem Report,* December 13, 1990, pp. 11-12.

18. *al-Majalla,* April 5-11, 1989, reported in *FBIS,* April 7, 1989.

19. Khalid al-Hasan warned that Palestinians in the territories may decide to establish their own "international popular leadership." Steinberg, "The Pragmatic Stream of Thought Within the PLO According to Khalid al-Hasan," *The Jerusalem Journal of International Relations,* vol. 11, no. 1 (March 1989), p. 45.

20. Palestinians in Kuwait included both refugees and West Bank residents. Palestinians in large numbers have never been welcome in Saudi Arabia and Egypt.

21. In 1971, Israeli Defense Minister Moshe Dayan wanted to let West Bank and Gaza delegates attend the PNC. Prime Minister Golda Meir refused. The deportee closest to Arafat was Akram Haniya, an al-Fatah activist who had been publisher of the PLO-subsidized East Jerusalem newspaper *al-Sha'b* and headed the Arab Journalists Association from 1983 to 1985. Israel expelled him from the West Bank in January 1987.

22. Indeed, at the 1991 PNC, Muhammad Milhim—a West Bank mayor elected in 1976 and expelled by Israel in 1980—was dropped from the Executive Committee.

23. *Middle East Mirror,* March 19, 1990. The two selected were Abdullah Franji, PLO envoy in West Germany, and Nabil Sha'th, an advisor to Arafat living in Egypt. The Central Committee could not agree on a third candidate but was said to favor a military aide to Arafat, Col. Abu al-Mu'tassim (Ahmad Affani). Franji had been in West Germany for most of the time since 1963 while Sha'th, chairman of the PNC's Political Committee, had gone to Egypt in 1948.

24. Nor should the continued radicalism of even West Bankers be underestimated. In a 1986 poll conducted by PLO supporters, West Bankers almost unanimously endorsed the PLO and Arafat as their leaders, while rejecting UN Resolution 242 and demanding a Palestinian state. Only a small

plurality was willing to accept a West Bank/Gaza state even as an interim solution. *al-Fajr,* September 12, 1986.

25. Leading notables in Gaza include: Fayiz Abu Rahma, head of the bar association and the late Abu Jihad's brother-in-law; Dr. Zakariya al-Agha, head of the Gaza Medical Association; Dr. Hatim Abu Ghazala; lawyer Zuhayr al-Rayyes, a veteran nationalist; Khalid al-Kudra of the bar association; Asad al-Siftawi, an independent-minded al-Fatah supporter; Mansur al-Shawwa, son of the late political boss; and Haydar Abd al-Shafi, the leading leftist eventually appointed head of the Palestinian negotiating team to the Madrid peace conference. In the West Bank, they include: Radwan Abu Ayyash, head of the Arab Journalists Association; Hanna Siniora, the (Christian) editor of the pro-PLO newspaper *al-Fajr*; Ziyad Abu Zayyad, editor of a Palestinian Hebrew-language newspaper; the Communist Ghassan al-Khatib, a lecturer at Bir Zayt University; Jamil al-Tarifi, a former deputy mayor; Ghassan al-Shaka, from a leading Nablus family; and pro-Jordan notables Elias Freij, (Christian) mayor of Bethlehem, and Said Kan'an, a Nablus businessman, as well as Muhammad Nasser an independent political strongman in Hebron. Also, see Emile Sahliyeh, *In Search of Leadership: West Bank Politics since 1967* (Washington: Brookings Institution, 1988); Moshe Ma'oz, *Palestinian Leadership on the West Bank* (London: Frank Cass, 1984); and *al-Ahram,* September 10, 1989, reported in *FBIS,* September 13, 1989.

26. *New York Times,* March 9, 1986; *Washington Post,* September 21, 1987.

27. *Middle East Mirror,* November 27, 1989.

28. Voice of Palestine (Sanaa), March 30, 1989, reported in *FBIS,* March 31, 1989. Ex-Israeli Arabs in the PLO hierarchy included Imad Shakur, Muhammad Darwish, and moderate Palestine Research Center director Sabri Jiryis. Elie Rekhess, "Arabs in a Jewish State: Images vs. Realities," *Middle East Insight,* (January-February 1990), pp. 3-9.

29. *Middle East,* May 1983; "From our perspective," Jordan's Crown Prince Hasan insisted, these "Palestinians are Jordanian citizens." Hasan was referring to a U.S. report estimating that there were 1.2 million Palestinians in Jordan. Address to The Washington Institute for Near East Policy, September 12, 1989.

30. Interview with author, July 1989. Aharon Levran et al, *The Middle East Military Balance, 1987-88* (Boulder, CO: Westview, 1988), p. 362; *al-Tadamun* (London), September 11, 1989, reported in *FBIS,* September 15, 1989.

31. Yusef Hasin, *al-Nadwa* (Saudi Arabia), October 1, 1990.

32. Middle East News Agency, October 12, 1989, reported in *FBIS,* October 13, 1989.

33. Jamal al-Surani in *al-Majalla,* November 21, 1989.

34. See Thomas L. Friedman. "West Bank Grows Critical of Arafat," *New York Times,* November 20, 1984; *al-Bayadir al-Siyasi* (East Jerusalem), March 28, 1984.

35. *al-Muharrir* (Paris), November 25, 1989, reported in *FBIS,* November 29, 1989; *Ukaz* (Jidda), November 16, 1989, reported in *FBIS,* November 27, 1989.

36. *al-Sharq al-Awsat,* December 3, 1983; *al-Watan al-Arabi,* January 13-19, 1984.

37. See, for example, *New York Times,* November 6, 1986. Labib had belonged to the Baghdad-based May 15 organization headed by Husayn al-Umari (Abu Ibrahim), who left the PFLP in 1979. In 1982, this group bombed a U.S. airliner en route to Hawaii, killing one and injuring fourteen passengers. In December 1983, it tried to blow up three airliners and, in January 1984, it attempted to bomb an El Al plane. The PLO blocked U.S. efforts to extradite a Hawari operative, Muhammad Rashid, from Greece for the 1982 bombing.

38. *al-Anba,* April 5, 1989, reported in *FBIS,* April 7, 1989; speech, December 11, 1989, text in *Middle East Mirror,* December 12, 1989.

39. Matti Steinberg, "The Pragmatic Stream," p. 48.

7

Israel: Political Change in a Democratic State

Marvin Feuerwerger

On June 23, 1992, Israel's electorate reversed a fifteen-year trend to the right by shifting leftward and returning the Labor party to power. This led to new Israeli approaches to the peace process, domestic affairs, and Israel's relationship with the United States.

While this shift followed the Gulf War, there is no indication that Iraq's Scud missile attacks and other aspects of the war experience were the decisive factors in ousting the governing Likud. Indeed, in the aftermath of the war the Israeli polity had continued its slow shift to the right, a steady trend that had marked Israeli politics since the landmark election which first brought the Likud bloc to power in 1977. Despite lackluster leadership by Yitzhak Shamir, the Likud was clearly the dominant element in the Israeli political landscape, and Shamir was well-positioned to lead the Likud to an electoral victory in 1992. However, a combination of political and demographic factors led to an erosion of support for the Likud and an enhancement of Labor's power. At the same time, taken as a whole, the shift to the left in Israel was extremely mild, with a majority of Jewish voters continuing to support right-wing and religious parties. Nonetheless, even a narrow Labor victory may have dramatic implications for the position of many elements in Israeli society. Clearly, many of the groups most closely associated with Likud policies—including settlement activists—will find themselves increasingly marginalized under a Rabin-led coalition.

Yitzhak Rabin entered office as a man in a hurry, claiming a clear mandate to change Israeli policies with respect to the two key issues, the peace process and economic priorities. On the former, he promised to accelerate peace negotiations and take a moderate stance on the substantive issues that had divided Israel from its Arab neighbors. On the economy, Rabin promised to alter priorities by ending expenditures on "political" settlements in the West Bank and Gaza, while focusing increased attention on employment and economic reform.

Looking to the future, the Likud has already embarked on the process of choosing a new leadership; given the age of senior party leaders Rabin and Shimon Peres, the Labor party cannot be very far behind. The course of Israeli politics for the next decade will probably depend on two factors: first, the degree of success which Rabin enjoys in promoting his security and domestic policy agenda and second, on the capacity of the Labor party to exploit its current opportunity to reshape its image in the eyes of the Israeli public.

Israel Elects Rabin

The government that emerged from the June 23 parliamentary elections is comprised of a center-left/religious coalition led by Yitzhak Rabin, who himself was only elected Labor party leader the previous February. Labor controls the most important ministries, including defense, foreign affairs, and finance, rendering it the dominant party within the ruling coalition. Inside the current government, Rabin has asserted a strong leadership role by retaining the critical defense ministry in his own hands. This was the common practice of Israel's first prime minister, David Ben Gurion, but of no one since. Rabin's retention of the defense portfolio gives him the leading operational role in key areas of Israeli national security policy, including control of all aspects of the army and military operations as well as all aspects of Israeli policy with respect to the Palestinians of the West Bank and Gaza. By virtue of his grip on the prime ministry and the defense ministry, Rabin has placed his fellow cabinet members in a clearly subordinate position.

Rabin's dominant role within the government was a logical culmination to the way in which he conducted Labor's election campaign. After winning Labor's first-ever primary election to lead the party, Rabin ran a campaign focused as much on his personality and leadership as it did on the general appeal of the Labor party and its declared policies. Labor's political campaign stressed Rabin's military and leadership experience and highlighted his commitment to pursue peace while preserving Israeli security. The implied message was that even voters disenchanted with the traditional Labor party or distrustful of dovish factions around Shimon Peres could now trust a reinvigorated party led by Rabin.[1]

Rabin's campaign pledges focused on two principal policy areas—the peace process and changing Israel's domestic priorities to improve the economy—and the used his election success as a mandate to follow through on his promises quickly. Despite the narrow margin of Labor's victory, Israel's parliamentary democracy permits a ruling coalition considerable leeway to implement its core policies. On the peace process, Rabin promised to accelerate negotiations and take a moderate stance on the substantive issues that have long divided Israel from its Arab neighbors. For example, Rabin proposed to reach an agreement on Palestinian self-rule within nine months; with the Syrians, he embraced the concept of territorial compromise and indicated that Israel would also consider territorial withdrawal on its border with Syria provided there was a Syrian commitment to real peace. Almost immediately upon taking office, Rabin halted new settlement activity in the West Bank and Gaza, canceled about half of the housing projects previously undertaken, removed incentives that the Likud had fostered to promote settlement activities, and approved a number of confidence-building measures toward the Palestinians, such as the release of detainees.

These initiatives had the effect of isolating some key groups which had been powerful forces in Israeli politics under Likud governments. Settlement activists, who had played a central role under Likud governments of the 1980s, found themselves completely excluded from political decision-making. Indeed, they complained bitterly that, thanks to Rabin's new policies, they could not even get Labor officials to answer their telephone calls or to assist them with some elemental problems. Similarly, the National Religious Party, which had been part of every Israeli government since Israel's declaration of independence in 1948, found itself for the first time sitting in opposition, unable to reconcile itself to Rabin's moderate views on the Arab-Israeli peace process.

With respect to the economy, Rabin promised to alter priorities by such measures as ending expenditures on "political" settlements in the West Bank and Gaza, while focusing increasing attention on employment and economic reform. Achieving success in the economic sphere would not be easy, given the challenge posed by the unprecedented levels of immigration from the former Soviet Union and Ethiopia and the great need for economic reform of a system that had been based on the principles of socialism. These problems were compounded by Israel's traditional requirement to maintain a large defense budget because of ongoing threats from its Arab neighbors. However, Rabin viewed the peace process as providing a window of opportunity to limit defense spending, especially in light of the military decline of regional antagonists Iraq and Iran in recent years. While growing military threats in the late 1990s might force Israel eventually to allocate far more to its defense budget, the opportunities afforded by the offer of loan guarantees from the United States and elsewhere, combined with the shrinkage of Israel's diplomatic isolation throughout the world, presented a rare chance to stimulate real and lasting economic growth. Here, too, Rabin felt the need for prompt action.

Beyond the peace process and the economy, Rabin placed great emphasis on improving relations with the United States. Under Shamir, those ties had been strained over the Likud government's settlement policies and the decision of the Bush administration to link the approval of $10 billion in loan guarantees for immigrant absorption to a freeze on Jewish settlement activity in the West Bank and Gaza. Just days after forming his government, Rabin welcomed Secretary of State James Baker to Jerusalem for intense consultations on reviving the peace process. Within weeks, Rabin travelled to Kennebunkport to meet with President Bush. Following an historic set of private meetings, the Israeli prime minister and American president announced agreement on the provision of loan guarantees and a procedure for addressing any future differences on settlement activity.

In the following weeks, Rabin and Bush also demonstrated an unusual degree of cooperation with respect to the sale of F-15 aircraft to Saudi Arabia. Although Rabin publicly opposed the sale of any advanced weapon system to states technically at war with Israel, he let it be known that Israel would not vigorously fight against an F-15 sale worth billions of dollars and thousands of American jobs. In return, the Bush administration took concrete steps in five areas to help Israel preserve its qualitative military edge over prospective Arab foes.[2]

The Labor Coalition

Yitzhak Rabin's government comprises a coalition controlling sixty-two seats of the 120-member Knesset (parliament). The coalition includes Labor's forty-four seats, twelve seats for the leftist Meretz coalition, and six seats for the predominantly Sephardic Shas party. (See Table 7.1) In addition, Labor can count on the tacit support of the five Knesset members from the two Arab-oriented parties in the Knesset, Hadash and the Arab Democratic Party. By contrast, the opposition Likud bloc and its right-wing allies control forty-three seats, augmented by the ten other seats of religious parties that have not joined the Labor-led coalition. Thus, despite the narrowness of the governing coalition, it appears relatively stable; under virtually all imaginable circumstances, there are at least sixty-one parliamentarians who would refuse to join a right-led coalition. Moreover, Labor retains the potential to bring additional partners into its coalition so as to broaden its political base. In particular, the Ahdut Hatorah and Tsomet parties were quite close to agreements with Labor during coalition negotiations in July 1992, and they may yet still come to terms.

On the other hand, the current government does have a number of fissures which could eventually lead to its collapse. The most serious of these are controversies over the relationship between religion and state. In initial coalition negotiations, Rabin made concessions to some ultra-orthodox groups by incorporating the Shas party into the government in return for Shas's general support for Rabin's primary objectives on the peace process and the economy. Despite criticism from many within his own party, Rabin continued to work closely with the Shas leadership because of its support of his stance on the peace talks. By contrast, negotiations with the secular, hawkish Tsomet party broke down in part because of Rabin's insistence on pursuing a policy of territorial compromise.

In the first months of the new government, conflict broke out between Minister of Education Shulamith Aloni, the avowedly secular head of the Meretz bloc, and the religious leadership of the Shas party. On one level, the confrontation reflected political differences as to the proper role of religion in Israeli schools; at another level, the conflict centered on Aloni herself and accusations that she had failed to observe Jewish religious practices during an official trip abroad. Though the conflict was settled in autumn 1992, it threatened to deteriorate into a full-fledged coalition crisis. Future problems with Shas could also plague the government, including the possibility that Shas Knesset members, including the current minister of the interior, might be indicted for criminal fraud during the prior Likud-led government.

In addition to these problems within the coalition, Rabin still faces potential challenges from inside his own party. Though Rabin defeated rival Shimon Peres for the party leadership in February 1992, it is clear he only owed his narrow victory to the support of some erstwhile Peres backers who came to the conclusion that, after four unsuccessful attempts, their man could not win at the polls. Their votes for Rabin were pragmatic, not enthusiastic, and it appears that the Peres camp still outnumbers Rabin's faction within the

TABLE 7.1   The Twenty-fifth Government of Israel

Yitzhak Rabin, *Prime Minister and Defense Minister (Labor)*
  b. 1922, Jerusalem. Served as chief of staff of the Israel Defense Forces; prime minister, 1974-1977; defense minister, 1984-1990.
Shimon Peres, *Foreign Affairs (Labor)*
  b. 1923, Poland; immigrated to Israel in 1934. Served as defense minister under Rabin; prime minister, 1984-1986; foreign minister, 1986-1988; and finance minister, 1988-1990.
Avraham (Beiga) Shohat, *Finance (Labor)*
  b. 1936, Tel Aviv. Former mayor of Arad, a development town; entered the Knesset in 1988; chairman of Finance Committee, 1988-1990.
Shulamith Aloni, *Education and Culture (Meretz)*
  b. 1929, Tel Aviv. Entered Knesset in 1965; has served continuously since 1974; leader of Meretz bloc, composed of her Citizens Rights Movement, the Shinui (Change) party, and Mapam.
Arye Der'i, *Interior (Shas)*
  b. 1962, Morocco. Served as minister of interior since 1988.
Micha Harish, *Industry and Trade (Labor)*
  b. 1936, Romania; immigrated to Israel in 1950. Entered Knesset in 1974; served as Labor party secretary-general prior to June 1992 election.
David Libai, *Justice (Labor)*
  b. 1934, Tel Aviv. Former professor of law, Tel Aviv University, and chairman, Israel Bar Association; entered Knesset in 1984.
Binyamin (Fuad) Ben-Eliezer, *Housing (Labor)*
  b. 1936, Iraq; immigrated to Israel in 1950. Retired brigadier general; entered Knesset in 1984.
Yisrael Kessar, *Transportation (Labor)*
  b. 1931, Yemen; immigrated to Israel in 1933. Served as secretary-general of the Histadrut labor federation; entered Knesset in 1984.
Haim Ramon, *Health (Labor)*
  b. 1950, Jaffa. Entered Knesset in 1983; served as chairman of Labor parliamentary faction, 1988-1992.
Moshe Shahal, *Police and Communications (Labor)*
  b. 1935, Iraq; immigrated to Israel in 1950. Served as minister of energy, 1984-1990; entered Knesset in 1971.

(continues)

TABLE 7.1 (*continued*)

Yaakov Tsur, *Agriculture (Labor)*
   b. 1937, Haifa. Served as minister of absorption, 1984-1988; minister of health, 1988-1990; entered Knesset in 1981.
Shimon Shitreet, *Economy (Labor)*
   b. 1946, Morocco; immigrated to Israel in 1949. Former professor of law, Hebrew University; entered Knesset in 1988.
Amnon Rubinstein, *Energy (Meretz)*
   b. 1931, Tel Aviv. Former dean, Tel Aviv University Law Faculty. Served as minister of communications, 1984-1988; entered Knesset in 1977; head of Shinui (Change) party.
Uzi Baram, *Tourism (Labor)*
   b. 1937, Jerusalem. Served as secretary-general of the Labor party, 1984-1988; entered Knesset in 1977.
Yair Tsaban, *Immigrant Absorption (Meretz)*
   b. 1930, Jerusalem. Entered Knesset in 1991, former political secretary of Mapam.
Ora Namir, *Environment (Labor)*
   b. 1930, Hadera. Entered Knesset in 1973; former chairwoman, Education and Labor and Social Affairs Committees.

party institutions and apparatus. Indeed, in a clear demonstration of political weakness, an intra-party election chose a Peres man over Rabin's preferred candidate in an October 1992 vote for secretary-general of the party. This division of power within the Labor party necessitates close cooperation between Rabin and Peres if Labor is to have any chance of achieve its stated goals during the life of this Knesset.

Rabin and Peres's rivalry is legendary, stemming both from their decades of competition inside the Labor party and differences over policy and personality. Early signs suggest, however, that the two antagonists are finding themselves able to find common ground on the critical issues. They agreed, for example, on an arrangement allocating authority between them with respect to the peace process. In addition, they concurred on the appointment of Professor Itamar Rabinovich to succeed Zalman Shoval as ambassador to the United States—the type of appointment that was frequently bottled up in the days of Likud-Labor National Unity Governments. However, Rabin continues to view Peres as a potential rival for national leadership, a fact which that undoubtedly colors their day-to-day interaction.

Trends in Israeli Voting Prior to 1992

Throughout the early history of the Jewish state, Mapai, predecessor of today's Labor party, was the dominant factor in electoral politics and the leading party in every government coalition. Mapai and its allies of the left, operating in a bloc known as the Alignment, peaked in 1969, when they won fifty-six seats in the Knesset. Thereafter, the Alignment fell to fifty-one seats in 1973 and then suffered a precipitous drop to thirty-two seats in 1977, when it finally lost the government to the Likud.

Israel's electorate was transformed during the 1950s and 1960s, largely as a result of the alienation of Jews of Sephardic origin from the Labor party and the demographic changes that took place in Israeli society as voters of Sephardic origin emerged as the majority.[3] Paul Abramson has pointed to seven factors that marked Israeli electoral politics up until 1992:

1. Entry into the electorate of young Ashkenazi voters with relatively low levels of support for the Alignment
2. Diminution of older Ashkenazi cohorts with high levels of Ashkenazi support
3. Entry into the electorate of young Sephardi voters with very low levels of support for the Alignment
4. Diminution of older Sephardi cohorts with relatively high levels of support for the Alignment
5. Relative stability of Alignment support among Ashkenazi cohorts
6. Substantial shift among all Sephardi cohorts toward the Likud
7. Differential ethnic composition of the younger and older cohorts.

The change in Israel's electorate was evident in the votes for the most prominent parties of the left and right since the late 1960s. Between 1969 and 1988, Israel's electorate expanded by almost 900,000 voters. During that period, the Likud doubled its vote, from 338,948 in 1969 to 709,305 in 1988. By contrast, Labor and its successors increased their strength by only 110,000 votes.

Interestingly, Labor's support among Sephardi voters continually fell, despite more aggressive efforts by Labor than Likud to move Sephardi candidates up on its Knesset list in recent years. In 1988, Sephardi Jews increased their representation in the Knesset from thirty-three to thirty-eight seats; of those, fourteen were Labor members, twelve were Likud.[4]

Religious Party Voting

The gradual rightward shift of the Israeli electorate never affected one of the fundamental bases of Israeli governmental formation since the founding of the state, i.e., the inclusion of some religious parties in any governing coalition. Indeed, while there was no inherent need to include religious parties in the National Unity Governments which evolved out of the 1984 and 1988 elections, each of the major, non-religious parties sought to maintain a coalition with religious parties in the hope that it could thereby establish a coalition in which it would be the dominant party.

Moreover, in the 1988 Knesset elections, religious parties dramatically increased their vote-getting power—much to the surprise of many observers. From a combined total of thirteen seats in the 1984 elections (239,604 votes), religious parties won eighteen seats in the 1988 elections (341,120 votes).[5] Shas, the largest religious party, challenged Likud support within the Sephardic community and halted the long-term trend of increased Sephardic support for the Likud that had marked every election since 1977.

Nonetheless, despite the growing strength of the religious parties, the central factor in Israeli politics during the 1980s was the Likud. The Likud demonstrated that it could ally with both religious parties and parties of the extreme right, or that it could turn to the Labor party in a National Unity Government.

The Labor party tried to reach coalition agreements with religious parties in both 1984 and 1988; however, given Labor's perceived weakness and the growing hawkishness of the religious community on both religious and national security issues, Labor could not reach a coalition agreement with the religious parties.

Arab Voters

In theory, Labor could have made up for a loss on the right by increasing its support among Arab voters. Between 1977 and 1988, the number of valid Arab votes cast in Knesset elections rose by 59.2 percent, compared with a rise of 30.6 percent in the total vote.[6] In the 1988 Knesset elections, eligible Israeli Arab voters theoretically had the potential to choose some fourteen Knesset members. Moreover, in 1988, neither the Palestine Liberation Organization nor Muslim fundamentalist leaders ruled out voting for mainstream Israeli parties.

But in 1988, Arab voters did not fully counterbalance the trend among Jewish Israelis away from Labor and its allies. In the first instance, Israeli Arabs voted at lower rates than their Jewish counterparts—a common phenomenon in Israeli politics. Second, many Israeli Arabs "wasted" their votes by sending them to a number of small parties, which in turn did not fully utilize the votes they received by failing to reach surplus vote agreements with other political parties.[7] Most importantly, in 1988 just as in 1984, about 47 percent of the Arab electorate voted for either the Democratic Front for Peace and Equality (Hadash, the former Communist party) or the Progressive List for Peace—parties with which neither Labor nor other mainstream Zionist parties could enter into a coalition. In total, non-Zionist Arab minority and radical parties received 58 percent of the total Arab vote, as opposed to 51 percent in 1984. Moreover, the Labor party vote among Arabs declined by 8 percent, despite the presence of two Arabs on Labor's list and the addition to the Labor party of Ezer Weizman, whose Yahad party had won 5.5 percent of the Arab vote in 1984.[8] By contrast, between 1984 and 1988, the Likud increased its share of the Arab/Druze vote by 60 percent, from 4.5 percent to 7.2 percent.[9]

It remained possible that Arab voters could play an increasingly important role in the Israeli electorate. However, this would require both increases in the percent of eligible Arab voters casting their ballots and increasing Arab support for "coalitionable" parties in the Israeli political landscape. It would also be important if the three predominantly Arab parties would consolidate, so that Arab votes would not be split. However, there was little indication in the late 1980s that any of these would occur.[10]

After the Gulf War

The Kuwait crisis, into which Iraq tried to draw Israel as a combattant by firing Scud missiles at Israeli population centers, had a mixed effect on the Israeli political psyche. According to a March 1991 survey by Jaffee Center of Strategic Studies at Tel Aviv University, 29 percent of Israelis said the war had changed their opinions on national security issues.[11] However, this group was split virtually down the middle, with just over half saying they were now more ready than before the war to negotiate some territory for peace and just less than half saying they were less ready than before to negotiate on the same terms.

Overall, however, a trend toward what Israeli political scientist and election analyst Asher Arian has called "creeping conciliation" has been maintained.[12] The Jaffee Center survey found that some 58 percent of Israelis favored returning at least some territories for peace, and 34 percent supported the creation of a Palestinian state with appropriate security guarantees for Israel. By contrast, fewer than 50 percent of Israelis supported territorial compromise in 1986, while fewer than 25 percent of Israelis supported a Palestinian state in 1987. Other surveys found that Israelis also supported in increasing numbers the concept of a peace conference sponsored by the United States and Soviet Union.[13] When the U.S. and Israeli governments came into conflict over the issue of settlement activity, two-thirds of Israeli Jews supported at least a temporary halt in settlements so as to probe Arab intentions.[14]

At the same time, in the wake of the war, there was a hardening of some other attitudes on security issues. For example, 91 percent of Israelis supported development of nuclear weapons, compared with 78 percent in a similar survey in 1987. Just under 50 percent of the sample thought that the Arabs wanted to destroy Israel and kill Jews, while another 23 percent thought the Arabs "only" sought to conquer Israel. About two-fifths of the Israeli electorate endorsed the concept of "transfer" of Arabs from the West Bank and Gaza.[15] And on a rather consistent basis, about 55 percent of the Israeli public opposed territorial compromise on the Golan Heights.[16]

Despite some long-term moderation in the views of Israelis toward the peace process, they still saw the Likud as the party best able to secure true peace. Shamir's policy of restraint during the Gulf War won great support among the Israeli public at the time, reinforcing Likud's perceived electoral strength. With respect to their choice for prime minister, respondents in the Jaffee Center survey overwhelming preferred Likud candidates to Labor candidates, 55 percent to 32 percent. (The individual breakdown was Shamir, 28 percent; Yitzhak Rabin, 15 percent; Shimon Peres, 14 percent; Moshe Arens and Ariel Sharon, 11 percent each; David Levy, 5 percent; Mordechai Gur, 2 percent; and Moshe Shahal, 1 percent.)

Moving Toward 1992

The shift in the Israeli electorate away from parties of the left/center and toward the parties of the right, right/center, and the religious parties continued after the 1988 Knesset elections. Likud made major gains in Israel's 1989 municipal elections, driving Labor from the leadership of many of its traditional strongholds. At the national level, poll data consistently indicated a reduction of support for parties of the left. For example, a Smith poll in June 1991 indicated that if the election were held then, a coalition of the right would defeat the left by a margin of 45.5 percent to 37.5 percent, a significant improvement from its 41.5 percent to 40 percent margin in 1988. Generally, polls found that the Likud would hold its own in elections, while the Labor party was facing a dramatic reduction in strength. (See Table 7.2)

Had no major political changes occurred, at least five Knesset seats would have shifted from Labor and its allies to the Likud and its allies in the 1992 Knesset elections. This expectation was grounded on two demographic developments: the replacement of older pro-Labor voters with younger pro-Likud voters and the near-term impact of Soviet Jewish immigration.

On the age factor, studies have shown that, in every election since 1977, younger voters have tended to favor the parties of the right to a larger extent than older voters. Naturally, if Labor and its allies had been unable to win

TABLE 7.2   Israeli Political Preferences *(in percentages)*

	1988 vote	*11/90*	*5/91*	*6/91*
Center/Right				
Likud	34.0	29.0	32.0	34.0
Tehiya	3.5	5.0	3.5	4.0
Tsomet	2 plus	5.0	5.0	4.5
Moledet	2 plus	5.5	4.0	3.0
Center/Left				
Labor	31.5	21.0	23.0	26.0
CRM	4.5	7.0	7.5	6.0
Mapam	2 plus	2 plus	3.0	—
Shinui	2 minus	3.5	2.5	2.5
Religious				
NRP	4.0	4.0	3.5	4.0
Shas	5 plus	3.0	4.0	4.0
Aguda/Degel Hatorah	6.5	5 minus	4.0	4.0
Other	2.0	2.0	2.0	1.0
Undecided	—	8.0	6.5	4.0

Source: Hanoch and Rafi Smith, "Likud and Right Riding Crest of Strong Support, Poll Finds," *Jerusalem Post,* July 7, 1991.

increased support among younger voters, their position among the electorate at large would have eroded as older voters died. This tended to occur at a rate of approximately two Knesset seats per election.

With respect to Soviet Jewish immigrants, poll data indicated that they leaned to the right and were likely to add to the strength of the Likud and its right-wing allies. One poll in the summer of 1991 found that Soviet immigrants shifted dramatically to the right in the first year following their arrival in Israel.[17] Assuming that about half of the 350,000 immigrants who had arrived in Israel by late summer of 1991 would vote in the 1992 Knesset elections, it was reasonable to expect that they would contribute three seats to the Likud and its allies.

More specifically, poll data through the summer of 1991 also indicated that Yitzhak Shamir stood an excellent chance of leading the Likud to victory in 1992. The only significant danger which Shamir appeared to face was a head-to-head, direct election for prime minister with the Labor party's Yitzhak Rabin. According to a Gallup poll conducted during summer 1991, more three-quarters of the Israeli public (including 66 percent of Likud voters) favored direct election of the prime minister.[18] However, Israelis vote for their prime minister on an indirect basis by party list, and Prime Minister Shamir deferred direct election to the prime minister until 1996.

Although the Israeli political landscape appeared relatively stable in late 1991, two issues appeared capable of shaking the system: a dramatic development in the peace process or severe economic difficulties. In addition, it appeared that the Labor party could improve its performance if it replaced perennially unpopular party leader Shimon Peres with Yitzhak Rabin.

In the context of the peace process, Israel faced a unique and historic situation—the prospect for face-to-face negotiations with its neighbors that could lead alternatively to peace, if successful, or to a heightening of the conflict between them. The last time that Israel faced a similar prospect, in the wake of Egyptian President Anwar al-Sadat's 1977 visit to Jerusalem, Likud leader Prime Minister Menachem Begin accepted full withdrawal from the Sinai and a framework for Palestinian autonomy in exchange for peace with Egypt. In the months after the October 1991 Madrid peace conference, the prospects for success had not yet looked so bright. Prime Minister Shamir's approach to the peace process led, on the one hand, to increased tensions with the United States over the loan guarantees issue and, on the other hand, to the breakup of his government over opposition by small right-wing factions to any discussion of autonomy for West Bank and Gazan Palestinians. The result of the scheduling of early elections for June 1992.

The other development which appeared capable of affecting the Israeli polity was the perception of a major setback in the economy. Unemployment in early 1992 reached near-record levels of about 12 percent, with the rate among new Soviet immigrants hovering around 50 percent. Uncertainty over the fate of the economy and the unease among the right regarding the government's position in the peace process combined to shake confidence in two of the Likud's core constituencies.

Analysis of the June 1992 Election

Whatever advantages Likud may have enjoyed at the beginning of 1992 dissipated by June, leading to a major electoral reversal and its first outright loss of power in fifteen years. (See Table 7.3) In 1992, the Likud received 60,000 votes fewer than it had in 1988, while Labor increased its total by some 220,000 votes. Taken as a whole, the left won about 50 percent of the vote, an increase of about 5 percent over its 1988 total.

TABLE 7.3   Comparison of 1988 and 1992 Knesset Election Results

Party	Votes	Percent	Seats
Labor	906,126 (685,363)	34.6 (30.0)	44 (39)
Likud	651,219 (709,305)	24.9 (31.1)	32 (40)
Meretz	250,206 (193,396)	9.5 (8.5)	12 (10)
Tsomet	166,247 (45,489)	6.3 (2.0)	8 (2)
National Religious	129,601 (89,720)	4.9 (3.9)	6 (5)
Shas	129,310 (107,709)	4.9 (4.7)	6 (6)
Ahdut Hatorah	86,138 (136,993)	3.2 (6.0)	4 (6)
Moledet	62,247 (44,174)	2.3 (1.9)	3 (2)
DFPE	62,138 (84,032)	2.3 (3.7)	3 (4)
Arab Democratic	40,799 (34,279)	1.5 (1.2)	2 (1)
Tehiya	31.938 (70,730)	1.2 (3.1)	0 (3)
Progressive List	24,069 (33,695)	0.9 (1.5)	0 (1)

Note: 1988 statistics are in parentheses.

Source: Central Elections Committee, Results of the Elections to the Knesset, 1988 and 1992.

From the aggregate numbers, it appears that the Likud lost support primarily to parties to its right, which gained four seats over their 1988 total. Secondarily, the Likud apparently lost some votes to Labor, now headed by Rabin. But critical to both Labor's success and the Likud's decline was the voting behavior of new Israeli voters, including recent immigrants and young people. Labor made impressive gains among the young, outpolling the Likud, for example, by a margin of 32 percent to 25 percent among Israeli soldiers. Yet while the Likud weakened among soldiers, the right (excluding religious parties) still outpolled the left by a margin of 49 percent to 46 percent.[19] Still, the most significant gains for the left occurred among new immigrants, especially Jews from the former Soviet Union. Here, Labor outpolled the Likud by a margin of 47 percent to 18 percent, and the left as a whole won a decisive majority of this segment, contributing a net gain of about three seats to the future governing coalition.[20]

Notwithstanding these gains, it is important to stress that the overall result was still a close affair. A shift of fewer than 20,000 votes would have given a majority of Knesset members to the right and religious parties. Had the Knesset not raised the threshold qualifying parties for a seat from 1 percent to 1.5 percent in 1992, the Tehiya party would have won one seat, producing a 60-60 tie between the two major blocs.

Nevertheless, the reversal of the rightward trend of the past two decades is unmistakable. In this regard, perhaps the most important factor was Labor's election of Rabin to head its list. Rabin has been Israel's most popular politician for many years, and his primary election victory in February 1992 immediately gave Labor a boost over Likud. A March 1992 Dahaf poll of Jewish voters, for example, showed Labor leading the Likud by a margin of forty-one seats to thirty-seven. This was the first lead Labor enjoyed over Likud, and one it never relinquished.[21]

In earlier Israeli elections, notably in 1984, majorities of the Israeli public had policy orientations closer to those of Labor on the economy and foreign policy but still resisted voting for the Peres-led party. With Rabin at the helm, some Likud voters believed that when they disagreed with their own party over policy matters, they could now vote for Labor without fearing for Israel's security. By mid-1992, many voters felt the time had come to turn out the Likud because of perceived failures on the peace process, the economy (unemployment stood at 12 percent), managerial competence, and the status of U.S.-Israel relations in the wake of the Bush administration's deferral of Israel's request for $10 billion in loan guarantees. Accordingly, internal Likud poll data indicated that more than 100,000 former Likud voters were wavering between support for Likud and Labor. Particularly vulnerable were immigrants from the former Soviet Union, who saw Likud policies on settlement and U.S.-Israeli relations as undermining their own economic prospects.

In addition, one should also not discount the performance of the Likud in the months leading up to the election. In contrast with the orderly and democratic procedures which seemed to characterize Labor process of choosing its party leadership and Knesset list, the Likud was racked by internal bickering and unseemly demonstrations of discord. In addition, accusations of incompetence and malfeasance, especially coming from sources like the comptroller-general, heightened popular disaffection with the Likud's performance.

Looking to the Future

Public Attitudes

It is too early to tell whether a Labor government will affect long-term Israeli attitudes towards the economy, party affiliation, or the peace process. Undoubtedly, such developments will depend in part on the degree of success which Rabin's government will enjoy.

In the early months of the new government, there were a number of concrete achievements which could have had some impact on political attitudes. Relations with the United States were dramatically improved, and the Bush administration and Congress agreed to provide Israel with $10 billion in loan guarantees. Negotiations with the Arab states became far more substantive and serious. Israel and Jordan agreed to a detailed agenda for future negotiations that read like a framework for a future peace treaty; Israel and Syria appeared to take small but significant steps toward bargaining about what would constitute peace between them. In addition, immigration from the former Soviet Union, which had begun to taper off as the economy worsened, again began to rise.[22]

Preliminary poll data indicated some moderation of Israeli public views, even on the sensitive question of territorial withdrawal on the Golan Heights. While close to 60 percent of Israelis have tended to oppose any change in Israel's border with Syria, this number dropped to about 50 percent in mid-1992.[23] Nonetheless, opposition to Israeli withdrawal in the Golan remained strong, including within parts of the Labor party, and tens of thousands of Israelis took to the streets in November 1992 to demonstrate against any possible withdrawal. By this time, however, Prime Minister Rabin had already begun to signal that Syria had not yet proven that it had taken the funda-mental decision in favor of peace with Israel that would make a successful negotiation possible. And the seeming inability of the Palestinians to utilize the negotiations to advance their own interests, combined with ongoing violence against Israelis and other Palestinians, reduced the prospects for dramatic changes in Israeli public opinion.

Succession

Looking to the next election and beyond, there are a variety of alternatives for succession within the Israeli democracy. This discussion can only speculate about the general parameters of future possibilities.

In the first instance, it is very possible that the 1992 Knesset election was the last of its kind. Should it come about, extensive electoral reform could alter the shape of the Israeli political landscape. The Labor party has expressed support for such reform, not only in the context of the direct election of Israel's next prime minister, but also in terms of promoting district elections for some Knesset members and raising the threshold required for parties to enter the Knesset. In addition, these positions are supported by significant parties of the left (Meretz) and right (Tsomet), as well as by prospective Likud leader Binyamin (Bibi) Netanyahu. Electoral reform of this sort is likely to reduce not only the importance of small parties, but it might also reduce the importance of party structures altogether, as has been the case in the United States. This area is virtually assured to remain one of critical analytical focus in the years ahead.

Within the traditional party context, the Likud is scheduled to replace party leader Yitzhak Shamir in early 1993, a process that often fuels internal turmoil and discontent within a party moving from government to the opposition. The decisions by Shamir and former Defense Minister Moshe Arens to retire from political life open the door for a major struggle for control of the heart of the party.

In November 1992, the Likud decided to reform its internal electoral system by adopting a primary system. The leader chosen in these elections will also be the Likud's candidate for prime minister when Israel holds its first direct election for that office sometime before 1996. Most observers believed that the most likely candidate to win the internal party leadership battle was Netanyahu, the young, U.S.-educated, former ambassador to the United Nations. As of late 1992, Netanyahu was the clear leader among public opinion polls of Likud voters.[24] His main rival for Likud leadership is another figure of his generation, the more reserved Binyamin (Benny) Begin, son of the former prime minister. Though possible, it appears highly unlikely that the party would turn to older stalwarts, such as Ariel Sharon or David Levy, to carry its banner in the 1996 election.

For its part, Labor is also likely to move to a new leadership by the mid-1990s, as septuagenarians Yitzhak Rabin and Shimon Peres pass from the scene. With the party assuming the mantle of leadership for the first time in fifteen years, it is too soon to predict who may emerge as the most popular or competent leader from among the current crop of ministers. Generally speaking, however, there are two separate "young generations" in Labor today. The first group consists of politicians in their fifties and sixties, including Finance Minister Shohat and Transport Minister Kessar. Despite their experience and seniority, they have not traditionally enjoyed popularity among the Israeli public, although this could change as they begin to wield ministerial authority for the first time. Labor's second "young generation" includes Knesset members in their thirties and forties, such as Health Minister Ramon, Deputy Foreign Minister Yossi Beilin, and Member of Knesset Avraham Burg. While such leaders offer Labor a potentially brighter future, they are not widely known within the body politic. Labor might also be able to incorporate senior military leaders—such as current Chief of Staff Ehud Barak—at or near the top of future lists.

Yitzhak Rabin has promoted some of his loyalists, such as Shohat and Housing Minister Ben-Eliezer, to senior ministerial positions. But his ability to cultivate a new leadership in the party will depend to a large extent on his policy successes and their own performance in office. So too will Labor's position within the Israeli political system as a whole. Labor has taken important steps in recent years to rid itself of socialist trappings and to demonstrate to the Israeli public that it offered a viable alternative to the Likud. Its membership registration and national primaries led to an impressive display of democracy, and its new young 1992 Knesset list won it wide respect.

Nonetheless, the outcome of the 1992 elections should be seen more as a rebuff of the Likud than as an endorsement of Labor. Labor regained power largely as a result of Likud's collapse and some special and unique circumstances. With everything working in its favor, Labor did not greatly exceed its vote-getting results in 1984, and it remains far below party popularity in the 1950s and 1960s. However, as the party of government, Labor will now have an excellent opportunity to burnish its image and improve its position. To do so will require success on three fronts: the economy, the peace process, and the maintenance of warm relations with the United States. These will remain Prime Minister Rabin's highest priorities.

Notes

1. Clyde Haberman, "Rabin Invokes Old Victory to Seek a New One in Israeli Election Campaign," *New York Times,* May 21, 1992.

2. Thomas L. Friedman, "U.S. and Israel Working Out Deal to Offset Warplane Sale to Saudis," *New York Times,* September 15, 1992.

3. Paul Abramson, "Generational Replacement, Ethnic Change, and Partisan Support in Israel," *Journal of Politics,* vol. 51, no. 3 (August 1989), pp. 545-574.

4. Don Peretz and Sammy Smooha, "Israel's Twelfth Knesset Election: An All-Loser Game," *Middle East Journal,* vol. 43, no. 3 (Summer 1989), p. 403.

5. Robert O. Freedman, "Religion, Politics, and the Israeli Elections of 1988," *Middle East Journal,* vol. 43, no. 3 (Summer 1989), pp. 406-422.

6. Ian S. Lustick, "The Changing Political Role of Israeli Arabs," in Asher Arian and Michal Shamir, eds., *The Elections in Israel-1988* (Boulder, CO: Westview, 1990), p. 125.

7. Surplus vote agreements are a mechanism by which remainder votes are allocated among parties to determine members of Knesset. In the 1988 elections, each Knesset seat required 18,563 votes; 112 seats were allocated in this manner, and eight seats were allocated by surplus vote agreements. Neither the DFPE, the PLP, nor the Arab Democratic Party entered into surplus vote agreements. Had they done so (depending upon the parties with whom they had allied), they could have garnered an additional one or two seats.

8. In 1984, Labor and Yahad won 31.5 percent of the Arab vote. In 1988, their successor parties, Labor and Mapam, won 22.5 percent of the Arab vote. Another reason the Labor party may have lost votes was that Yossi Sarid, a popular figure in Israel's Arab community, moved from Labor to the Citizens Rights Movement between 1984 and 1988. The CRM increased its share of the Arab vote from 1 percent in 1984 to 4 percent in 1988.

9. Joseph Ginat, "The Elections in the Arab Sector: Voting Patterns and Political Behavior," *The Jerusalem Quarterly,* No. 53 (Winter 1990), pp. 27-55.

10. Indeed, there are indications that additional Arab parties may be formed. See, for example, "New Arab Party to Run in Knesset," Voice of Israel, October 2, 1991, cited in *Foreign Broadcast Information Service-Near East and South Asia (FBIS)*, October 3, 1991.

11. Asher Arian, "Israeli Public Opinion on Security Issues and the Peace Process in the Aftermath of the Gulf War," Jaffee Center for Strategic Studies, mimeo, April 14, 1991.

12. Ibid.

13. Two polls in July 1991 found that over 70 percent favored such an approach; support rose to over 80 percent in August 1991. "Over 70 Percent Favor Giving an Unequivocal 'Yes' to Baker," *Mideast Mirror*, July 26, 1991; "86 Percent Support Government Decision to Go to Peace Conference in October, According to Phone Poll in *Ma'ariv*," *Mideast Mirror*, August 9, 1991.

14. "Poll Probes Attitudes Toward Settlement, Peace," *Al Hamishmar* (Tel Aviv), September 12, 1991, reported in FBIS, September 17, 1991.

15. Hanoch Smith cited in *Mideast Mirror*, May 3, 1991; for earlier poll data, see "Poll: 49 percent lean towards 'transfer' of Arabs from areas," *Jerusalem Post*, December 8, 1988; Reuven Ben-Tsvi, "Poll: 59 percent in Israel Favor Lean Towards Transfer," *Ma'ariv* (Tel Aviv), June 6, 1990.

16. Hanoch and Rafi Smith, "Polls Find Majority Against Giving Up Golan," *Jerusalem Post*, July 22, 1991; "Poll Shows More Readiness for Golan Concessions," *Davar* (Tel Aviv), September 8, 1991, reported in *FBIS*, September 10, 1991.

17. Yaron London, "The Immigrants Lean to the Right," *Yediot Aharonot* (Tel Aviv), June 18, 1991. By contrast, a Dahaf Institute poll in spring 1991 found that 63 percent of new immigrants defined themselves politically as belonging to the left, despite the fact that 60 percent believed the territories should not be returned. "Only 18 percent of immigrants say they are right-wing but 60 percent oppose territorial compromise." *Mideast Mirror*, May 3, 1991.

18. Dan Izenberg, "Wide Support Found for Direct Election of Premier," *Jerusalem Post*, July 3, 1991.

19. Leslie Susser, "Rabin's Master Plan," *Jerusalem Report,* July 16, 1992.

20. Susser, "Rabin's Master Plan."

21. "Labor Ahead But Lacks Majority, Poll Shows," *Mideast Mirror,* March 20, 1992.

22. Clyde Haberman, "Ex-Soviet Immigration to Israel Picking Up Again," *New York Times,* November 22, 1992.

23. "50 percent of Israelis oppose any concessions on Golan," *Mideast Mirror,* October 16, 1992.

24. Clyde Haberman, "Israel's Likud Puts Hope in U.S.-Style Changes," *New York Times,* November 17, 1992.

8

Egypt's Political Order: Continuity and Challenges

Ami Ayalon

Continuity and stability have long marked Egypt's political development. They are likely, though not necessarily certain, to remain the dominant themes in the foreseeable future. Heavy economic pressures, problems of political and cultural orientation, the advent of an aggressive opposition, and a volatile international environment, all combine to form a scene which contains a potential for unpredictable developments. This chapter will examine the structure and basic tenets of the Egyptian regime, discuss the various challenges facing it, and assess its durability.

Mubarak's Presidency

The Egyptian state of the early 1990s is a hybrid system: it is at once an authoritarian state and a state of institutions. As an authoritarian-presidential system, it carries certain marks of patrimonial rule. The authority of the head-of-state is paramount, rooted in age-old popular conventions, backed by the country's all-powerful military, and assisted by a group of loyal aides. At the same time, this authoritarian government also leans on an elaborate system of civilian institutions.

While the system's authoritarian government and its military underpinning are as old as Egyptian civilization, the institutions are relatively new. Introduced in embryonic form in the nineteenth century, they have been consolidated in the twentieth, particularly during the last two decades. They

195

include an appointed cabinet, governing a massive bureaucratic apparatus; a parliament elected periodically by a multi-party system; and an increasingly autonomous judiciary. Outside the official system there are other political forces acting legally, semi-legally, or illegally. This includes Islamic movements, both open and clandestine, alongside organizations of the secular-minded intelligentsia, acting in cooperation with, or in opposition to, the government.

The authoritarian principle still plays a dominant role in the Egyptian system. The president is the author of all important decisions in domestic and foreign matters and makes all major appointments to civilian and military posts. While his government is not hereditary, the rules governing the transfer of power have the effect of firmly securing his stay on the throne for as long as he wishes. Nor is the constitutional basis for his rule its most important guarantee; far more significant are the unshaken support of the military and civilian establishments and, perhaps equally vital, the traditional acceptance of this status quo by the massive majority of the people. In a sense, the Egyptian head of state is, thus, a "presidential monarch." More than just a president, he is a *ra'is* (literally "head")—a term implying uncontestable leadership and a call for obedience. The system's other components are, in the final account, subordinate to him.

Bases of Legitimacy

Egypt has long been viewed as a classical model of an "hydraulic society."[1] A riverain country, it has developed an hierarchical state in which the ruled have always looked up to the ruler, expecting him to care for their needs and defend them against enemies. This does not necessarily mean total passivity and submission; Egypt has known rebellion in both ancient and modern times. But for Egyptians, that the state should be headed by a mighty leader has been the most natural order of things. This traditional concept had been prevalent in the pre-modern era, and while it has recently been eroded by modern developments, it has remained broadly popular. It has yet to be effectively replaced by a more pluralistic alternative.

That the system should be led by a single, powerful authority is not merely an offshoot of the "hydraulic" philosophy. It is also an idea that stems from Islamic political thought, the faith of some 90 percent of Egypt's population. Islam requires believers to obey the ruler, whoever he may be; more than merely a political duty, obedience is an article of faith.[2] Like the hydraulic concept, the Islamic principle of obedience has undergone considerable erosion under the impact of modernization. Yet in a society still largely religious, it is still a widely held view that the welfare of the community demands authoritarian leadership.

Traditional concepts, shaped by geography and Islamic teachings, combine to give the head of the Egyptian state a unique standing. The very fact of his being the *ra'is* buys him solid legitimacy, perhaps more so in Egypt than in many other places. Such an attitude seems to be shared not merely by the lower, more traditionally minded segments of Egyptian society but also, to a large extent, by the political and intellectual elite. This was borne out, for example, during President Anwar al-Sadat's struggle against political rivals soon after his ascent to power in 1970. The very fact that Sadat occupied the presidential throne bought him the critical support of the army and politicians against the other, formidable contenders.[3] Likewise, when Sadat was assassinated, the shock shared by supporters and critics alike was, in large part, because the attack on him was viewed as an assault on the institution of the presidency itself.

Another important source of legitimacy is the July 1952 revolution which overthrew the royalist regime of King Farouk and established the modern republic. The revolution's original ideals are highly revered by virtually all Egyptians; it was a redeeming movement, designed to liberate the country from foreign domination and the evils of a corrupt government, to redistribute wealth and opportunities, and lead Egypt to international grandeur. Though the glory of the revolution and the popular admiration accorded its first leaders have been tarnished over the years, some of its splendor has remained. Four decades later, Husni Mubarak is still bearing the revolutionary banner to accrue prestige. Revolutionary symbols and ceremonies, the memory of its heroes, and its emotional jargon are an inseparable part of the state's political style. No less a part of the state's style is its ongoing struggle against the revolution's external enemies, who, everyone agrees, have by no means disappeared. The present regime, therefore, continues to pose as the country's shield against their threat, a safeguard of Egypt's honor. And Mubarak, as its head, still enjoys a special standing. An eminent son of the revolution's "October [1973] generation," he is widely viewed as leader of the continuing struggle to secure for Egypt a respectable place under the sun in the modern world.

Mubarak: Effective Control and Uninspiring Leadership

Husni Mubarak (b. 1928) was fifty-three years old when he succeeded the slain Sadat in 1981. He apparently accepted the presidential assignment with reluctance, showing signs of hesitation; it was quite evident that, at first, he felt uncomfortable in his new role. Half-way into his first six-year term, however, it had become clear that he was prepared to carry on beyond one term. Since then, Mubarak has developed much of the craftiness necessary to succeed in international diplomacy. More important, not only has he earned the public's esteem for his businesslike management of the domestic scene, but he has also built a solid position within the regime, safe from any rivals or challengers. On the other hand, it seems that Mubarak lacks one important virtue, namely charisma.

In post-revolutionary Egypt, the notion of charisma has been synonymous with Nasser. His magnetic personality was an invaluable asset at an historical juncture where old institutions crumbled and new ones had yet to evolve. Nasser's charisma seemed to obviate the need for state institutions throughout most of his tenure. It was a unique attribute; neither Muhammad Naguib before him nor Sadat thereafter were similarly blessed.

Mubarak is not a charismatic leader, especially if judged by Nasser's standards (and perhaps even by Sadat's). In the cautious words of one Arab observer, Mubarak's is "a low key, businesslike style that [is] unlikely to generate strong emotions among the populace."[4] A bright man with sharp political instincts but a somewhat reserved personal style, he had to labor hard to build himself a popular standing. With a reputation as a war hero but unexperienced politician, Mubarak started from a low point, a subject of street jokes focusing on his awkward manners and apparent lack of political wit. But his assiduity, clean handedness, frankness and, more important, political achievements—chiefly on the foreign front—have gradually bought him popular esteem. Esteem, though does not extend as far as to include admiration; the public's view of Mubarak seems to be devoid of emotion. His integrity and diligence win him the appreciation, but not veneration, of supporters and critics alike.

Mubarak inherited the leadership of Egypt after a long and exhausting period of intensive political action. Nasser combatted imperialism, led wars against Israel, and inspired a grand vision of Arab unity. Sadat, always fond of drama, fought his own war and then brought peace with Israel, quarreled with the Arabs, and reformed the political system. Mubarak's government, by contrast, so far seems to offer Egypt an anticlimactic respite. Mubarak chooses to engage in the unexciting projects of improving infrastructure, expanding democracy, and slowly building Egypt's regional position, always through gradual evolution, never through "electric shocks." This approach reflects his personal style; he is a man of moderation and patience, of deliberate consideration and not of particularly grand vision. Under his government, the notion of grand vision has given way to pragmatism, no-nonsense efficiency, and a realistic encounter with the often-gloomy realities of economics. These circumstances, and Mubarak's personality, combine to form an uninspiring leadership.

Are charisma and vision indispensable requisites for governing Egypt? As for the former, the answer is apparently no. But when the leader is not charismatic, his government must rely more heavily on other props, most notably the loyalty of the president's confidants and the military and civilian institutions. As for vision, the answer is more complicated. When present realities are harsh, a vision of a better future—even if mere illusion—may alleviate mass suffering and strengthen the government's authority. A tough present and a bleak future might prove a hazardous blend. When charisma and vision are replaced by down-to-earth pragmatism, popular support could erode. Such a development could give ground to centrifugal political forces.

Mubarak's Lieutenants

In the original sense of the term 'lieutenant'—"one holding the place of another"—Mubarak has none. Through clever management of government", he has molded a system in which he has no obvious replacement, challengers, or even would-be challengers among his chief aides.

Throughout Mubarak's years in power, he has consistently refused to appoint a deputy. In Egypt the role of vice president has long been regarded as equal to that of heir-apparent, a fact of which Mubarak is acutely aware, having served as Sadat's deputy before succeeding him. (Similarly, Sadat was Nasser's vice president when the latter died.) This has made the issue of vice presidential appointment a focus of much public interest and endless speculation. Mubarak has chosen to leave the post vacant, saying that he had "not found an appropriate candidate" for it. In recent years speculation has grown rarer, apparently indicating that Mubarak's solitude in government has become an accepted reality.

Is Mubarak's consistent refusal to appoint a deputy a mark of his resolve to retain exclusive authority in his own hands? Is it a sign of excessive self-confidence? It is difficult to assess what his motives were during the early years of his tenure, but it is safe to assume that today Mubarak feels quite comfortable as president and may not entertain any thoughts of stepping down in the foreseeable future.

One sign of Mubarak's self-confidence was his removal of Abd al-Halim Abu Ghazala, deputy prime minister and defense minister, from his post in April 1989. Abu Ghazala was powerful figure who enjoyed a unique standing thanks both to his status as Mubarak's longtime comrade-in-arms as well as his effective control of the army, where he had "established something of a personal fief."[5] As a result, he was regarded as the undisputed "number two" in Egypt, second only to the president. When Mubarak deposed him abruptly, appointing him to the vaguely defined and largely ceremonial post of "special presidential assistant," it was a surprise to outside observers and to the Egyptian political establishment alike that Mubarak was attempting to weed out any potential challengers (or even successors). This idea, however, seemed to be confirmed by his choice of General Yusef Sabri Abu Talib, a professional officer lacking in popular standing and political connections, as Abu Ghazala's replacement. (Abu Talib himself was later removed from office.) Mubarak thus further consolidated his grip on the government; in the words of Tahsin Bashir, a seasoned Egyptian diplomat, Mubarak was "making public that he is the king and master."[6]

Abu Ghazala's ouster opened a big gap between the president, now without any conceivable challengers or even peers, and a group of subordinate leaders, none of whom was politically prominent or particularly well known. This group includes a number of senior officials whose experience and talent are highly regarded by the president, who consults them regularly in their respective fields of expertise. They are not all in the limelight; some, commanding powerful apparatuses, occupy posts requiring anonymity. Among them are the chief of civil intelligence and (somewhat less powerful) chief of military intelligence. Others who receive more press coverage included, at the time of this writing, the following:

- *Usama al-Baz,* first undersecretary in the foreign ministry and Mubarak's *eminence grise* and chief political adviser since the latter's vice presidential days. al-Baz, who holds a doctorate in international relations from Harvard, is a shrewd political tactician and gifted administrator. His power stems from his talent for acting behind the scenes, which he prefers to holding a senior post with more ceremony but less influence. He seems to have as much staying power as any of the others inside Mubarak's inner circle.
- *Dr. Atif Sidqi,* prime minister since 1986. Like most other cabinet ministers, Sidqi is not a politician but a technocrat, a professional economist appointed to lead the fight against the country's economic ills. As such, Sidqi does not represent any independent power base. But given Egypt's centralized government, his post allows him control of the huge civil bureaucracy and, with it, significant administrative power.

- *Gen. Muhammad Husayn Tantawi,* minister of defense since May 1991. A professional officer with an impressive, 36-year record of service in the military, Tantawi fought in all of Egypt's wars since 1956. He commanded the elite Republican Guard before acting as chief liaison officer with U.S. forces during the Gulf War, after which he was elevated to head the defense ministry. The very fact that he holds this position places him as a senior member of the leadership team. In principle, it would also give him the latitude to nurture his own power base, but given Mubarak's handling of Abu Ghazala, is not likely that the president would allow this to occur.
- *Amru Musa,* foreign minister since May 1991. A career diplomat with an extensive record of international experience, Musa served as Egypt's ambassador to the United Nations before replacing Ismet Abd al-Meguid, who was appointed as secretary-general of the Arab League. Though gifted and popular, Musa has little political experience and his position does not give him the opportunity to build much of a base.
- *Dr. Ismet Abd al-Meguid,* Arab League secretary-general and, until May 1991, deputy prime minister and minister of foreign affairs. A veteran diplomat and politician, highly regarded by Mubarak and popularly respected, Abd al-Meguid's vast experience in foreign affairs, rather than a power base within the Egyptian system, buys him his senior standing in the president's inner circle.
- *Dr. Yusef Wali,* deputy prime minister, minister of agriculture and food security, and secretary-general of the ruling National Democratic Party (NDP). Though Wali's position is influential—controlling much of the patronage that makes Egypt's system function—it is not clear to what extent his influence translates into real political power.

In addition to this group of high-ranking officials, the following personalities of lesser influence should be mentioned.

- *General Abd al-Halim Musa,* minister of the interior, a critical position in terms of responsibility for confronting the domestic opposition, but one that tends to wear down its incumbent. (Musa is the fifth interior minister to serve under Mubarak).
- *Ahmad Fathi Surur,* speaker of the People's Assembly since December 1990, a post of considerable political leverage. According to the Egyptian constitution, should the presidency become vacant for any reason, in the absence of a vice president, the speaker serves in that position until a new president is elected.

- *Butrus Butrus-Ghali,* secretary-general of the United Nations and former deputy prime minister for foreign liaison. Ghali, a Copt, is respected for his experience in foreign affairs but lacks independent power.
- *Kamal Ahmad al-Ganzuri,* deputy prime minister and minister of planning.

Some or most of these men could be involved in a possible transfer of power, in circumstances to be discussed below.

The Regime's Backbone: The Army

The army, which brought the present regime to power in 1952, still serves as its chief support. The regime would not survive without the army's backing; discontent in the army's ranks would certainly imperil its stability. While the political arena has been expanding in recent years to include other forces as active players, the role of the regime's backbone still remains with the armed forces, a well-organized, 450,000-man institution.[7] This is so even when the army's visibility is low, as it is today, both in the number of military officers occupying ministerial posts and in the daily atmosphere on the Egyptian street. The government's dependence on the armed forces, and the latter's unreserved loyalty to the civilian authorities, were demonstrated convincingly during the mutiny of the security forces in February 1986, when the army moved to quell the riots, restored order, and then returned to its barracks.[8]

The relationship between army and government is a symbiotic phenomenon; just as the government needs the armed forces' backing, so the army has a vested interest in the government's survival. All Egyptian presidents, from Naguib to Mubarak, have been ex-armed forces men, and the army views the government as its civilian wing assigned to administer state affairs. In exchange for its commitment to support the government, the army expects the regime to safeguard its privileged position in the distribution of national resources and to ensure the perpetuation of these privileges. The government finds the deal acceptable—officers, soldiers, and their families enjoy better material conditions than their civilian counterparts; sizeable portions of the national budget are spent on modernizing military equipment and on purchasing sophisticated and expensive weapons, to give the corps professional satisfaction; and, to keep the moral of the troops high, state leaders miss no opportunity to praise them and express the nation's gratitude to them for preserving its security and stability. Even in times of growing national hardship, the army is always materially one step ahead of the civil sector. So far, the government has managed to keep the troops happy and therefore loyal.[9]

This is not to suggest that the regime has hermetically shielded the military from the economic misery that affects most Egyptians and could be a source of discontent and doubt. Army men and their families, even when protected by their privileged position, are still often exposed to the troubles of economic distress and hence, potentially, to the message of those purporting to offer "an alternative way," primarily the fundamentalists. When the country's general circumstances are harsh, it is doubtful whether the government's efforts to quarantine the military in separate, comfortable cities and to monitor signs of dissent among its personnel could provide a foolproof guarantee against the percolation of negative sentiments into the ranks. The conscripts' revolt in 1986, which was at least partly the result of socioeconomic malaise, could be seen as illustrating the difficulties in isolating another vital supporting pillar of the regime from such sources of trouble.[10]

Another problem, paradoxical yet real, with keeping the armed forces content lies in the absence of actual combat for long periods of time. Aside from a border clash with Libya in 1977, nearly two decades passed, from the 1973 October War to the 1991 Gulf War, in which the military saw no action. Even in the Gulf War, only 36,000 men participated, less than one-tenth of the army's total. Sensitive to the potential frustration of endless training toward no well-defined objective, the government has tried to involve the armed forces in civilian projects that it hopes would generate satisfaction and pride, such as building bridges and operating bakeries.

On a more conventional level, the army regularly undertakes large-scale maneuvers and exercises. This has created a sense of the need for preparedness for an imminent confrontation—either war with Israel or some other state in the region[11]—something which the war against Iraq has evidently borne out. In line with this approach, the two senior officers in charge of Egypt's effort in the Gulf War, Tantawi and General Salah Halabi, were elevated to the posts of defense minister and chief of staff respectively, a mark of gratitude to the army for successfully executing the government's policy.[12] This strategy has hitherto proven most effective.

The army will remain loyal to the government as long as the latter protects its interests. Once the government appears unable to do so, the army's power could conceivably be transformed from an asset into a threat.

The Civil Bureaucracy

The civil bureaucracy, another pillar of the regime, is an hierarchical system of ministries, agencies, and branches administered by the president's appointed officials and their subordinates. It governs every important aspect of public life. The huge public sector of government employees, built under Nasser's interventionist economic policy and preserved by his successors, is fully controlled by this bureaucracy. To a significant though lesser extent, the private sector is also dependent on the bureaucracy. And the public at large must rely on it for all public services, from food supply to health and education and from road-building to business-licensing. In the countryside, perhaps more than in the cities, the population depends on the system's local representatives in everything but their most private affairs. Based on a hierarchy of loyalties, the system is topped by the general directors of ministries who answer to their ministers who, in turn, answer to the president. Like the concept of centralized authoritarian rule, the reality of heavy-handed bureaucracy meets popular Egyptian expectations.

The civil bureaucracy is the government's main tool in implementing its policies at home. But because of its legendary unwieldiness and inefficiency, it often serves as a disruptive rather than constructive force. Like most bureaucratic systems, or perhaps more than most, the Egyptian system is more effective in blocking progress than in generating it. This kind of effect, which often seriously hinders the government's performance, could be useful to whoever commands any part of the system; properly manipulated it could be used to thwart undesirable initiatives of the central authorities. Thus, though under the government's direct command, the bureaucracy also has a certain autonomous power of its own.

State Institutions

The Cabinet. The Egyptian cabinet can hardly be considered an inde-pendent political force. Under Mubarak, as under Sadat, the cabinet has been little more than an assembly of technocrats assigned to run the different branches of government on the basis of their professional experience. Very few politicians serve as cabinet ministers; most come from academia, business, or extensive service in their ministries. Typical of modern Egyptian cabinets, Mubarak's cabinet (as of mid-1991) contained thirty-one members, of whom eighteen held doctorates and five were engineers; only two, the minister of defense and the interior minister (also in charge of police) were ranking military officers. The prime minister himself was an economist by training, brought to the post after serving as head of the Central Auditing Agency. Cabinet reshuffles, an effective means for preventing the formation of independent power bases, are frequent; only nine of those thirty-one ministers were leftovers from Mubarak's first cabinet, formed in 1982, and they held purely technical portfolios like transport, housing, and social insurance. Indeed, Sidqi himself is the fifth prime minister to serve under Mubarak.

Under Mubarak, as with his predecessors, the cabinet does not operate as a corporate forum that makes political decisions. Rather, it functions as a group of appointed officials who implement policies. Its chief importance, therefore, lies in its authority over the civil bureaucracy. Politically and constitutionally, it has little role in matters relating to the presidency, to the executive authority of the state, or to the succession or transfer of power.

The Legislature. Since 1980, the Egyptian legislature has been bicameral, consisting of the People's Assembly (parliament, or *majlis*) and the Consultative Council (*shura*). The latter body is of negligible political consequence. A deliberating forum, its members include ex-politicians and non-political public figures such as prominent authors, professors, artists, and Coptic representatives, some of whom are elected while others are nominated by the president.

The People's Assembly is a more important institution. With 444 elected members and ten nominated by the president, it is officially the state's chief legislative body. It is also designed to fulfill another important function, as the main arena for political encounter between the government and its critics. The assembly is thus the forum in which the agenda of public debate is both reflected and, to a large extent, shaped. The constitution also allots to it a crucial role in electing the president—it is this body which nominates the one candidate to be confirmed in a popular referendum.

Despite its considerable constitutional authority, however, the assembly's practical power is much more limited. The government, represented by a large majority, often employs the assembly as an instrument of the state, using it to sanction decisions made elsewhere. Having delegated extensive constitutional power to the assembly, the regime is careful to retain firm hold over it.

The Judicial System. The judicial system is mentioned here not so much for being a branch of the government but, more important, because of the possible political significance of its palpably growing autonomy. Both Nasser and Sadat were prone to manipulate this system to serve political ends. Mubarak, in contrast, seems to adhere to his oft-proclaimed commitment to the full independence of the judiciary. The courts have ruled against the government and for its rivals on a surprisingly high number of occasions; especially prominent were cases concerning the rights of political groups to organize as parties and the constitutionality of election laws.[13] The government has uniformly complied with these judicial decisions.

Continued governmental commitment to the autonomy of the courts is bound to create standards of conduct and popular expectations. These may evolve into a problematic constraint should the regime wish to change its course in this matter. In such an event, the government, without necessarily losing control of the system, might find itself forced to pay an undesirable political price. If the freedom of the judiciary is as yet still reversible—Mubarak may choose not to comply with legal rulings—its slow but steady consolidation might make such disregard for the courts increasingly difficult in the future.

The Multi-Party System and the NDP. The multi-party system, inaugurated by Sadat and expanded under Mubarak, has grown into an integral part of the governmental structure. Parties are allowed to function, organize, publish their own newspapers, criticize the government, and compete with each other for parliamentary seats in general elections. From the regime's point of view, the system serves several important purposes. As a "safety valve"—Mubarak's term—for popular dissent, it renders much opposition activity harmless while satisfying at least some of the political expectations of the small but influential Egyptian intelligentsia and boosting the regime's democratic credentials.[14] At the same time, the system helps the government identify many of its domestic opponents and trace their complaints. With the government's blessing, the democratization process has made impressive strides in Egypt over the past fifteen years, reaching a point without parallel in the Arab world.[15] An expanding process of pluralism, however, may also involve certain risks which will be examined below.

The National Democratic Party was founded by Sadat in 1978 to represent the government in the pluralistic game. It was designed to play a role similar to that of its predecessor, the Arab Socialist Union, the regime's mobilizing organization in the old single-party system. That role is to win legitimacy through popular participation in political action. The NDP represents the regime in the open contest against the opposition parties, a contest which, however, everyone admits is weighed heavily in the NDP's favor. The NDP is chaired by Mubarak himself, who recognizes that traditional attitudes prevent most Egyptians from voting against "the president's party" and has thus refused to give up this position despite repeated opposition protests. Senior party positions are held by leading ministers and other state officials, and the party's provincial branches are headed by state functionaries. No less significant for the way the democratic game is played in Egypt is the fact that government agencies—many of which are led by current or former NDP party-men—are responsible for administering elections and declaring the winners. The government is both a player and a referee in the game.

The NDP is also a tool for controlling the legislature. Having always enjoyed a majority of three-quarters or more of assembly seats, the party serves as the channel to obtain legal sanction for the regime's policies. The NDP political bureau, comprising thirteen members and chaired by Mubarak, serves as their party's executive, decision-making forum, complementary to the smaller informal forum of the president and a handful of his confidants. As is evident, there are no clear lines that distinguish regime from party; having been created by the regime, the party continues to be operated from above, a government-made and government-controlled apparatus.

Challenges to the Stability of the System

The Egyptian government appears to be stable. Its different constituents seem to act in harmony, a promising recipe for durability. There are, however, forces outside the system which challenge this stability. The challenges come principally from two quarters: the Islamic fundamentalist movement and, to a lesser extent, the political-intellectual elite operating within the multi-party system. What makes these challenges dangerous is a double crisis, material and spiritual, with which the country has to contend. In addition, Egypt's international environment, in particular the Arab arena, displays a high potential for instability which might have an impact on Egypt's domestic scene. Such challenges had existed in the past, and the country's political system had survived them. However, they have not disappeared, and they seem no less threatening today than ever before.

A Twofold Crisis: Material and Spiritual

Socioeconomic Troubles. By all standard economic indicators, Egypt faces a serious socioeconomic crisis. The basic structural problem is clear—approximately 50,000 square kilometers of fertile land in Egypt (about 5 percent of the country's total land area) are already fully exploited and cannot accommodate the fifty-seven million people that now live in the country, let alone the million more that are added through natural increase every nine months or so. On top of the daunting problems spawned by an untenable relationship between land and people, Egypt is plagued by an inefficient economic structure that only exacerbates its economic woes.

According to varying estimates, Egypt imports 50 percent to 70 percent of its food and is dependant on a ceaseless string of ships that daily unload essential supplies from abroad. The country makes great efforts to stretch its income from exports (pre-Gulf War estimate, about $6 billion) to finance some $10 billion of imports, including foodstuffs, raw materials, and military equipment.[16] This results in a huge foreign debt, which was estimated at $50 billion prior to the Gulf crisis and which was swelling even faster than the population. Servicing this debt means a heavy burden on the Egyptian budget. Prior to the Gulf War, Cairo's efforts to reach agreement with the International Monetary Fund that would allow rescheduling of its debt repayments had produced poor results. A previous, May 1987 agreement with the IMF collapsed several months later, as the government refused to accept the fund's conditions for substantial changes in its economic structure and policies.[17] Those changes, according to Mubarak, "would make hell in the country."[18] By the summer of 1990, the Egyptian economy was in dire straits, with little relief in sight.

The figures mentioned here are no mere matter of budget books and balance-of-payment tables. They reflect a gloomy reality that affects the lives of tens of millions of Egyptians on a daily basis. For the poor, society's largest segment, the national economic crisis means an almost impossible task of keeping up with inflation on the most basic staples.[19] But even those who do not belong to the poorest classes suffer. A general sense of malaise is the product of periodic shortages of foodstuffs; scarcity of housing; unemployment for skilled and educated workers; inadequate public services; and even more aggravating, the conspicuous gap between the majority of the population and a small group of the sumptuously wealthy, some of them enriched by the government's open-door economic policy. The present is bad enough, and the future portends even more troubles. While a substantial increase in the country's wealth is hardly a realistic possibility, the population is sure to continue growing rapidly, reaching some seventy million people by the end of the 1990s. A number that huge would vastly increase the pressure on Egypt's limited resources. To those who are not familiar with the probable scenarios for the future, Mubarak spells it out loud and clear.

> What will happen when there are seventy million of us, keeping in mind that resources do not increase at the same rate as population? ... What about houses, food, education, medical treatment, and many other needs for [these] millions? Where will we get these things?[20]

What makes the scene especially complicated is the cumbersome system of government subsidies, mostly for basic food and petroleum. This system, begun under Nasser and expanded under Sadat, has created a heavy dependence on the government and, by extension, an inextricable bond between the economy and political stability. The subsidies have become a racking liability for the regime. By the mid-1980s, Egypt was spending an estimated $4 billion annually, or 7 percent of its gross national product, on food and fuel subsidies. Committing a sizeable portion of its revenues to sustaining especially the poor, the government cannot cut subsidies substantially without risking dangerous outbursts of social unrest. Yet as long as subsidies remain at such high levels, the country's economic structure will remain unhealthy and a source of many risks.

There is another aspect to the direct correlation between economic and political troubles. In recent years, Egypt's needs have made the country increasingly dependent on U.S. financial aid, on U.S. influence upon other western industrial states, and on the goodwill of these other creditors themselves.[21] Such heavy reliance on the West, especially on Washington, is irritating to many Egyptians, even when cloaked with statements of friendship and common interests. Dependence is embarrassing and evokes unpleasant memories from the days of foreign occupation. Egyptian sensitivity is roused whenever the United States and Egypt disagree occurs on whatever issue. Though everyone in Egypt knows that the relationship with the United States is essential for Egypt's survival, it does not make the bitter pill of dependence any easier to swallow. This factor contributes to the antagonism between the regime and its critics, thereby enhancing domestic tensions.

The Gulf War, a watershed event in so many ways, created unexpected new opportunities for Egypt's economy. Basically, Egypt benefited from it in two ways. First, a considerable portion of Egypt's foreign debts were written off by its international coalition allies, primarily the United States (approximately $7 billion) and the wealthy Gulf states ($6 billion to $8 billion). Other allies contributed more emergency aid worth hundreds of millions of dollars. Equally important, these developments facilitated a new Egyptian agreement with the IMF, ratified in April 1991, which allowed the gradual rescheduling of another large part of its debt. Consequently, Egypt's total foreign debt could, by 1994, be reduced to a reasonably manageable $25 billion, just half its pre-war total. The effect of these financial boons was to alleviate the debt servicing burden, relaxing the country's overly strained budget.[22] Second, these changes in the financial scene, combined with a strengthened popularity of Mubarak and his government at home, created circumstances perhaps more convenient than at any time in recent years for introducing extensive economic reforms. If successfully implemented, such reforms could mark a new and promising departure for Egypt's economy.

It will be years before a full assessment of the impact of these developments, though a preliminary balance sheet shows promising indications, including a decrease in state subsidies. Wise handling of the new opportunities could produce a historic change in Egypt's economy. These opportunities, however, could fizzle, if the government is unable to overcome the tremendous obstacles still ahead. In that case, the structural problems would return with a vigor.

Finally, there is another angle to the economic question. By standard economic indicators, the Egyptian economic system could very well collapse; it is conceivable that the growing gap between revenues and expenditures, chronic shortage in cash for buying food, and soaring prices at home could combine to cause a breakdown even before the population reaches the frightening seventy-million mark. However, standard economic rules, neatly applicable elsewhere, may not be the best yardstick for assessing the Egyptian situation. Indeed, the "imminent collapse" of the Egyptian economy has often been prophesied but has never come to pass. This is accounted for by three factors that are essential elements of the country's economic picture: the "hidden economy," the resilience of the Egyptian people, and the regional interest in Egyptian stability.

Alongside the "official" economy, which serves as the basis for conventional analyses, there exists a lively "hidden economy." Many Egyptians—there is no telling exactly how many—have more than one job and sometimes more than two, thereby increasing their otherwise tiny incomes through channels which leave no trace in government statistics. Large amounts of foreign currency, perhaps as much as $40 billion, are held in banks abroad and offer a safety net to many Egyptians. Thus, there is a considerable gap between the official information on the Egyptian economy and the actual situation.[23]

At the same time, economic data do not adequately take into account the impact of the natural optimism and resilience that are not just part of the Egyptian stereotype but are very real components of society. Egyptian society has long been known as remarkably tolerant, accustomed to meet trouble of all kinds with patience and a unique sense of humor. This proverbial tenacity has often been ascribed to two factors: first, the somewhat mysterious impact of the Nile, a mighty and until recently untamed giant, on those inhabiting its banks; and second, the profound religious faith of most Egyptians, which teaches believers to accept God's will without question. This tolerance is largely responsible for the fact that Egypt's economy bends but does not break, in contrast to other economies that would surely suffer collapse or upheaval if faced with Egypt's enduring problems. Optimism and resilience are elusive factors, unknown quantities of tremendous force, that are often not factored into predictions of future economic behavior.

In a larger sense, it is important to note that sustaining the Egyptian economy is not solely an Egyptian interest, but it is also a vital interest of countries that support Egypt. Issues of debt repayment and continued foreign aid are not determined solely by economic logic but also by a variety of other considerations. Egypt's economy, therefore, may not really be—and perhaps has not been in the past—heading toward an inevitable breakdown. Nevertheless, there is no doubt that, when combined with other factors, the currently grave situation contains a serious potential for sociopolitical agitation.

Spiritual-Ideological Dilemmas. In recent decades Egypt has been facing an ideological predicament, often described as a crisis of disorientation. In part, it derives from sharing the broader crisis of Middle Eastern society, yet to carve its own niche in the modern world and find a satisfactory substitute for the long-gone caliphate after 150 years of Western domination and then several decades of independence. For Egypt, there is also the disenchantment with the July 1952 revolution, now four-decades old, whose gains have failed to match its initial promise. At one time, the country was offered a grand vision of pan-Arab leadership coupled with sociopolitical justice at home, a formula that seemed to fit Egypt's great past and a suitable response to the challenges of the time. The dream died, leaving the country somewhat confused. Sadat's efforts to devise a substitute vision, primarily by highlighting Egypt's magnificent pharaonic past, seem to have further puzzled Egyptians without leading anywhere. Mubarak, as we have seen, is not inclined to advance any grand plan and often paints a bleak picture when pressed on his vision of the country's future.

Egypt's cultural problem is often described as one of identity. Islam, which for centuries had offered an adequate spiritual support in times of material hardship and political difficulty, is no longer the only available formula, nor is it the one which the government itself propounds. Secular concepts, such as Arabism, pragmatic Egyptian nationalism, and marginally collectivist options such as socialism, are also available. For the state, secularist and modernizing in its essence, Islam is at best irrelevant to the country's present needs; at worst, it is an obstacle. But what the state itself is offering instead is hardly as total an answer to Egypt's problems as Islam ever was. Consequently, while in the past there was harmony between needs and responses, today there is a bewildering disharmony.

The premises underlying the new orientations are not only very different from each other, but they are also often mutually exclusive; what the rationalistic-pragmatic government may define as Egypt's vital national interest could be unacceptable from a pan-Arab (e.g., peace with Israel) or an Islamic (e.g., family planning) point of view. The assortment of ideological options that have become available alongside Islam are thus often a source of perplexity, particularly troublesome as material conditions deteriorate.

One recent mark of this confusion is a growing yearning for the exciting times and leadership of Nasser. It is evident in a multitude of forms: in movies, literature, public discourse, and a proliferation of Nasser's portrait in private homes and public places. It also finds political expressions, such as in the repeated attempts to establish a legal "Nasserist" party; the adoption of "Nasserist" principles by existing parties; and, lately, in the popular sympathy for the "Egyptian Revolution" leftist terrorist group, exposed in 1987 with Nasser's own son as one of its leaders. "These men are heroes," was one intellectual's response to their arrest, "they are the sons of Egypt. They have raised guns against ... those who attack the Arabs, in order to defend our dignity and honor.[24] Such selective attachment to a past period of great hope—as well as pain, now largely overlooked—best epitomizes the spiritual dilemmas of the present.

The Challenge of Islamic Fundamentalism

Of the forces challenging the regime, the Islamic fundamentalist movement is the most significant. The fundamentalists' goal is to apply traditional Islamic values as a comprehensive remedy to the country's ills; they do not seek deliberately to destabilize the state. But forming the main channel for popular protest, they pose a threat to the political order. Under the existing harsh circumstances, the fundamentalist alternative is a problem the regime must confront on a daily basis.

The background to and various expressions of the fundamentalist phenomenon in Egypt and elsewhere are the subjects of an extensive literature and need not detain us here.[25] Basically, the movement signifies the revitalization of a puritanical trend which has always lived in Islam, now grown attractive to the community in the face of recent troubles. It is not a socioeconomic protest movement which happens to phrase its complaint in Islamic terms, as has sometimes been suggested. Rather, it is a religious movement which is gaining ground due to socioeconomic and spiritual circumstances.

The fundamentalist challenge takes on different forms. The Muslim Brotherhood, representing the movement's mainstream, has been depicted as "moderate" since it chooses to employ political and educational rather than violent means in attaining their goal of implementing Islamic law. It uses its influence in mosques and a host of publications to disseminate its message and support an extensive network of welfare institutions to increase its popular constituency. The Brotherhood also associates itself with political parties, though often via shifting alliances, in order to take advantage of the officially sanctioned political contest. Having opted to act from within the system, it has already achieved some impact on shaping the agenda of public debate on political, social, and cultural issues and has gained headway in forcing the government to react to its call. The Brotherhood's temperate style, consonant with basic Egyptian values, makes it far more popular than its more extreme colleagues. This moderation, however, should not be mistaken; they do pose a problem for the system. By engaging the government in a debate over religious principles, and sometimes forcing it to adapt itself to its demands, the Brotherhood constricts the already limited range of options at the government's disposal and thwarts many of its efforts to address the country's difficulties.

The radical, and much smaller, wing of the movement presents a more immediate problem. Groups (*gama'at*) of angry youth in their twenties and thirties openly defy the government as they seek to impose an Islamic way of life upon state and society. They start by introducing Islamic patterns in their immediate environment, at the universities, neighborhoods, and public places, and by conducting demonstrations, disrupting public order, and clashing with security forces. Such clashes have been reported with monotonous regularity, particularly in upper Egypt, where the relatively large concentration of Christian Copts serves as a catalyst, but also elsewhere, provoking popular tension and nervousness. Some ultra-radical groups, entertaining millenarian ideas, totally reject the existing political system and act clandestinely to replace it through violence and revolution. On the whole, the radical trend is small, perhaps just several hundred in the ultra-radical groups, several thousand in the other *gama'at*. But the actual numbers matter little when it comes to groups which would resort to terror, as Egypt learned in such a dramatic way in the assassination of Sadat.

The fundamentalists, both moderates and extremists, challenge the government by presenting an alternative way. Their formula, like the government's, does not offer a visible, effective, and specific solution to all problems. However, it does seem to provide at least the comfort and warmth of communal solidarity, rationalizing suffering in terms of God's ultimate justice and giving hope for a better future by God's grace. This is an outlet, if an illusory one, from the troubles of the present; if plight is as much a state of mind as it is an objective situation, the fundamentalist message is a psychological answer where no practical solution is in sight. As such, their call in itself may seem to contain no danger to the regime; in a way it may even be viewed as complementing the government's efforts. Nonetheless, it is problematic. Egyptians, still highly receptive to this kind of message, might be convinced that acting in an "Islamic way" may bail them out of their troubles. They would then be prone to taking their cue from religious leaders rather than from state officials. This could lead to an erosion of the government's authority.

It is important to note the inherent weakness of the movement. It is badly divided, has no coherent organization, and has no strong and inspiring leadership. Even if it offers a potentially attractive doctrine, its political power is, on the whole, rather limited. There are also limits to its popular appeal. While the public may be open to the Islamic call, it will also, for the most part, be reluctant to join or support a movement set to defy the legitimate government. The fundamentalist challenge is, therefore, mainly disruptive in nature. The fundamentalists may present an attractive message to the public, question the government's authority, and force it to react to their demands, but they do not as yet form a real political alternative.

The government handles the fundamentalists by countering each shade of the movement on its own terms. With the moderates, the government wages a complex struggle, through public debates and parliamentary battles, for which it enlists the official religious establishment to support its case. Although the regime is more powerful and perhaps better equipped for this encounter than its rivals, the results are not always in its favor. Here and there the government seems to lose ground, grudgingly adapting itself to the fundamentalists' demands. It is, however, still too early to assess the significance of concessions that still seem minor.

As for the radicals, the government's answer is more direct and simple: a combination of persuasion and, failing that, a constant effort to disrupt their organization and, if possible, eliminate them. "It is a grave error to deal with these people through dialogue," said Zaki Badr, a former interior minister. "I see them as mad dogs, with all due respect to dogs." Instead, Badr's preferred means were "killing, amputation, and live ammunition."[26] The government's effective intelligence units have penetrated the groups and, when this seemed desirable, the equally effective security forces have confronted them and hit them hard.

This battle, though, is not of the kind that cay be won conclusively. With its different branches, the fundamentalist movement draws its vitality from old religious beliefs and from the country's intricate socioeconomic realities. Complete elimination of the fundamentalist phenomenon, and perhaps even of its more violent form, is therefore hardly a realistic objective.

The Problematic Potential of Political Pluralism

The risks that may be inherent in Egypt's processes of democratization and liberalization are of a very different kind and magnitude. Basically, as we have seen, democratization is a positive process which largely benefits the government and helps stabilize the political system. But under certain circumstances, in the long run, it could also contain some dangers.

By definition, democratization leads to the weakening of centralized government, shifting authority from the ruler to the ruled. The farther the process advances and the more people it involves, the greater its momentum grows and the harder it is to stem. As more people participate in public affairs—as active politicians, voters, or just interested citizens—and free political action and speech become customary, the public grows more appreciative of these rights and more aware of the limitations to even fuller participation. This is a process that, once begun, is likely to feed on itself as people press for ever greater political liberties.

In Egypt, where the process began in the mid-1970s, there are signs that it is beginning to gather such momentum. The government, under Mubarak more so than under Sadat, has been committed not merely to retaining the existing level of freedom but also to expanding it. Such commitment has been reflected in more than just proclamations. During Mubarak's tenure, more parties have been licenced, more opposition newspapers have been published, and more and harsher criticism has been targeted against the government. True, political parties are still less popular as conduits for protest than fundamentalist movements, which are more closely compatible with old modes of social and political action, but party activity and open political debate are clearly on the ascendance.[27]

There is no particular reason for the Egyptian government to rue the dawn of democracy as having opened an inexorable process that will lead to its own demise. Indeed, from the way the government treats parties, it is evident that it views them as little more than a nuisance, whose harm is far less than the advantages gained from their existence. For all their recent gains, parties in

Egypt are regarded as politically insignificant, unable to pose a serious threat to the regime any time in the foreseeable future. The government believes that democratization is bound to remain a readily reversible process for a long time to come; if necessary, it would be possible to neutralize whatever danger the parties pose by hitting selectively at opposition groups and leaders. As for the long-term effect of expanding freedom, Mubarak seems to assess that it is a very long term indeed. The great majority of Egyptians, a largely illiterate society, have no interest in political life, and the process required to change this popular attitude would be so protracted that it need not worry the present government or any government in this generation.

Such an appraisal makes sense. Indeed, the Egyptian authorities may be best equipped to assess the situation regarding the elusive point-of-no-return. Yet if we place the democratic process in the broader, and very real, context of Egypt's harsh economic circumstances, we may see that the pluralistic system could also be problematic in the shorter run. An exacerbated economic crisis might compel the government to employ tough and unpopular measures that would, in turn, kindle social unrest. In that case, opposition parties might conceivably turn into standard bearers in a struggle that may not be limited to words alone, contributing their organizational apparatuses and publications to the anti-government effort. Their impact would become significant should they operate in coalition with other, extra-parliamentary forces, articulating their grievances and enhancing the sense of national crisis. The regime would then find itself forced to circumscribe political freedoms, taking away something it had previously given, thus undermining its own credibility and aggravating the tension between government and governed. In an environment as harsh as Egypt's, it is not to be ruled out that democratization, beyond advancing with great difficulty, could also backfire.

The Dangers of Regional Instability

Although Egypt's international relations and their impact on domestic Egyptian politics are beyond the scope of this study, it is important to mention regional politics briefly, given that the tensions which characterize the regional situation may have a destabilizing effect on the country itself.

The Middle Eastern system is in flux. As has been customarily the case, local conflicts which die out are succeeded by new encounters. The end of the Iraq-Iran War in 1988 marked the rekindling of the struggle for primacy in the Arab world, involving Egypt once again in the contest. This struggle came to a head in the Gulf crisis which, despite its unprecedented scope, did not necessarily resolve much. Similarly, Egypt's return to the Arab fold, which coincided with the outbreak of the uprising in the West Bank and Gaza, has not only failed to solve Egypt's regional problems, but it may have actually complicated them. The combination of a stalled peace process in which Egypt has a vital stake, an increasingly dangerous regional arms race, growing conflicts over resources such as oil and water, and the still-unclear impact of the demise of the Soviet Union creates a volatile situation with which Egypt is profoundly involved.

The Egyptian leadership is well familiar with situations in which regional developments prompt it to make decisions unpalatable to its domestic constituency. One may readily imagine how an open clash between Israel and another Arab state, sharp deterioration in the Palestinian problem, or another American intervention in a regional dispute would engender pressures on the government and create tension inside Egypt. During the Gulf crisis, the government was remarkably successful in maintaining domestic tranquility and an appearance of national cohesion despite popular discontent, even some agitation, over its close alignment with the United States. Should another crisis of the magnitude of the Gulf War occur, a repetition of that success cannot be guaranteed. It is impossible to predict the results of such an eventuality, but one may assume that it will not solve any of the country's major problems. At best, it would alleviate them temporarily; it is more likely to complicate them.

Assessment
Continuity is not the sole option for the state's future. As discussed above, growing economic, demographic, political and cultural pressures do pose a threat to the durability of the regime. How is this threat to be assessed? And how strong are the forces which seek to assure stability?

Determinants of Continuity and Change
The Egyptian regime, backed by the army and in firm control of the bureaucracy, is infinitely mightier than any other actor on the scene. The fundamentalists, the only other force with some potential, are divided, disorganized, and poorly led. They pose a challenge to the regime in more ways than one, but they are a far cry from forming a viable alternative. All other actors on this stage, including opposition party politicians, are of secondary or marginal weight.

The regime's strength is the single most important determinant in the country's political evolution. Like all governments, Mubarak's has a strong survival instinct, coupled with a deep belief in the exclusive validity of its message to the country. Subtle management of its relations with the armed forces would assure their continued support. Likewise, the persistent dependence of the bureaucracy on the government for employment and resource distribution should guarantee its continued cooperation. Such unity of interests among the most important apparatuses renders the Egyptian system of government highly resilient. This, coupled with the traditional Egyptian subservience to central authority and the support of the country's foreign allies, ought to permit the existing regime to remain in power for the foreseeable future.

On the other side of the ledger, a combination of forces pulls Egypt in the opposite direction. The association of economic exigency and fundamentalism, along with the absence of an attractive vision for the future, could form a dangerous brew that would jeopardize this stability. The growing malaise, the disaffection of much of the younger generation, and the spawning of militant variations of fundamentalism are all factors that seem to increase the menace. It is conceivable that the pressure on the government by those offering their own outlet from the crisis would grow. The government would either have to adapt its ways to those of the fundamentalists or confront them ever more forcefully. Either response could be painful and risky.

Egypt's famed deference to authority is surely not unlimited. Experience has shown that, in moments of extreme distress, Egyptians may react with an eruption of rage and violence, letting out steam that had accumulated over a long period of restraint. Dramatic outbursts in 1977, 1981, 1986, and, on a smaller scale, on several other occasions, marked the threshold of tolerance. They showed that once Egyptians lose their patience they are capable of exploding and of forcing the powers-that-be into a reactive posture. Such an explosion could be triggered by a sharp rise in the price of staples (prominently, though not exclusively, bread), by the cumulative effect of a series of more moderate price hikes, or by an abrupt change in Egypt's international environment in a manner that would stir powerful emotions. Where exactly is the breaking point is impossible to discern.

Prospect

Certain basic facts about Egypt's future are, however, abundantly clear. It is obvious that the adverse trend of population growth will persist through the rest of the decade and beyond. The economic situation is likely to remain difficult for a long time, post-Gulf War developments notwithstanding, and this will continue to serve as a potential source of tension and crisis. Opposition forces, primarily Islamic fundamentalism, will therefore continue to gain popular support as an outlet (real or imaginary) from these frustrations.

The most likely scenario would have the present regime continuing to govern Egypt well into the future. Mubarak, known to be healthy and fit, might himself even continue to rule for the rest of this decade. The army would continue to support the government, ensuring that it, in turn, defends the army's interests. If unable to solve or substantially alleviate the people's material problems, the regime could face increasing sociopolitical protests expressed frequently, though not solely, through fundamentalist channels. The popular attraction of the religious outlet might grow, rendering Egypt more pious as a whole. The government would have to be on the alert, allowing fundamentalist sentiments to expand popularly but checking signs of threat to its legitimacy and stability, if necessary by force. As for the multi-party system, the government would be able to broaden its basis, making it a partner to the responsibility for the existing state of affairs. But, if the parties become excessively critical, the government has a number of ways to silence them. All in all, this is not an easy prospect for Egypt. Even if the government remains stable, it has good reasons to look forward with some concern.

The number of other possible scenarios is endless and depends on the observer's imagination. The following are three options which are as probable as any other:

1. *A change of government due to Mubarak's disappearance from the scene.* If Mubarak disappears from the scene in circumstances not involving the overthrowing of the regime—due to illness, sudden death or even assassination—a likely development would be an otherwise smooth transfer of power. If past experience (1970 and 1981) is any indication, and if one considers that the regime has a powerful instinct of survival and a strong inclination for continuity, then one may expect to see the following: in accordance with the constitution the presidency would pass to the speaker of the People's Assembly, who would govern until a new president is appointed by the Assembly and confirmed in a national referendum. Until a successor is in place, and perhaps also shortly thereafter, the state may be governed by a collective forum of leading generals and technocrats. (If this occurs in the foreseeable future, such a forum would probably include the men listed earlier as well as the heads of civilian and military intelligence, the army chief of staff, and a handful of top army commanders behind the scenes.) Mubarak's successor would be a person appointed by this forum, though not necessarily one of its number.

2. *A prolonged period of instability.* An acute economic crisis, prompted by sharp food price hikes or severe shortage of staples, could lead to an explosion of violence, with or without a fundamentalist attempt to lead the protest. In this such, the government would have to rely heavily on the military and security forces to retain control. If Mubarak's (or his successor's) government would appear to be losing command, the army (or certain elements in it) might move to replace the political leadership by a team more able to restore control. The army-backed regime would remain in power, but its legitimacy would be based on sheer force amidst an atmosphere of tension and terror.

3. *A fundamentalist-military takeover.* This is a variation of the previous scenario, but one that at this point looks still less likely. The fundamentalists, who lack the power to depose and replace the present regime, might be more successful if they join hands with elements within the army or security forces. Since the total shielding of these forces from economic hardship and the radicals' message cannot be guaranteed, this is a possible scenario, although a remote one.

Implications for Egypt's International Orientation

Egypt's international policy is strongly influenced by the constraints dominating its domestic front. Because it badly needs foreign assistance, Egypt seeks to retain good relations with as many sources of potential aid as possible. Because it cannot afford to spend its meager resources on foreign adventures, Egypt seeks stability and peace in its regional neighborhood. These basic guidelines have been reflected in the following principles in Egypt's international strategy:

- Preserving the close alliance with the United States, Egypt's chief and indispensable supporter and with other Western industrial states is a high priority. Staying on friendly terms with the successor states to the Soviet Union is also important, though considerably less so.
- Pursuing good relations with all members of the inter-Arab system, including the Palestine Liberation Organization. Egypt's historical tradition and self-image drive it to look for a leading position in this system, but it has no ambition for territorial expansion nor a desire to be involved in a regional war. The moderating role which Cairo under Mubarak has been playing in this arena has bought it much prestige and has thus proven a desirable course of action.

• Retaining its peace with Israel is a strategic interest. The peace has been highly beneficial to Egypt, for economic and other reasons. The alternative could be costly and, on the whole, objectionable. Egypt would rather use resources for domestic needs than for returning to a war footing.

The present regime will most likely continue to have a vested interest in adhering to these principles and will gear its foreign policy to safeguard them. It will endeavor to foster its friendship with the United States and retain the image of Washington's faithful Middle Eastern ally. Cairo's stance as a stabilizing and moderating force in the region will serve to enhance this image and to secure a peaceful international environment that Egypt badly needs. To this end, Cairo under the present regime will also prefer to remain committed to peace with Israel and further work to expand the peace by trying to bring other Arab states and the Palestinians into the peace-making process.

Notes

1. According to the theory of "hydraulic societies," the political system in countries where life depends on a central water artery tends to be centralistic and authoritarian, as people are dependent on a central "water council." Subordination to a strong government becomes a typical characteristic of society's basic political philosophy. Such countries are also relatively easy to rule: whoever controls the river controls the population living along it. For the relevance of this theory to Egypt, see Nazih Ayubi, *Bureaucracy and Politics in Contemporary Egypt* (London: Ithaca Press, 1980), especially pp. 77-136.

2. See Bernard Lewis, "Islamic Concepts of Revolution," in his *Islam in History* (London: Alcove Press, 1973), pp. 253-58. The initial Islamic concept indeed commended the removal of an impious ruler by force, holding that this was not only the subjects' right but also their duty, for they were not to put up with a sinful government. Fundamentalists nowadays return to this formula (based on a saying ascribed to the Prophet, that there should be "no obedience to a creature in disobeying the Creator") to justify clandestine efforts to topple the government. This old concept, however, was abandoned as early as the eleventh century, giving way to a principle, sanctioned by Islamic jurists, that government, however tyrannical, should always be obeyed provided it was Islamic.

3. See Raymond A. Hinnebusch, *Egyptian Politics under Sadat* (Cambridge: Cambridge University Press, 1985), pp. 44-45.

4. Nazih Ayubi, "Government and the state in Egypt today," in Charles Tripp and Roger Owen, eds., *Egypt under Mubarak* (London: Routledge, 1989), p. 13.

5. *Financial Times*, April 18, 1989.

6. Quoted in ibid.

7. International Institute for Strategic Studies, *The Military Balance 1990-1991* (London: IISS, 1990), p. 102.

8. For a detailed description of these events, see the chapter on Egypt in Itamar Rabinovich and Haim Shaked, eds., *Middle East Contemporary Survey* (*MECS*), vol. 10 (Boulder, CO: Westview, 1986), pp. 263-289.

9. For a more extensive discussion see, Robert Satloff, *Army and Politics in Mubarak's Egypt*, Policy Paper Number Ten (Washington: The Washington Institute for Near East Policy, 1988).

10. Ibid., chapter three.

11. Ibid., pp. 46-54.

12. In the war, Tantawi served as chief liaison officer with U.S. forces, and Halabi was commander of the Egyptian expeditionary force. They were moved to their new posts in May 1991.

13. See, for example, in *MECS* 1983-84, 1987, and 1990, chapters on Egypt.

14. Mubarak's interview in *al-Majalla* (London), July 12-18, 1989.

15. See Ali al-Din Hilal, *al-Tatawwur al-dimuqrati fi misr* [Democratic Development in Egypt] (Cairo, 1986) and Mona Makram-Ebeid, "Political Opposition in Egypt: Democratic Myth or Reality?" *The Middle East Journal*, vol. 43, no. 3 (Summer 1989), pp. 423-36.

16. Mubarak's speech, text in *al-Ahram*, November 12, 1989. The figure for earnings quoted by Mubarak, if correct, marks a steep decline from Egypt's foreign currency revenues of about $11 billion in fiscal year 1987-88; see Economist Intelligence Unit, *Country Report-Egypt*, No. 4, 1989, pp. 9-10.

According to William B. Quandt, *The United States and Egypt* (Washington: The Brookings Institution, 1990), p. 50, Egyptian imports in 1988-89 exceeded exports by $8 billion.

17. For details, see *MECS* 1987, p. 333, and *MECS* 1988, p. 391.

18. Mubarak, quoted in *New York Times*, July 9, 1990.

19. See, for example, ibid., Alan Cowell's description.

20. Mubarak's May Day speeches, Radio Cairo, May 1, 1988, translated in *Foreign Broadcast Information Service-Near East and South Asia (FBIS)*, May 3, 1988; Radio Cairo, May 1, 1989, translated in *FBIS*, May 3, 1989.

21. For details, see Quandt, pp. 40-49, pp. 76-77.

22. For details, see *Financial Times* (London), October 30, 1990; Middle East News Agency (Cairo), October 30, 1990, reported in *FBIS*, October 30, 1990; Economist Intelligence Unit, *Country Report-Egypt*, no. 4, 1990, pp. 17-19; *Middle East Report*, January-February 1991, p. 20; *Middle East International*, April 19, 1991, p. 17 and May 31, 1991, p. 13.

23. See Quandt, p. 52; *New York Times*, July 9, 1990; *The Middle East*, July 1990, pp. 29-30.

24. *al-Wafd* (Cairo), December 26, 1988. For details on the group, see Ami Ayalon, "Regime, opposition and terrorism in Egypt," in Barry Rubin, ed., *The Politics of Terrorism* (Washington: The Johns Hopkins University Foreign Policy Institute, 1989), pp. 81-85.

25. For a recent study, see Barry Rubin, *Islamic Fundamentalism in Egyptian Politics* (New York: St. Martin's, 1990).

26. Badr's interview in *al-Watan al-Arabi* (Paris), February 3, 1989.

27. See Gudrun Kramer, "The change of paradigm—political pluralism in contemporary Egypt," *Peuples Mediterranees*, nos. 41-42 (October 1987-March 1988), pp. 283-302; Ayubi, "Government and the state in Egypt today," pp. 7ff; and Mona Makram-Ebeid, "Political opposition in Egypt."

About the Contributors

Ami Ayalon is chairman of the Department of Middle Eastern and African History at Tel Aviv University and senior research fellow at the university's Moshe Dayan Center for Middle Eastern and African Studies. He serves as editor of the Dayan Center's annual *Middle East Contemporary Survey* and is the author of *Language and Change in the Arab Middle East* (1987).

Shaul Bakhash is the Clarence J. Robinson Professor of History at George Mason University, Fairfax, VA, and the author of numerous works on Iranian history and politics. A revised edition of his *The Reign of the Ayatollahs: Iran and the Islamic Revolution* was published in 1990.

Amatzia Baram is senior lecturer in the Department of Middle Eastern History at the University of Haifa. His most recent book is *Culture, History, and Ideology in the Formation of Ba'thist Iraq, 1968-89* (1991).

Marvin Feuerwerger served as first secretary at the U.S. Embassy in Tel Aviv and as senior strategic fellow at The Washington Institute for Near East Policy. The author of *Congress and Israel* (1979), he is now director of defense and strategic issues at the American-Israel Public Affairs Committee.

Adam Garfinkle is coordinator of political studies at the Foreign Policy Research Institute in Philadelphia, PA. He is the author of *Israel and Jordan in the Shadow of War* (1991) and coeditor of *Friendly Tyrants: An American Dilemma* (1991).

Emile A. Nakhleh is the John L. Morrison Professor of International Studies and chairman of the Department of Government and International Studies at Mount Saint Mary's College, Emmitsburg, MD. His books include *The Gulf Cooperation Council: Politics, Problems, and Prospects* (1986) and *The Persian Gulf and American Policy* (1982).

Itamar Rabinovich was appointed head of Israel's delegation to peace negotiations with Syria in July 1992 and, subsequently, as Israel's ambassador to the United States. A noted scholar of Syria and Lebanon, he served previously as rector of Tel Aviv University and head of the Moshe Dayan Center.

Barry Rubin is a fellow at the Foreign Policy Institute of the Paul H. Nitze School of Advanced International Studies. The author of numerous volumes on Middle East politics and U.S. foreign policy, his most recent book is *Cauldron of Turmoil: The United States in the Middle East* (1992).

Robert B. Satloff is deputy director of The Washington Institute for Near East Policy and a specialist on Arab and Islamic politics. He is the author of *From Abdullah to Hussein: Jordan in Transition* (forthcoming, 1994) and *Troubles on the East Bank: Challenges to the Domestic Stability of Jordan* (1986).

Index

227

About the Book and Editor

Examining regime stability and political change in the heartland of the Middle East, this book focuses on the main actors in the two confrontations that have historically engaged Western, and particularly American, interests in the region—the Arab-Israeli conflict and the battle for control of the Persian Gulf. In particular, the contributors discuss the distribution of power within each regime; the sources of regime legitimacy and challenges to it; and the social, economic, and ideological trends influencing change in the region. Probable scenarios for regime succession are also explored.

Although states in the Middle East have proven themselves surprisingly resilient in recent decades, these essays paint a portrait of a region in flux. In the absence of the Cold War, in the shadow of the Gulf War, and in the era of historic Arab-Israeli negotiations, the Middle East emerges as a region in which governments and citizens are being forced to grapple with internal problems that have long been shunted aside.

Robert B. Satloff is deputy director of The Washington Institute for Near East Policy, a specialist on Arab and Islamic politics, and a professorial lecturer at The Johns Hopkins School for Advanced and International Studies. He is the author of *From Abdullah to Hussein: Jordan in Transition* (forthcoming, 1994) and *Troubles on the East Bank: Challenges to the Domestic Stability of Jordan* (1986).